One Alliance, Two Lenses

D0890491

**THE WALTER H. SHORENSTEIN
ASIA-PACIFIC RESEARCH CENTER**

SHORENSTEIN
APARC
STANFORD

Studies of the Walter H. Shorenstein Asia-Pacific Research Center

Andrew G. Walder, General Editor

The Walter H. Shorenstein Asia-Pacific Research Center in the Freeman
Spogli Institute for International Studies at Stanford University sponsors
interdisciplinary research on the politics, economies, and societies of
contemporary Asia. This monograph series features academic and policy-
oriented research by Stanford faculty and other scholars associated with
the Center.

One Alliance, Two Lenses

U.S.-KOREA RELATIONS IN A NEW ERA

Gi-Wook Shin

Stanford University Press

Stanford, California

Stanford University Press
Stanford, California

© 2010 by the Board of Trustees of the Leland Stanford Junior University. All rights
reserved.

No part of this book may be reproduced or transmitted in any form or by any
means, electronic or mechanical, including photocopying and recording, or in any
information storage or retrieval system without the prior written permission of
Stanford University Press.

This book is published with the generous support of the International Center for
Korean Studies, Korea University's Center for research, publication, and development
in Korean Studies. The International Center for Korean Studies was established in
2003 to support scholarship and exploration of Korea in the humanities and social
sciences, and to promote new research in Korean Studies to a wide international
audience.

Printed in the United States of America on acid-free, archival-quality paper

Library of Congress Cataloging-in-Publication Data
Shin, Gi-Wook.
    One alliance, two lenses : U.S.-Korea relations in a new era / Gi-Wook Shin.
        p. cm. — (Studies of the Walter H. Shorenstein Asia-Pacific Research Center)
    Includes bibliographical references and index.
    ISBN 978-0-8047-6368-4 (cloth : alk. paper) — ISBN 978-0-8047-6369-1
(pbk. : alk. paper)
        1. United States—Foreign relations—Korea (South)   2. Korea (South)—Foreign
relations—United States.   3. United States—Foreign relations—Korea (South)—
Press coverage.   4. Korea (South)—Foreign relations—United States—Press
coverage.   5. United State—Foreign relations—1989–   6. Korea (South)—Foreign
relations—2002–   I. Title.   II. Series: Studies of the Walter H. Shorenstein
Asia-Pacific Research Center.
    E183.8.K6S55 2010
    327.730519—dc22   2009025675

Typeset by Publishers' Design and Production Services, Inc. in 11/14 Adobe Garamond

Contents

Illustrations

Acknowledgments

"Are you ever going back to Korea?" This is one of the questions that I have been asked most frequently for the last two decades while teaching in the United States. I usually respond, "Well, I could, but I believe I have more things to do here."

This question does not come as a surprise to me, since I came to the United States as a foreign student with every intention to return to Korea following my graduate education. My parents anxiously awaited my return to Korea with my doctorate. When I got my first teaching position at the University of Iowa in 1991 and even when I moved to UCLA a few years later, I still harbored the thought that I would go back to Korea after gaining some teaching and research experiences in American academia. Over the years, however, I have come to the conclusion that I stand to make more of a contribution by staying in the United States. Looking back, it was not an easy decision to make, but it is one that I have not regretted.

Korea is my homeland and the place that I grew up. I have great affection for and pride in this great nation. Korea is also a topic in which I claim professional expertise.

The United States has become my second home. It is the place that has given me educational and professional opportunities and the place that I am raising my children. I am honored to be on the faculty of a great American world-class university, Stanford.

As a Korean American scholar, I have a sense of mission to accomplish: improving the relations of the two countries to which I am most attached. Accordingly, I have been trying to promote a better understanding of Korean affairs and the development of constructive relations between the United States and Korea in both research and praxis. As a scholar of sociology and Korean studies, my primary tasks are research and writing on Korean affairs and the U.S.-Korea relationship. Yet I have also been attempting to facilitate better relations between the two allies by convening conferences (academic and policy) and establishing fellowships that are designed to enhance mutual understanding of the bilateral relationship and to promote networking among experts and policy makers in both countries.

This book is an outcome of my long-standing interests and efforts to better understand U.S.-Korea relations. It examines the bilateral alliance during a period that may very well come to be considered the height of identity politics in South Korea, as well as the policy discord that existed between the two countries. My hope for this work is that it will help enhance understanding of the difficult times that have characterized the bilateral relationship in recent years.

I would not have been able to produce this book without wonderful support from so many people, at Stanford and elsewhere. I have been truly blessed with an enormous pool of talented individuals, who have helped me carry out this project for the last five years. The following four people were particularly instrumental in completing the project in various stages: Kyu S. Hahn (research design and data collection), Jeong-Woo Koo (data analysis), Kristin Burke (research and writing), and Hilary Izatt (editing and publication). Many undergraduate and graduate students at Stanford and in Korea have diligently worked on the tedious task of data coding. They include Eun Sang Hwang, Sung-Jin Lee, David Juan, Susan Lee, Katie Barracloug, Jin Yoon, Joon-Seok Hong, Gloria Kim, Suh-Young Shin, Stella Shin, Young-Joo Kim, and Jung-Eun Lee.

This was such a large project that it took me about two years just to collect and code the data. That would not have been possible without strong financial support. I am very grateful for having received a generous grant from the Korea International Trade Association and would like to thank its chairman, Kim Jaecheol, who saw the merit of the project and had no reservations about it. Support from the Pantech Korean Studies Fund and the Shorenstein Asia-Pacific Research Center Faculty Grant also greatly aided completion of the project. Finally, a grant from the International Center for Korean Studies at Korea University in Seoul helped me to complete the writing of this book.

I have also greatly benefited from valuable comments provided by the following people: Michael Armacost, David Straub, Daniel Sneider, Gil Rozman, Donald Keyser, John Merrill, Young-Kwan Yoon, Jong-Seok Lee, Mary Connor, John G. Fallon, Myoung-Koo Kang, John Ciorciari, Joon-Seok Hong, Joon-Nak Choi, Soo-Kyung Kim, and Seo-Hyun Park. Many of these individuals are my colleagues at the Shorenstein APARC, which offers a wonderful intellectual community that I truly appreciate. I also feel fortunate to have received valuable comments during the study period from those who were directly involved in policy making about the U.S.-ROK relationship on both sides of the Pacific.

Three readers for the Stanford University Press (SUP) offered extensive comments that proved very useful to my revision. Stacy Wagner, Jessica Walsh, and Carolyn Brown at SUP and Denise A. Botelho provided wonderful assistance to me, from the review process to the production stage. Susan M. Freese deserves credit for her excellent editing of my writings here. My able and dedicated staff at Shorenstein APARC—especially Heather Ahn, Debbie Warren, and Sabrina Ishimatsu—have made my professional life as a scholar, teacher, and administrator much more enjoyable.

Any acknowledgment of gratitude would be incomplete without mentioning the support of my family. My mother, who lives in Korea, has made the sacrifice of seeing her son only once in a while but fully understands and supports my work toward U.S.-ROK relations. My family in the United States—Michelle (Mee-Sun), Kelley, Ashley, and William—have endured my busy schedule and frequent absences from home. Kelley just started college, and I hope that she will follow in the footsteps of her father by studying Korean affairs.

Last but not least, it is my great honor and pleasure to acknowledge the friendship and support of Byeong-Yeop Park, my close friend and a long-time benefactor of the Korean Studies Program at Stanford, which I established in the fall of 2001. He clearly understands my efforts to promote better relations between the United States and Korea and has given me almost unconditional support. His contributions have established the now well-known Pantech Fellowship in Korean Studies at Stanford and supported many academic and policy conferences on Korean affairs. As such, it is only fitting to dedicate this book to him.

One Alliance, Two Lenses

ONE

Identity Politics and Policy Disputes in U.S.-Korea Relations

During the South Korean presidential campaign of 2007, President Lee Myung Bak pledged to prioritize and strengthen a United States–Republic of Korea (U.S.-ROK) alliance widely regarded as strained. "Disagreement over North Korea was always the main obstacle to good relations [with the United States]," one of Lee's foreign policy advisors asserted upon the new president's inauguration. Such disagreement did not exist between President Lee and President Bush, the advisor insisted, paving the way for a better bilateral relationship.[1] Indeed, only weeks into Lee Myung Bak's presidency, longtime Korea observer Michael Breen noted it was immediately clear that the new government was not going to treat North Korea as a special case, as its predecessors had. According to Breen, "This government sees the North Korea issue as a foreign policy issue—and not even the most important one."[2]

Although the 2007 campaign did not turn on these issues, Lee's campaign pledges for improved relations with the United States and a tougher line toward North Korea were significant. Only five years earlier, during the 2002 presidential race, such rhetoric would have proved untenable. At that time, a second North Korean nuclear crisis had just occurred, and candidate Roh Moo Hyun's vows to continue engagement with the North despite the crisis were clearly at odds with the Bush administration's desire to isolate Pyongyang. Also preceding the 2002 election, a massive wave of anti-American sentiment erupted in response to the handling of a U.S. military training accident that killed two Korean schoolgirls. Catholic priests went on a hunger strike, and tens of thousands of Koreans—not just activists but middle-class adults—protested against the United States. At the same time,

Roh gave a campaign speech under a banner reading "Yankee Go Home!"[3] Even conservative candidate Lee Hoi Chang, who had proudly demonstrated his ties to the United States by visiting Washington, DC, early in the campaign, later distanced himself from his country's traditional ally in response to the clear sentiment of the nation. On the eve of the U.S.-ROK alliance's fiftieth anniversary, South Korea—long perceived to be one of the United States' most stalwart partners—was dubbed by the *New York Times* as "one of the Bush administration's biggest foreign policy problems."[4]

The tumult of demonstrations drew to a close soon after Roh Moo Hyun's inauguration,[5] but anti-American sentiment persisted. According to a 2003 Pew survey, aside from the Arab states, South Korea was identified as one of the most anti-American countries, along with France and Russia.[6] Similarly, a 2004 RAND report showed that many Koreans who had previously held a favorable view of the United States had abandoned this position and joined the ranks of those holding an unfavorable view.[7] As new progressive policy elites sought to reassess history and the United States' role in inter-Korean relations and unification, the alliance became a subject of intense debate within the South. Although it may be a myth that there was ever a "golden age" in U.S.-ROK relations[8] and both Washington and Seoul officials made a habit of denying any signs of tension,[9] developments in U.S.-Korean relations during these years led many scholars and experts on Korean affairs to question the future of the U.S.-ROK alliance.[10]

Over these years, political change had come to Washington, DC, as well. From its inception, the Bush administration had been deeply skeptical of efforts to engage North Korea, including the Clinton administration's 1994 Agreed Framework and the South's Sunshine Policy. The new U.S. president conveyed these views in a March 2001 meeting with Kim Dae Jung, whose diplomatic mission to Washington, DC, was widely perceived as a failure.[11] Subsequently, the September 11 terrorist attacks focused U.S. attention on the dangerous potential nexus between rogue states with weapons of mass destruction (WMD) capabilities and terrorists seeking to strike the American homeland. From the perspective of the Bush administration, which said it had new evidence that North Korea was pursuing an enriched uranium route to nuclear weapons, this regime presented a grave security threat to the United States and was to be isolated until it reversed course.

This thinking would collide with ROK policies and sentiments. Seoul advocated continuing inter-Korean cooperation, despite the nuclear problem, which it assigned to the realm of U.S.-DPRK (Democratic People's Republic of Korea) relations. In contrast to the U.S. view, many in the ROK had come to see their northern neighbor as a poor sibling in need of assistance, rather than a dangerous state building up its asymmetric threat capabilities.

No anti-Koreanism appeared in the United States comparable to the anti-Americanism seen in the ROK, but many U.S. experts and observers of Korean affairs—champions of the alliance—reacted strongly to the Roh government and the wave of sentiment that had lifted it to power. Michael Armacost, former ambassador to Japan and longtime Korean affairs observer, noted that even "conservative commentators who [had] long supported the alliance with South Korea—e.g., William Safire, Dick Allen, Ken Adelman, and Charles Krauthammer—[had] expressed sharp criticism of recent ROK policies."[12] Initially drawn to Seoul by the story of anti-American demonstrations, the U.S. news media had, by early 2003, begun to focus on the growing U.S.-ROK policy rift over North Korea and the best approach to its apparently renewed pursuit of nuclear weapons.

What had happened to fifty years of robust alliance relations? Had they been irreparably damaged? Or were the strains merely "growing pains," bound to emerge in the maturation process of such an unequal relationship forged in the cold war? If the mood of the Korean public changed, would U.S.-ROK relations get back on track? Could administrations in Seoul and Washington with similar policy approaches to the North restore relations? Had the alliance entered a new era? Was the alliance really in need of a new strategic rationale?

Since the election of Lee Myung Bak in late 2007, expectations have been high on both sides of the Pacific that this change in leadership would revive the troubled alliance. The Lee administration has promised to stress the importance of the U.S.-ROK alliance and has declared its intention to pursue a "pragmatic" course in foreign policy, in contrast to the ideologically driven Roh administration.[13] The replacement of Bush with Obama has likewise increased expectations for a bright future for the alliance. Indeed, one could argue that the overlap of Roh and his team of "386" advisors[14] with Bush and the neoconservatives was the least workable combination of leadership and that those days are now over.

Unwarranted optimism must be avoided, however, and Lee's first year in office proved the need for caution. Lee's presidency has gone forward in a context transformed in recent years, and returning to any other (fondly remembered) point in time seems impossible. The Obama administration also has to deal with many daunting tasks inherited from the Bush administration (e.g., war on terrorism, financial crisis), and the North Korean nuclear problem remains as a key policy challenge for both nations. The events, disagreements, and policies of recent years were not simply the outcomes of a mismatch between U.S. and Korean administrations or of a particular policy dispute (e.g., over North Korea) but rather reflections of larger trends and changes in both nations.

Although the alliance should focus on the future, rather than the past, in moving forward, it is imperative to understand the underlying causes of strains in the bilateral relationship from the early 1990s to more recent years—a critical period that may well be remembered as the height of identity politics and policy discord. This study seeks to explain how the U.S.-ROK relationship has been affected by seminal changes in these allies' environments: the end of the cold war, the South Korean transition from authoritarianism to democracy, and the strategic reorientation spurred by the September 11 terrorist attacks. The main goal of the study is not simply to trace responses to events during this critical period but rather to offer analytical perspectives that will be useful in understanding the perceptions and implications borne of these changes. As the Lee government and the newly established Obama administration seek to find ways to enhance their alliance, the past experiences and lessons that this book addresses should be given serious consideration.

Sources of the Strain: Anti-Americanism or Policy Rift?

From the end of the cold war through the years of the Sunshine Policy and the elections of Bush and Roh, various developments contributed to straining U.S.-ROK relations and provoked serious debate over their origins and repercussions. In basic terms, two major arguments have been advanced to explain the strained relationship during this period.

The first argument is the *anti-Americanism thesis*, which points to the ostensible rising tide of anti-Americanism in South Korea as the principal source of bilateral tension. Literature that focuses on anti-Americanism in South Korea connects the phenomenon to a multitude of factors: the generational divide and demographic change in the South, the U.S. war on terror and other Bush administration policies, Korean nationalism, reduced threat perceptions of North Korea, views of China as a viable strategic partner alternative, supposed historic U.S. complicity in the suppression of Korean democracy, and a perception of U.S. arrogance based on events ranging from the U.S. military's alleged disregard for South Korean citizens to a perceived unfair judgment in speed-skating contest in the 2002 Winter Olympics in Utah.[15]

In particular, two events in 2002 sparked major outpourings of anti-American sentiment in Korea: first, President Bush's characterization of North Korea as a member of the "axis of evil" during his State of the Union address in January, and second, a U.S. military training accident in June, in which two South Korean schoolgirls died after being crushed by an armored vehicle. In line with these events, public opinion polls showed a clear deterioration in South Koreans' views of the United States. Many in the South, especially those in their twenties and thirties, contended that not only had the United States failed to appreciate Korean interests, but it had also actively pursued policies running *counter* to them. As a U.S. expert on Korean affairs noted, "The Korean brand of anti-U.S. sentiment exhibits the notion that the United States blocked the national will of the people, reflected in the perceived lack of American respect for [Korean] foreign and domestic concerns," especially inter-Korean engagement.[16]

To be sure, this recent wave of anti-Americanism was neither entirely new nor unique to Korea. Similar sentiment had roiled U.S.-Korea relations in the past, including during the U.S. occupation following the end of colonial rule (1945–1948), when the Carter administration intended to withdraw U.S. troops from the South in the late 1970s, and during the democracy movement of the mid-1980s.[17] After 2001, anti-American sentiment rose in other parts of the world, as well. As the sole superpower of the post–cold war era, the United States has been criticized by many nations, including traditional allies, for unilateralism, especially in connection with the war on terror.[18] Joseph Nye, chairman of the National Intelligence Council and an assistant secretary of defense in the Clinton administration, concurred with these foreign critics when he pointed to "increasing evidence that the policies and tone of the new unilateralists were directly responsible for the decline of America's attractiveness abroad."[19]

Yet the fundamental challenge that recent Korean protests posed to the alliance distinguished it from prior instances of anti-Americanism. In the past, bouts of anti-Americanism had rarely questioned the basic rationale for the alliance; rather, security-related provocations from the North had spurred ever-closer cooperation between Seoul and Washington. However, in the fall of 2002, anti-U.S. sentiment did not abate with the resurrection of the nuclear threat from North Korea. Instead of cooperating more with the United States, the government in Seoul advocated an autonomous defense and pressed for continuing inter-Korean cooperation.[20] In years past, Korean governments had been quick to suppress anti-American movements led by dissident intellectuals, activists, and opposition politicians, but in 2003, many of the figures who had previously taken to the streets in protest became newly minted policy elites of the Roh administration. Just as these individuals were absorbed into institutional politics, it has been argued, the anti-American themes they advocated transcended dissidence into influence on government policies.[21]

The second explanation for recent problems in the U.S.-ROK relationship can be termed the *policy rift thesis*, as it refers to the allies' diverging perceptions of the North Korean threat and the consequent policy rift over how to deal with North Korea pursuing nuclear weapons. For example, a study by the Center for Strategic and International Studies in Washington, DC, entitled "South Korean Views of the United States and the U.S.-ROK Alliance," concluded that "it is the apparent difference in perceptions of and policy toward North Korea, that is challenging most seriously the foundations of the alliance."[22] Similarly, a report from an opinion leaders' seminar convened by a Washington-based think tank, the Korea Economic Institute, noted South Korea's "decline in trust of the United States" and warned that "if the United States and South Korea could not reach agreement on how they viewed the North Korean threat, the U.S.-ROK alliance would be in grave trouble."[23]

According to the policy rift thesis, the end of the cold war and new inter-Korean engagement (epitomized by the 2000 Korea summit) brought important changes in how South Koreans viewed the North and, consequently, the U.S. role in their national defense. From the U.S. perspective, the September 11 attacks changed the landscape of national security policy, placing even greater emphasis on nonproliferation. As such, the United States regarded North Korea as a serious regional and even global security threat, whereas many South Koreans came to perceive the North—now a partner in inter-Korean reconciliation—as a weak state with severely diminished capacity to threaten ROK national security.[24] Thus, the traditional allies no longer viewed the North Korean nuclear issue through the same lens, and this difference allegedly strained the alliance. Divergent views and approaches to the North Korean issue posed a fundamental challenge to the U.S.-ROK alliance, as experts of international relations held that alliances must rest on a congruence of strategic interests and a willingness to share risks and costs.[25]

In more specific terms, the policy rift thesis maintains that it was the conflict between progressive Korean governments and a conservative U.S. administration over North Korea that strained the alliance. Upon entering office, President Bush demonstrated a decided reluctance to engage the North and readily expressed skepticism over South Korea's Sunshine Policy, most notably during President Kim Dae Jung's visit to the White House in the spring of 2001. The new U.S. administration's characterizations of North Korea—first as part of an "axis of evil" and later as an "outpost of tyranny"—angered not only North Koreans but also many in the South, creating noticeable tension at the policy level. By early 2002, even *before* the beginning of the current nuclear standoff, the U.S. media began to report on a growing policy rift between the once-close allies. Whereas North Korea had earlier stood as the threat that necessitated and galvanized cooperation in the alliance, very different perceptions and policy approaches toward the regime now tested U.S.-ROK relations.

Both theses make many valid points, and they are not mutually exclusive. Yet a series of unanswered questions remain.

First, a more complete answer is needed to the question of why only *recent* anti-Americanism, and not past spikes in such sentiment, has had a significant impact on the alliance. Anti-American sentiment and movements in the South were more widespread and violent in the 1980s but had little, if any, jeopardizing effect on the future of the U.S.-ROK alliance.

Second, the question remains why there was no anti-Koreanism in the United States comparable to the anti-Americanism that appeared in South Korea. As noted earlier, U.S. policy makers and experts in Korean affairs have voiced their concern over tension in the alliance, but no broad anti-Koreanism can be found in the American public.

Third, in a related vein, some explanation is needed for why the alliance has become a subject of intense debate within South Korea, whereas no comparable contention has appeared within the United States. In other words, why was the Korean debate over the purpose and terms of the alliance more widespread and intense, while American examinations of these issues were limited in scope and largely confined to academic and policy circles?

Fourth, the reason for the alliance becoming a subject of concern in the United States only in recent years, when its rationale has been challenged by Korean progressives over a much longer period, needs to be addressed. Why have Koreans, not Americans, led the questioning and even the challenging of this enduring, decades-old relationship?

The final question to be addressed is whether the U.S.-ROK relationship can dispel the label of being "strained" and once again be characterized by robust cooperation. The anti-Americanism thesis suggests this can happen once anti-American sentiment has dissipated. The policy rift thesis, on the other hand, asserts that cooperation can be restored once congruous U.S.-ROK perceptions of the North have been established and/or the North Korean nuclear issue has been resolved.

In sum, neither the anti-Americanism thesis nor the policy rift thesis sufficiently addresses these critical questions; both have limited explanatory power. Instead, the answers must come from a careful examination of the ways in which Koreans and Americans view U.S.-ROK relations, because, as mentioned earlier, they appear to employ different lenses, or frameworks, in understanding the relationship. That is, not only should the examination address how Koreans and Americans have assessed their bilateral relationship over time, but, more importantly, it must also discern the conceptual frameworks wherein such assessments have been made. If there is strong evidence that Koreans and Americans indeed utilize different frameworks, then an explanation must be provided as to why. Doing so must involve a nuanced examination of sentiment, conceptually separating that which is critical of the other country from that which is critical of the bilateral relationship or the alliance.

This study examines changing U.S.-ROK relations in the context of American and South Korean views about each other, their bilateral relationship, and the DPRK, as recorded through the print media from 1992 to 2003. The study is based on the premises that perceptions matter in international relations and that the news media offer insights into the influence of perception.

Identity Versus Policy in the U.S.-ROK Relationship

Although the U.S.-ROK relationship has become more comprehensive over the years, a military alliance still forms its core. Alliance formation is a critical tool in international politics, and nations establish alliances to increase their security by merging their capabilities against a common enemy.

According to the *neorealist theory* of international relations, the way in which power is distributed determines the nature of the system (e.g., unipolar, bipolar, multipolar) and, in turn, shapes how states will pursue their interests within that system (balancing or bandwagoning).[26] This theory also explains how shifts in power disparities between allies can challenge alliances and how alliance commitments may become more fluid in a multipolar world (rather than a bipolar one).[27] Alliances can be symmetric or asymmetic, depending on the relative power of the involved partners, and, like many other institutions, alliances change over time.

In neorealist terms, the U.S.-ROK alliance has been asymmetric. Although South Korea is a sovereign state, the United States acted as its patron, in both military and economic terms, for decades. The existing literature on alliance politics has addressed this type of asymmetry in power between allies. James Morrow, for instance, lays out a basic theoretical framework for alliances between unequal partners, emphasizing the trade-off between autonomy and security that each partner accepts as part of an alliance bargain. In his view, asymmetrical alliances are easier to form and tend to last longer, because each side receives different (complementary) benefits and can deliver its end of the bargain.[28] Glenn Snyder also details how the relative balance of power and degree of dependence among allies can determine the course of alliance management. In his view, the more dependent a state is, the more likely the costs and risks of abandonment (defection) will outweigh those of entrapment (being committed to a situtation wherein the interests of one side are not necessarily served).[29]

Therefore, in an asymmetric alliance, such as the U.S.-ROK relationship, it is reasonable to expect the partners to have different interests and to approach the alliance accordingly. As Morrow points out, both the patron (larger state) and client (smaller state) view each other through diverse lenses that are driven by different motivations based on notions of power and alliance. In more general terms, one can argue that the client views the alliance in larger terms than does the patron. For the client state, the patron is not just a partner in sharing common interests. Instead, it often functions as a "significant other" in forming its national identity, and discussions tend to focus on the overarching purpose of the alliance. On the other hand, for the patron state, the alliance is more narrowly defined as a policy issue, and the scope and depth of discussions are limited.

In other words, as this study shows, for the client state, the alliance is often related to the larger question of identity, while for the patron state, it is

TABLE I.I
Power disparity, perception, and frameworks in alliance

Power status	Relationship	Framework for conceptualizing alliance
Minor power	Sees partner as significant other	Linked to identity issue
Major power	Does not see partner as significant other	Interest-based policy issue

a matter of a specific policy. Table I.I summarizes this dynamic, which will be expanded throughout this book.

In understanding the U.S.-ROK relationship, one must consider the dynamics arising from power disparities that exist between the two nations. To South Korea, in particular, the United States is not simply another state in the international system with which it shares interests. Rather, the United States has been a significant other, shaping South Korea's national identity in the post-1945 era;[30] from its position as patron, the United States and its anticommunist banner heavily influenced South Korea's constructed identity.[31] For the United States, however, South Korea served principally as a strategic bulwark against regional communist advancement during the cold war era. Thus, while U.S.-ROK relations became a pillar of national identity for Koreans, for Americans, the alliance was a matter of policy with little, if any, particular bearing on the national psyche. The alliance was one of several similar security arrangements constructed to serve larger strategic goals. These different perceptions of the alliance stem from a basic power disparity that initially existed between the two states.

Accordingly, the evolution of South Korean views on U.S.-ROK relations over the last 15 years must be placed in the context of identity politics, reflecting a larger societal effort or trend, led by progressives, to redefine South Korea's position in the emergent post–cold war and postauthoritarian era and a newly developing Asian regional order featuring the rise of China.[32] Although the power disparity between the allies has decreased, for South Koreans, who are considering their nation's new place in the region and in the world, the United States is not just another country but one that has significantly shaped their past and will shape their future as well. As sociological theory suggests, formation of a social identity presupposes the existence of one or more significant others, and the United States is one such other shaping the national identity of South Koreans.

Yet the converse does not fit this mold: Americans do not view Korea as a significant other impacting their national identity. Under these terms, perhaps only England, during the American struggle for independence and the early years of the republic, and the Soviet Union, during the cold war, have been prominent enough others to be capable of affecting Americans' concept of national identity. Instead, for Americans, relations with South Korea are largely based on policy concerns and strategic interests in the region. It can even be argued that Korean policy is only part of the larger U.S. policy approach to East Asia, in which Japan and China are the foremost considerations. Thus, from the American perspective, it is understandable that the strain in the alliance has largely been perceived and explained as stemming from a rift over divergent policy approaches to North Korea.

To adequately understand the ways in which South Koreans approach issues related to U.S.-ROK relations, one first needs to acknowledge that the significance of the issues extends beyond policy and domestic politics[33] to deeper questions of national identity. Accordingly, the anti-Americanism thesis must be expanded and reframed to fit the larger context of identity politics. This expanded analytical framework can be termed the *identity thesis.* At the same time, the policy rift thesis has explanatory power in terms of the U.S. approach to U.S.-ROK relations, since Americans tend to conceive of these issues in the context of policy.

It is the central contention of this book that the U.S.-ROK relationship is linked to the issue of national identity for Koreans, while it is largely a matter of policy for Americans. The difference in these respective frameworks for U.S.-ROK relations stems from these two nations' relative levels of power and roles in the international system and has important implications in understanding the nature and evolution of the bilateral relationship.

Identity Politics in Korea's Relations with the United States

Korea's geographic location has long meant that Koreans have had to be keenly aware of their bigger neighbors, who, at different times, have dominated the peninsula and used it as a battlefield. This was the case during the Sino-Japanese War of 1894–1895, the Russo-Japanese War of 1904–1905, and the Korean War of 1950–1953. Despite centuries of attempted foreign influence, the Korean people were able to retain their territory and sovereignty (except under Japanese rule in the first half of the twentieth century) as well as their identity. After World War II, however, the peninsula was broken into two competing states, and throughout the cold war, both vied to be the sole legitimate representative of the Korean (ethnic) nation. Korea's national identity politics, which underlies the recently changing orientation of South Korean views toward the North and the United States, is grounded in these geographical and historical contexts.

It is illustrative to compare the current Korean identity politics to that of a century ago. Like South Koreans today, Koreans then were seeking to reposition their nation in relation to a newly emerging regional and world order. Their quest reflected the decline of China, the rise of Japan, and the increasing presence of the West (especially Russia) in Northeast Asia.[34] It was during this period that the concept of *nation* emerged as the crucial foundation of a new collective identity among Koreans. Nationalism—especially *ethnic nationalism,* stressing the shared bloodline and ancestry of the Korean people—became dominant. After 1910, as Korea endured the oppressive rule of Japanese colonialism, the politics of national identity intensified. Koreans resisted colonial assimilation, which threatened to impose Japanese culture and identity, by stressing the purity and uniqueness of the Korean nation. Indeed, Japanese rule neither erased nor weakened Korea's national identity but rather reinforced its sense of ethnic national identity based on a shared bloodline—a concept that remains powerful today in both North and South Korea.[35]

During this time, the United States was not a significant other against which Koreans shaped their sense of national identity. Rather, in the late-nineteenth and early twentieth centuries, the key influences on Korean identity were China, Japan, and Russia (representing the West). This is not to say that the United States did not have any effect on the Korean peninsula during this time. As is often cited in Korea, under the 1905 Taft-Katsura Agreement, the United States recognized Japan's control of Korea (essentially violating an earlier commitment to the Korean kingdom) in return for Japan's acknowledgment of U.S. rights to the Philippines. The United States also maintained a significant but largely nonpolitical presence in terms of American missionaries and educators, who played a key role in building modern institutions such as schools and hospitals.

Only after 1945 did the United States become involved in Korean affairs in earnest. It established a military government in the South (1945–1948) and fought the communists in defense of the Southern regime during the Korean War (1950–1953). In the process, the United States became a major (and arguably, the most important) significant other, shaping identity in both the North and the South. As North Korea was proclaimed to be built on anti-imperialist credentials, anti-Americanism became an indispensable element of national identity.[36] In the South, however, the United States was considered the savior of the Korean nation, having liberated the country from the shackles of colonialism and prevented it from falling under communist rule. South Koreans also widely regarded the United States as an important partner in Korean modernization.

Since this time, the main pillar of U.S.-ROK relations has been the military alliance. Formed as a response to a common threat—communist North Korea—at the end of the Korean War, the alliance developed into a prosperous, robust, and successful relationship in the following half century. The U.S.-ROK alliance, along with the U.S.-Japan alliance, formed the hub-and-spoke basis of U.S. security arrangements in East Asia, a region where no multilateral security architecture existed, as in Europe (e.g., NATO).[37] For much of the cold war, the U.S.-ROK alliance stood strong and remained vital.

Empowered by the U.S. security guarantee and large amounts of economic and military aid,[38] the ROK accomplished impressive economic growth, making the nation, in one expert's view, "Asia's next giant" after Japan.[39] Under U.S. pressure, South Korea normalized its relations with Japan in 1965 and became a partner in the virtual trilateral security alliance with the United States and Japan. The United States enjoyed rights to a strategically significant forward deployed location (at the conjuncture of three major powers in the Northeast Asian region: Japan, China, and Russia) at a relatively low cost, and South Korea sent troops to Vietnam in support of the U.S. fight against communism. For decades, the U.S.-ROK alliance represented an exemplary military partnership, not only because it continued to successfully deter the North but also because both governments and their constituents believed that the alliance continued to serve their respective interests.[40]

Until the early 1980s, most South Koreans viewed the United States and the alliance quite positively. A 1982 poll taken by the newspaper *Donga Ilbo*, for instance, showed that the country most liked by Koreans was clearly the United States (61.6%) and that more than half of Koreans (58.1%) rated U.S.-ROK relations as "satisfactory." As Tim Shorrock points out, "The legacy of anti-communism and memories of the Korea war . . . [produced a] feeling of genuine warmth toward the U.S. for supporting South Korea with the sacrifice of thousands of young men and millions of dollars in aid."[41] Even dissidents and activists opposed to the authoritarian regimes generally believed the United States to be a friendly power that would support their efforts for democratizing Korea.

Crucial to deteriorating views of the United States among South Koreans was the Kwangju uprising and massacre in May 1980. Initially a student demonstration in this southwestern city of South Korea, the uprising escalated into an armed struggle that mobilized hundreds of thousands of citizens against the seizure of power by General Chun Doo Hwan, who responded with brutal suppression. Many Koreans expected that the United States would—or indeed, believed the United States had an obligation to—actively intervene to stop the armed confrontation and support their movement. Instead, the U.S. military command was alleged to have released South Korean paratroopers for redeployment to Kwangju, where they killed hundreds of civilian protestors. This perceived U.S. involvement in the suppression of a civic uprising and alleged support of the Chun dictatorship unleashed an anti-American movement in the 1980s as part of Korea's prodemocracy movement, even though U.S. officials later denied most of the allegations.[42]

Beyond this specific event, anti-Americanism reflected a growing Korean resentment of U.S. political and economic dominance in the South.[43] In a sense, this changing view was inevitable, since Korea was becoming economically prosperous and seeking enhanced international status. Yet even through this resentment, most Koreans continued to believe in the importance of opposing communism, and they did not question the necessity of the alliance. Anti-American sentiment did *not* translate into anti-alliance sentiment and was not seen in institutional politics. The looming threat of an aggressive, formidable, communist North during the cold war years, concentrated in South Korean minds by sporadic terrorism and hostile actions against South Koreans, continued to motivate the ROK to seek solidarity with its protector and benefactor.

The late 1980s and early 1990s brought important structural changes to South Korea. Internally, the ROK democratized, and externally, it witnessed the collapse of the Soviet empire. In the post–cold war context, the imperative and power of anticommunist ideology was weakened significantly, and the Korean government pursued a Northern policy, normalizing relations with Russia and China. At the same time, South Korea was becoming a democracy and developing into a vibrant civil society, thus expanding and diversifying national discourse on a number of key issues, including the North and U.S.-ROK relations.[44] These changes led South Koreans to re-think their position and identity built during the authoritarian, cold war years.

A turning point in South Korea's politics of national identity that had great implications for the U.S.-ROK relationship occurred with the imple-mentation of Kim Dae Jung's Sunshine Policy. The election of Kim Dae Jung, a longtime opposition leader, to the presidency not only signaled a maturing democracy in the South but also marked a new policy toward the North. Since President Kim's inauguration in early 1998, he had force-fully promoted his vision for bringing reconciliation, peace, and eventual reunification to the Korean peninsula. South Koreans in the 1990s were increasingly concerned by the prospect of a heavy financial burden if a hasty reunification occurred, having seen the costly unification process of Ger-many. The Sunshine Policy was inspired by this new thinking, and support-ers argued that it would be prudent to extend a peaceful coexistence for a lengthy period, during which the North's economy could be strengthened to minimize the financial consequences of eventual reunification.

Two key assumptions underpinned this policy: first, the two Koreas would not continue their cold war animosity and confrontation, and sec-ond, the Northern regime would be reasonable enough to accept changes to improve the quality of life for its people and to appreciate its common ethnicity with the South.[45] President Kim's policy set business and political relations on separate tracks and advocated economic aid to the North to foster and support DPRK efforts at reform. As stated by Kim's minister of foreign affairs and trade, Hong Soon Young, "Seoul's constructive engage-ment policies aim for peaceful coexistence. . . . The immediate priorities are to alleviate the human pain caused by division, to secure peace and stability, and to promote the common *identity* of all Koreans" (emphasis added).[46]

Kim Dae Jung's engagement policy toward the North led to a series of landmark diplomatic achievements and concrete projects, including South Korean tourism to Mt. Kumgang in the North. Most notably, the June 2000 Pyongyang summit between President Kim Dae Jung and DPRK National Defense Commission Chairman Kim Jong Il marked the first meeting be-tween the top leaders of the two Koreas since the peninsula was partitioned in 1945. Similarly unprecedented high-level military talks between the North and South Korean delegations followed. These achievements led to a change in the tenor of the relationship, and in the South, the North came to be viewed less as a threat and more as a compatriot.[47] A Korean Broadcasting System (KBS) survey conducted soon after the summit showed that 50.2 percent of South Koreans believed Kim Jong Il was politically trustworthy, compared to only 15.1 percent before the summit. Koreans were surprised that the figure they had been taught to regard as a dangerous communist seemed like a "modern, practical and intelligent man."[48] Even by the time the euphoria had dissipated, approximately six months after the summit, polls still showed that more than 40 percent of South Koreans believed the North had become an "equal cooperation partner" (down from 50 percent directly after the summit).[49]

This shifting view of the North triggered a corresponding change in South Korean views of the United States and the U.S.-ROK alliance. Because the alliance was built on the threat from the North, views of the two were inevitably related. More specifically, North Korea's economic decline led many South Koreans to perceive their neighbor as weak, while new contact with the North decreased the threat felt by South Koreans. The South's long-held notions of the North as a strong, threatening other were shattered.

These developments meant that the need for the U.S. security guarantee was not felt as strongly as it had been in the past.[50] United States troops became less valued as a deterrent, and the social and political consequences of U.S. military deployment in South Korea, especially in increasingly urban areas, seemed less tolerable. Under these new circumstances, U.S. forces appeared to some as an unnecessary inconvenience or, even worse, as an infringement on South Korean sovereignty, a source of interference in Korean politics, and a symbol of national stigma. Some in the South even came to portray the United States and the alliance as the essential obstacle to improvement in inter-Korean relations and eventual unification. Although one of President Roh's closest advisors strongly refuted these ideas, he asserted that it was widely perceived that "the core of bilateral friction lies in . . . [the] trade-off between inter-Korean engagement and the ROK-U.S. alliance."[51]

The Roh Moo Hyun administration went a step further in seeking to reorient Korean identity away from the nation's close ties with the United States.[52] While continuing his predecessor's policy of engagement with the North, President Roh also pressed for a more region-centered foreign policy.

Proclaiming an "era of Northeast Asia" (*tongpuk a sidae*), he asserted that the Republic of Korea must actively participate in the new era by becoming a hub in the region, going so far as to make the case that Korea could serve as a "balancer" in Northeast Asia. This initiative was widely interpreted as a veiled strategy to weaken the U.S.-ROK alliance and move closer to China, and it proved controversial both within and outside South Korea.[53] Even legislative leaders seemed to support this regionalist orientation. An April 2004 survey of members of the ruling Uri Party, taken immediately after general elections, showed that 50 percent listed China as Korea's most important ally, while only 42 percent believed that their nation's treaty ally, the United States, continued to occupy this position. This pro-China attitude marked a significant departure from the previous focus on the United States as Korea's most important ally and could be seen as reflecting the discontent with the United States harbored by a new generation of policy elites.[54]

This new outlook was not simply a matter of policy or strategy but rather was underpinned by Korea's new politics of identity. As Gilbert Rozman points out in his book on Northeast Asian regionalism, "National identity is the foundation of state power and foreign policy. To accept regionalism means to redefine one's country's identity."[55] South Koreans, led by progressives, have been actively seeking to redefine their position vis-à-vis foreign powers such as the United States and China, in addition to the DPRK. Their evolving view of how their relationships with these nations contributes to their sense of themselves as a nation is closely related to a changing regional and global order.[56]

However, not all Koreans' views have shifted in this way. Evolving perceptions of the kind of relationship that South Korea should have with the North and the United States, led by progressives and the administrations of Kim Dae Jung and Roh Moo Hyun, have provoked strong reactions and dissent from conservatives in the South. Although not necessarily opposed to engagement per se with the North,[57] conservatives remained skeptical that the North would change, and they have demanded greater reciprocity within inter-Korean relations.[58] In their view, North Korea's nuclear activities are a clear violation of the bilateral North-South agreements of the early 1990s, and the North Korean threat has not yet diminished. Accordingly, the pursuit of rapprochement under these conditions seems disconcerting, at best. As such, Korean conservatives have come to underline the importance of the U.S.-ROK alliance in even stronger terms than was traditionally the case. The bitter contention between progressives and conservatives on North Korea and alliance issues has been referred as <u>the "South-South conflict" or "a house divided."</u>[59]

Spurred by intense debate over how to approach North Korea and the alliance, the politics of identity reemerged in the South in earnest. As political scientist J. J. Suh asserts, South Korea has been "caught between two conflicting identities: the alliance identity that sees the United States as a friendly provider and the nationalist identity that pits Korean identity against the United States."[60] The former represents an established viewpoint that conservatives have maintained, while the latter is a new relationship framework that progressives promote in addition to being a reaction to the past. Despite having very different points of view, both groups seek to define their vision for national identity with reference to the United States and the DPRK. The nationalist identity, especially in the form of progressive presidential administrations, clashed with the Bush administration's tough line on the DPRK, engendering tension in U.S.-ROK relations. Seen this way, the allies' rift over DPRK policy was the most recent manifestation of alliance discord that is tied to shifting attitudes about Korea's place in the region and the world and its reassessment of its role in its asymmetric alliance with the United States.

Anti-American sentiment and policy incongruity are thus only part of the larger identity story that explains the strain in U.S.-ROK relations. What is required is a broader and more contextual explanation of identity politics and Korean efforts, led by progressive forces, to redefine their position in relation to significant others, such as the United States, in the postauthoritarian, post–cold war environment.

U.S. Policy Toward the Korean Peninsula

The modern U.S.-ROK relationship has far exceeded the expectations that any American present at its 1945 inception may have had. At that time, the United States was largely unprepared to address Korea's needs in the wake of Japan's surrender.

In fact, before the Korean War, South Korea had not figured prominently into U.S. strategic thinking about the region, as evidenced by its location outside Dean Acheson's famous "defense perimeter." According to Victor Cha, "Even after the Truman administration committed to defend the

South after the North's invasion in June 1950, Korea remained a remote, unknown, alien place that was strategically important to defend (i.e., keep out of communist hands), but intrinsically meaningless to Americans."[61] Yet out of the Korean War, an alliance was forged, and it would come to be a centerpiece of U.S. security in Asia during the cold war and beyond. Buoyed by the shared threat of North Korea, U.S. and ROK leaders worked together to strengthen deterrence, while simultaneously developing strong economic and political ties.

As the cold war intensified in East Asia, the United States went one step further to consolidate its military cooperation architecture by melding its separate alliance relationships with South Korea and Japan into a new security triangle. The United States needed a more robust and coordinated security strategy in its fight against international communism in East Asia, but the contentious history between Japan and South Korea made accomplishing this difficult. The United States persistently pushed for the triangular quasi-alliance, taking on the role of a security patron to its East Asian clients, and South Korea and Japan normalized their relations in 1965, two decades after the end of colonial rule. As Cha describes, the resulting triangular relationship was an "anti-Communist defense network in Northeast Asia" that would persist throughout the cold war.[62]

The power of the United States to shape the alliance agenda was proven again when the ROK government was asked to send its troops to support the U.S. war effort in Vietnam during the late 1960s and early 1970s. Yet despite a commitment of South Korean troops to Vietnam, the period was marked by considerable uncertainty regarding the definition and future of the U.S. role in the peninsula. Due to the U.S. overextension of military forces (and national wealth) to the Indochina conflict, President Nixon issued the Guam Doctrine, which called for rationalizing the U.S. military presence in East Asia and shifting certain roles, missions, and costs to U.S. allies. South Koreans reacted with surprise and concern to this policy and the U.S. troop reductions in South Korea that were a part of it. As Cha describes, "At the heart of ROK concerns was therefore a proliferation of doubt regarding U.S. dependability as a great power patron. Korea could no longer take for granted the notion of an automatic intervention which had underpinned the United States-ROK alliance for decades."[63]

This general sense of uncertainty was only aggravated by the incoming Carter administration's professed intent to withdraw all U.S. ground forces from the ROK by 1982. The Carter Plan was a product of its times: a national mood of despair and neoisolationism in the wake of the Vietnam defeat, a military retrenchment, a result of economic challenges arising both from the protracted war effort and the "oil shock" administered by the oil producers' cartel (OPEC), and a conviction that U.S. allies could and should assume a greater share of the costs associated with defending freedom against communist advances. While the plan was ultimately shelved in the face of congressional opposition and negative reactions by U.S. allies and friends, the U.S.-ROK alliance was visibly tested on a whole new level. South Koreans, fearing U.S. abandonment, began to consider adjustments that would serve to insulate the ROK against the consequences of U.S. action or inaction.

By the late 1970s and 1980s, other significant changes were transforming the shape and dynamics of the U.S.-ROK alliance. South Korea remained a security client, but it was also becoming important to the United States as a trading partner. The military authoritarian regime of Park Chung Hee, which took power in 1961 and was cushioned by the U.S. security umbrella as it pursued its strategic objectives on the peninsula and in Asia, pursued a top-down economic development strategy that produced speedy, successful modernization. By the late 1980s, South Korea had attained a kind of parity in its relationship with the United States, and by the 1990s, it had become the United States' seventh-largest trading partner. With its rising economic power, the ROK increased its burden sharing in the alliance, while U.S. defense aid was gradually phased out.

Despite these emerging new dynamics, security based on mutual cooperation remained a top priority to both the United States and South Korea as they focused on the North Korean nuclear challenge, which became apparent in the early 1990s. Although the alliance had been well aware of the DPRK's stealth plan for developing atomic weapons since the 1970s, it was not until 1992 that intelligence yielded a clear picture of the North's emerging nuclear capability. After a series of tense, high-level meetings involving Washington, the United Nations, and Pyongyang, DPRK nuclear endeavors were left unstopped by their reneging on Nuclear Non-Proliferation Treaty (NPT) commitments, including their resistance to International Atomic Energy Agency (IAEA) inspections. The nuclear standoff reached a climax when North Korea announced its withdrawal from the NPT and the United States began to consider a military response.

Through all of this, the ROK government was alarmed both at the on-rushing nature of events and the apparent disposition of the United States to ignore its counsel and interests. A crisis was averted at the eleventh hour due to former President Jimmy Carter's private mission to the DPRK. In the course of his meeting with Kim Il Sung, Carter successfully negotiated the North's willingness to freeze its nuclear activities in exchange for another round of talks with the United States and a North-South summit.

Although initially perturbed by President Carter's private diplomacy, the Clinton administration embraced the results and quickly launched a diplomatic negotiating process that resulted in the signing of an Agreed Framework to address all issues relating to North Korea's nuclear program. Joel Wit, the State Department's Agreed Framework coordinator, recalls that the process sorely tested the U.S.-ROK alliance:

> For the Clinton administration, the politics in Washington and with Seoul were often as challenging as dealing with the North. South Korean president Kim Young Sam dealt with the nuclear crisis as a critical domestic issue for his government, which it surely was. But his political needs led him at times to take positions or make inflammatory statements that undermined his American ally in its negotiations with the North, if they played well in the South. And more often than not, they did.[64]

Although policy coordination was often imperfect—as it was during President Carter's bid to downsize the U.S. troop presence on the peninsula and during the Clinton administration's handling of a DPRK submarine incursion and negotiations over its nuclear programs—both sides remained cognizant of their relationship's larger strategic rationale. More often than not, U.S. administrations strongly supported South Korean leaders' nascent efforts at engagement with the North, from the Red Cross talks through President Roh Tae Woo's 1988 policy to draw North Korea into the international system (what a State Department memo at the time called "a major—indeed historic—reversal of traditional ROK government policy").[65] Even when Washington viewed Pyongyang's aggressive development of nuclear and missile capabilities as a major security threat, the Bush (George H. W.) and Clinton administrations believed that engaging North Korea, while maintaining a deterrent posture and tight policy coordination with Seoul, was the best way to address this threat and had to be made the default U.S. policy.

The 1994 Agreed Framework came under heavy fire from conservative critics in the United States, especially Republicans in Congress. In 1999, a House Republican advisory group on North Korea issued a report that questioned the merits of engagement and claimed that "the comprehensive threat posed by North Korea to our national security has increased since 1994 . . . [as there are] a number of serious weaknesses concerning current U.S. policy toward North Korea."[66] Another 1999 report by Asia specialists and more moderate Republicans (who would be appointed to key positions in the State Department under the administration of George W. Bush) called the Clinton administration's approach to North Korea "politically unsustainable." It urged for a more comprehensive approach that conceptualized the Agreed Framework as the *beginning* of formulating a coherent, disciplined North Korea policy, rather than as any kind of resolution. This report also recommended greater consultation with allies South Korea and Japan and the presentation of an integrated deal to North Korea.[67]

Not surprisingly, when the new Bush administration came into power, it pursued a so-called ABC ("anything but Clinton") approach in its policy toward the DPRK. However, some time passed before the new government clearly established its North Korea policy. Even when President Kim Dae Jung visited the White House in March 2001 to meet with the newly inaugurated President Bush, key posts such as deputy secretary of state and assistant secretary of state for East Asia and Pacific affairs were still unfilled, as appointees remained locked in congressional approval processes. During this meeting, the new U.S. president lent rhetorical support to Kim Dae Jung's Sunshine Policy, but he unequivocally expressed his lack of trust of North Korea and asserted that there must be a better verification mechanism for nuclear compliance. The result of the meeting was colored by sensationalized media accounts, poor timing, and a lack of policy on the U.S. side. President Bush had spoken only in general terms, as his government had not yet formulated a policy on North Korea.[68] Statements of U.S. policy had apparently come into conflict with inter-Korean relations and the interests of the progressive Kim government.

The Bush administration announced the conclusion of its DPRK policy review in June 2001, confirming that this White House would take a harder line on North Korea. While the review concluded that the 1994 Agreed Framework should not be scrapped or renegotiated, as some Republicans had called for, it expanded the agenda for negotiations (to include conventional arms control) and advocated more rigorous verification measures related to the North's ballistic missile programs.[69] This more comprehensive approach officially raised the bar for progress in U.S.-DPRK relations.

Three months later, the terrorist attacks of September 11 transformed U.S. strategic thinking. The greatest threat came to be perceived as the nexus of rogue states with WMD capabilities and terrorist intent to strike the U.S. homeland and its interests abroad. Thus, when the second North Korean nuclear crisis broke out in October 2002, it was immediately couched in terms of nonproliferation. The administration eventually engaged in multilateral diplomacy and accepted a "carrot-and-stick" approach. However, Washington refused to talk to North Korea for months, insisting that it abandon its nuclear weapons program, and instead pursued a policy of isolation.[70] At the same time, South Korea vowed to continue inter-Korean engagement, despite the nuclear crisis.

The two governments were out of sync. While Washington viewed the North as part of an axis of evil and pursued a policy to contain this threat, Seoul had no intention of suspending or even toughening its engagement policy, which implicitly assumed (correctly or incorrectly) that DPRK belligerence derived from insecurity, and therefore aid and security assurances would reduce this threat. This was not simply a matter of poor coordination but rather a case of diametrically opposed policy approaches on the very issue that formed the basis of the alliance: the threat from North Korea. The South was no longer willing just to follow the U.S. lead in addressing its security affairs. According to Cha, "At the heart of this gap [were] parallel paradigm shifts in foreign policy that [had] taken place in Washington and Seoul" in the post–September 11, post–Sunshine Policy era, respectively.

Thus, even after policy coordination had been ostensibly restored, as the ROK agreed to press for the U.S.-formulated CVID (complete, verifiable, irreversible dismantlement) approach to North Korea's nuclear weapons development, the two governments remained suspicious of each other's intentions (i.e., Seoul's apparent desire to prop up Pyongyang at almost any cost and Washington's inclination toward regime change). The ROK's lack of participation in U.S. programs such as missile defense and the Proliferation Security Initiative (PSI) further reduced "Washington's confidence in Seoul's capacity as an ally."[71] Although the ROK was able to make deployments in support of the U.S. war on terror,[72] the DPRK was a clear case in which Seoul and Washington's interests, as defined by these shifts in the foreign policy paradigm, came into direct conflict.[73]

In contrast to the Korean perspective, the U.S. perspective saw differences in approaches to the DPRK—between the Clinton and Bush administrations, within the Bush administration, and between the United States and the ROK—as being based on varying preferences (informed by interpretation of interests, threats, and the effectiveness of various tools) for a range of possible programs of government action. Although differences of opinion on how best to approach North Korea may be sharp within the United States, this is a rather esoteric issue, generally debated within the policy arena and not within the context of U.S. national identity. The United States' sense of national identity most assuredly impacts its foreign policy, but this connection is tangential, at best, in the case of Korea. This explains, at least in part, why no broad anti-Koreanism existed in American society, even when anti-Americanism erupted in the South and captured U.S. media attention in 2002.

About This Book

This book examines U.S.-ROK relations from 1992 to 2003, a period that may very well come to be remembered as the height of both identity politics in South Korea and policy discord between the two allies. This period witnessed the end of the cold war, Korean full democratization, inter-Korean engagement, two nuclear crises, and the beginning of the U.S. war on terror—all occurring in the span of a decade. This period thus offers a good window to test this book's principal arguments regarding the identity and policy rift theses.

In South Korea, democratization and the end of the cold war led South Koreans to rethink their place in the region and the world, a process that prompted questioning of conventional views of their nation's relationships with the United States and North Korea. During the study period, the United States has dealt with two nuclear standoffs with the DPRK, with the second crisis occurring in the context of the war on terror. As North Korean issues are said to be at the heart of changes in the U.S.-ROK relationship from both countries' perspectives, this period presents a fascinating opportunity to examine how differing frameworks for conceptualizing North Korea and the alliance have affected U.S.-ROK relations and what kind of indelible mark such a disparity may have left on the future of the relationship.

In examining U.S.-ROK relations during the study period, newly collected data from three major U.S. daily newspapers—the *New York Times*, the *Washington Post*, and the *Wall Street Journal*—as well as two Korean daily newspapers—*Chosun Ilbo* and *Hankyoreh Shinmoon*—were used. If one is to believe that news is a kind of "first draft of history" and that perception matters in politics and international relations, then media analysis can serve as an important gauge of the bilateral relationship. In addition, the news media chronicle political positions and can impact foreign policy making. Therefore, content analysis of news coverage can offer insights into policy orientations and constraints in the two nations. (See Chapter 2 for a detailed discussion of the value of media data.)

More specifically, the following research questions are addressed in this book:

First, the book addresses how U.S. and South Korean newspapers have depicted the U.S.-ROK relationship since the early 1990s by measuring media attention (or news *volume*) and media sentiments (or news *tone*) in the two nations. In particular, the research is interested in identifying main issues and problem areas in U.S.-ROK relations presented in the press during the height of identity politics and policy discord (i.e., those issues that have received the most media attention and the most negative coverage in the United States and Korea). With this, the book seeks to show whether and where any gaps exist in coverage and/or perception between the two allies.

Second, the book examines temporal fluctuations in press coverage of U.S.-ROK relations in both countries. Here, the research is particularly interested in investigating if media attention was event specific or certain identifiable trends in news volume occurred over the years. This examination has crucial implications for the future, because if increased press coverage reflected a certain identifiable trend, then one must ask whether that trend is likely to continue and, if so, whether it will exert any significant impact on the U.S.-ROK relationship in coming years. Likewise, temporal changes in news media tone are assessed, with particular interest in evaluating whether the news media have turned more negative toward U.S.-ROK relations in recent years, as many experts have argued, and, if so, what this might mean for the future of the bilateral relationship.

Third, since changing views of the DPRK are perceived to be closely related to changing views of U.S.-ROK relations, the book analyzes media views of the North in both countries. More specifically, the research seeks to assess whether from the South Korean perspective, the DPRK is inherently tied to national identity, and whether from the U.S. perspective, the DPRK is indeed more narrowly defined as a policy issue, as argued earlier. This study also examines temporal fluctuations in press coverage of the DPRK in both the United States and South Korea to evaluate the validity of the prevailing argument that DPRK issues lie at the heart of changing views of U.S.-ROK relations.

Fourth, the book attempts to isolate a certain point after which the tone of the media coverage of U.S.-ROK relations has changed definitively. To do so, the research undertakes a comparative analysis of media attention and sentiments during various combinations of South Korean and U.S. administrations—first, Kim Young Sam and Clinton; second, Kim Dae Jung and Clinton; third, Kim Dae Jung and Bush; and fourth, Roh and Bush. If the arguments presented earlier are indeed valid, then one would expect the period of overlap between the Kim Dae Jung administration and the Bush administration to be a significant turning point in the U.S. press (per the policy rift thesis), after which the news volume increases, the focus on issues associated with conflicts in the alliance intensifies, and the news tone turns increasingly negative. On the other hand, one would expect a different pattern in the Korean press: consistently negative views of U.S.-ROK relations in the progressive newspaper throughout the 1990s, with the disparity in news tone between progressive and conservative newspapers increasing over time (per the identity thesis).

Fifth, the book tests the central argument of the study—namely, that during the years of the study, the alliance was enmeshed in issues of national identity for South Koreans but issues of national security policy for Americans. Using the Korean data, the research examines how progressives and conservatives have collided over the question of identity and how this conflict intensified with the election of the Kim Dae Jung government and the implementation of the Sunshine Policy. To test the policy rift thesis, the U.S. data are used to compare views on U.S.-ROK relations during the two nuclear crises. Here, the expectation is that relations were not negatively affected during the first nuclear crisis, since the allies took a common approach to the nuclear issue. In contrast, U.S.-ROK relations can be expected to have deteriorated during the current nuclear standoff, due to divergent perceptions of the North Korean threat and the resulting disagreement over the appropriate policy approach.

As a whole, this book is intended to offer rich, empirical data and analysis that will contribute to greater understanding of views of U.S.-ROK relations, as depicted in the news media, over years that may well prove crucial to the future of the alliance. The book will also demonstrate how identity politics has affected Korean views of the alliance and how the policy rift has impacted American views of the relationship. Based on the key empirical findings of this research, the book offers policy suggestions to improve or constructively redefine security-focused U.S.-ROK relations, which after 50 years have come under more sustained and serious criticism than ever before.

To build a future-oriented alliance, it is necessary to understand the underlying causes of strain in the bilateral relationship during these critical years. Although the past must be used as a foundation, building a revitalized relationship should not and cannot mean re-creating past circumstances. What is required is a careful examination of what has happened to the alliance, why it has happened, and how it will affect its future. After discussing policy implications of key findings of this study, this book concludes by offering larger theoretical implications, especially on the role of the news media in international relations and how power asymmetry, or imbalance, shapes perception, which, in turn, affects relations between countries.

TWO

Why the News Media? Data and Methods

This chapter describes in detail the data-collection process, including sampling and coding methods, and assesses the validity and reliability of the data used in this study. First, however, the chapter explains why this study utilizes the news media in examining United States–Republic of Korea (U.S.-ROK) relations and discusses the respective media environments in these two nations.

Why Look to the News Media?

While many experts and pundits have addressed the existence and sources of tension in U.S.-ROK relations, as laid out in the previous chapter, robust empirical data and analytical studies are still needed to thoroughly and systematically understand these dynamics and processes. Many pundits have addressed these issues through opinion-editorials in newspapers largely based on events of the day, their own ideological positions for or against certain administrations or policy factions, experiences in past administrations, anecdotal evidence, or impressionistic observations. In addition, notable studies in this area have tended to rely on public polls taken in either South Korea or the United States.[1] Survey data can be useful in capturing the popular sentiment or perception at a certain time on a particular event or issue, and when carefully assembled, they can also reveal general trends in public views of certain issues over time.

However, using only survey data, it is difficult to capture the *processes* by which the particular views of a foreign nation are discussed, debated, established, and reformulated. Public polls are most often taken in response to significant events or issues of concern and the "snapshot" nature of survey data makes it difficult to identify the causes that have led to the alleged strains in the U.S.-ROK alliance. For instance, there are still no convincing empirical data and analyses to prove or disprove the argument that divergent views of the North Korean nuclear issue strained the bilateral alliance.[2] Moreover, in those studies that utilize survey data, the principal inquiry often relates to how citizens of one country view the policies and actions of another country (e.g., anti-American sentiments in South Korea) and overlooks the *interactive* processes between nations in the formation of public opinion and foreign policy. This study seeks to assess key changes that have occurred in the relationship between the two allies through accounts in the news media. Like any data, media data are far from perfect (i.e., newspapers have their own biases, and content analysis is prone to human subjectivity), but they can offer fresh insight into the questions at hand.

By and large, the news media address issues and events in two principal ways. First, they offer basic *descriptive* or *factual* statements and stories. Descriptive statements and stories are those in which the reporter narrates key events or issues and summarizes recent developments related to them. In addition, the news media offer *evaluative* or *analytical* statements, in which reporters interpret or judge developing events, government policies, foreign nations' actions and motivations, and so on. Often, evaluative statements deal in norms and values; they assess phenomena, suggesting how something should or should not be.

A news story may contain both descriptive and evaluative statements. For instance, if part of a story states that the Democratic People's Republic of Korea (DPRK) has announced it possesses a nuclear weapon and that story goes on to speculate about Kim Jong Il's motivation for developing nuclear weapons, then this story has both descriptive and evaluative elements. Editorials and guest columns carried in newspapers are largely evaluative.

Through these forms of news coverage, the media play a number of important roles. Besides providing readers with factual or descriptive information on key events and issues, news coverage casts the spotlight of public attention on previously obscure or undisputed issues. Quite significantly, the media can frame the terms on which the public debates and evaluates specific policies. Through these priming and framing roles, the news media often set the agenda for public discussion and debate of key policy issues.[3]

A body of literature demonstrates that exposure to news can significantly influence public opinion on foreign policy issues as well as perceptions of other nations.[4]

In both reflecting and shaping public opinion, the mass media can influence foreign policy–making processes. Public opinion, long thought to be largely irrelevant to foreign policy making, has increasingly been accepted as a significant factor in policy decisions.[5] A number of case studies have established the role of public opinion in particular policy areas, such as U.S. relations with China and arms control issues.[6] In the Monroe study, foreign policy corresponded with the policy favored by the majority of Americans in more than 90 percent of the cases examined, and changes in collective public opinion were followed by congruent changes in policy approximately two-thirds of the time.[7] Both Cohen's and Powlick's studies showed that many foreign policy makers see major U.S. newspapers as surrogates for public opinion and often pay particular attention to editorials and opinion columns, which may offer useful ideas or reflect partisan reactions to policies from various segments of the political spectrum.[8]

Most people in the United States and South Korea learn about issues of foreign affairs through the mass media, rather than by direct association or involvement. In the case of South Korea, many suspect that the news media have, at least in part, contributed to the public's changing perceptions of North Korea and the United States.[9] In the United States as well, the news media likely have some influence on Americans' views of Korea, although probably to a lesser degree (for reasons that will be specified later). Despite the media's documented influence in the realm of foreign affairs, the role it plays in shaping issues related to the U.S.-ROK alliance is still not fully understood.[10] This book seeks to fill this research gap by examining press coverage of U.S.-ROK relations in *both* countries.[11]

In offering these media data and analysis, this book aims to lay down a robust empirical foundation for assessing U.S.-ROK relations during the study period, as reflected in the two nations' leading daily newspapers. If one is to believe that news reflects and influences public opinion and national debates over policy and that perception matters in foreign affairs, then these findings can serve as an important gauge of the bilateral relationship. Additionally, these media data can help identify the principal causes of the changes in U.S.-ROK relations. Provided that the news media reflect and influence foreign policy making, as discussed earlier, content analysis of news coverage can also offer a reasonable estimate of policy orientations and constraints in the United States and South Korea.

Media Environments in South Korea and the United States

In considering the media data presented in this book, it is crucial to note the different media environments in the United States and South Korea. In the nineteenth-century United States, most newspapers had an informal party affiliation and openly advocated for their parties' candidates. To publishers such as Joseph Pulitzer, Robert McCormick, and Otis Chandler, providing fiercely partisan coverage was more of a sacred duty than a cause for embarrassment—and it was not a duty that was shirked any more in the news columns than on the editorial pages.[12] The U.S. media environment has evolved significantly since that time, however, and objectivity, nonpartisanship, and high standards of journalistic ethics are now the aims of mainstream media organizations.[13]

In contrast, the media environment in South Korea today is not much different from that of the nineteenth-century United States. The South Korean news media are sharply divided on key policy issues—both domestic and foreign—in accordance with their ideological leanings. As many observers of Korean affairs have noted, a particular Korean media outlet often reflects only one side of a given issue, espousing almost entirely conservative or progressive views, depending on its leadership, orientation, and/ or audience.[14] This sharp division includes views of the North Korea issue and South Korea's relationship with the United States. Most progressive newspapers characterize themselves as nationalist and seek to expedite the inter-Korean reconciliation process while questioning the rationale for the presence of U.S. troops on the Korean peninsula.[15] In contrast, conservative newspapers generally insist that the South Korean government should demand greater reciprocity from North Korea while stressing the strategic importance of the U.S.-ROK alliance in resolving the North Korea problem. Korean newspapers' deep divide and heated debates on key policy issues enhance the importance of analyzing the Korean press to understand South Koreans' changing views of the alliance.

Given these differing degrees of acceptable media partisanship in the United States and Korea, it logically follows that media outlets have quite different relationships with the governments of the two countries. In news reporting, the U.S. media largely maintain a politically neutral stance toward the government. On the editorial pages, outlets can be critical or supportive of specific policies, and some newspapers, such as the *New York Times*, are generally perceived to be more liberal than others, such as the *Wall Street Journal*. But all things considered, as news sources, they are hardly partisan.[16] In sharp contrast, the Korean media are highly partisan, and they maintain relationships with the administration in power according to their ideological leanings. For instance, conservative newspapers supported government policies during the authoritarian years,[17] but they have been highly critical of recent progressive governments. On the other hand, progressive newspapers have maintained congenial relations with the Kim Dae Jung and Roh Moo Hyun administrations in accordance with their ideology.[18]

The U.S. and South Korean news media also differ in terms of the capacity to reach their respective national publics. Compared with their Korean counterparts, U.S. newspapers generally have much smaller circulations. For instance, the *New York Times*, the self-proclaimed U.S. paper of record, has a weekday circulation of only about 1 million. Moreover, in the United States, there is no national newspaper in a strict sense.[19] In contrast, many major news media in South Korea are larger in circulation and national in scope. *Chosun Ilbo* has a daily circulation of more than 2 million, thus reaching a significant portion of the ROK's approximately 47 million people (as of 2005). Even though *Hankyoreh* cannot claim the same volume of circulation, it has strongly influenced policy making, owing to its close association with the progressive governments. The large circulations of the Korean newspapers intensifies the dynamics associated with the politics of identity, as will be shown in later chapters.

Korean and U.S. newspapers cover their nations' relationship in very different ways. It is important to note that Korea (i.e., the U.S.-ROK relationship) is not a main subject of U.S. media attention. In this asymmetric alliance of nations, there is also an asymmetry of attention. As data presented in Chapter 5 will show, major U.S. newspapers accord the ROK about one-quarter the coverage of Japan; the frequency of articles about South Korea is more comparable to that of Italy, Argentina, or Indonesia. Most coverage of Korea comes from Tokyo-based bureaus or news stringers in Seoul.[20] However, coverage of the United States exceeds South Korean media coverage of foreign countries, garnering more attention than even North Korea or China. South Korean newspapers maintain news staff in Washington, DC (and in some cases, also in New York and/or Los Angeles), and these correspondents often write not only news articles but also opinion-editorials on the United States and its relationship with Korea. From July 1992 to July 2003, data show that the number of articles carried by the two Korean newspapers about the United States was three times greater than the number of articles carried by all three U.S. newspapers about *both* Koreas.

Similarly, the nature of U.S. and Korean media coverage of their alliance counterpart is quite different. Among U.S. media, coverage of Korean affairs is largely composed of descriptive articles that feature some news analysis; there is not a sizeable number of editorials or columns on Korean affairs (i.e., fewer than 200 in the 12-year U.S. sample of news on both Koreas). Korean news about the United States features more evaluative content, with a much larger number of editorials and columns (almost 2,000). Thus, even a cursory examination of the data reveals that the United States' place in the Korean media is far more prominent than Korea's place in the U.S. media (see Chapter 5).

These differences in the U.S. and Korean news media have crucial implications for understanding both the research findings and the arguments presented in this book. Overall, the United States is featured much more prominently in the Korean media than Korea is in the U.S. press; this supports the earlier claim that the United States is a "significant other" for Koreans, while Korea is not as important to Americans. In addition, the Korean news media are often evaluative in their coverage of U.S.-related issues, while the U.S. media's coverage of Korean affairs is largely descriptive. The Korean press is highly partisan and far better at reaching the national public. In light of these factors, it is logical to expect more heated debates on U.S.-ROK relations in Korean newspapers than in U.S. newspapers.

News Data

To examine the U.S.-ROK relationship as portrayed in the mass media, newspaper articles were chosen for analysis. Both substantive and practical reasons can be offered for analyzing newspaper content, as opposed to alternative forms of media content, such as network and cable news coverage. On the substantive side, studies illustrate that newspaper accounts of foreign affairs are more comprehensive than those in television news stories (both network and cable). Furthermore, the newspapers chosen for the current study—in both the United States and South Korea—are known to set the agenda for other news outlets.[21] Few local U.S. daily newspapers (dailies) and television stations maintain overseas bureaus or conduct independent coverage of foreign affairs; instead, these outlets rely heavily on the coverage of elite newspapers and news services.[22]

Practical considerations also influenced the decision to examine newspapers. Newspapers are routinely saved and readily searchable in computerized databases. Tapes and transcripts of television news, in contrast, are less accessible, making a systematic and exhaustive examination of television news more difficult. Finally, the presence of visual cues further complicates the task of coding television news.

In studying international news and its effects, it is essential to have extensive, reliable data on news content. For this study, three U.S. dailies and two Korean dailies were selected. The U.S. data were drawn from the *New York Times*, the *Washington Post*, and the *Wall Street Journal*. The *Times* truly has a unique status and is known to influence the agenda of other media outlets in the United States, especially in the domain of foreign affairs. The *Post* is another authoritative source in foreign affairs coverage and the major newspaper in the nation's capital. Therefore, these newspapers' coverage of Korea should be highly correlated with that in other (less prestigious) news outlets in terms of news attention and tone.

In addition, the *Wall Street Journal*, a leading conservative newspaper, was included to represent a wider spectrum of ideological perspectives, as the other two newspapers are perceived to be liberal, to some degree. The *Journal* is also the most influential U.S. financial news source and thus can capture coverage of an important aspect of U.S.-ROK relations: economics and trade.[23] Table 2.1 displays basic statistics and descriptive facts about these three U.S. newspapers.

For the Korean data, the newspapers selected were *Chosun Ilbo* (Chosŏn ilbo) and *Hankyoreh Shinmoon* (Han'gyŏreh sinmun). As noted earlier, the South Korean news media are sharply divided along ideological lines, and this includes their views toward the U.S.-ROK relationship. To account for the current media environment in South Korea, these two newspapers were selected as representations of conservative and progressive views. Conservative *Chosun* has the largest circulation of all Korean newspapers, while *Hankyoreh* is largely considered the most influential progressive newspaper in South Korea.[24] Table 2.2 displays basic statistics about these two South Korean newspapers.

TABLE 2.1
U.S. newspapers

	New York Times	Washington Post	Wall Street Journal
Established	1851	1877	1889
Circulation	1,066,600 Weekday	715,181 Mon.–Fri.	1.7 million
		660,182 Saturday	
	1,529,700 Sunday	983,243 Sunday	
Employees (news staff)	1,200	784	750
Number of foreign bureaus	26	16	42
Bureau in Seoul	No	No	Yes
Bureau in Tokyo*	Yes	Yes	Yes

SOURCES: *New York Times* data (2007): www.nytco.com/investors/financials/nyt-circulation.html; *Washington Post* data (Oct. 2004–Oct. 2005): www.washpost.com/gen_info/quickfacts/info_circ.shtml (Audit Bureau of Circulation data); *Wall Street Journal* data (2007): www.dowjones.com/Products_Services/PrintPublishing/WSJ.htm.

*U.S. foreign correspondents in Tokyo normally have responsibility for Japan, the Koreas, and the Russian Far East, unless the associated newspaper has additional correspondents in these locations.

TABLE 2.2
South Korean newspapers

	Chosun Ilbo	Hankyoreh Shinmoon
Founded	1920	1988
2003 circulation	2,061,928	—*
2003 sales (million won)	438,673	81,798
U.S. bureaus	Washington, DC; New York	Washington, DC

SOURCE: Korea Newspaper Association (KNA).

Hankyoreh does not report its circulation figures to the Korean Newspaper Association.

In this study, the principal data are full-text articles on U.S.-ROK relations in both U.S. and South Korean newspapers ("US DATA ON ROK" and "KOREAN DATA ON US"). To supplement the Korean news data and facilitate examination of the impact of the North Korea issue on U.S.-ROK relations, full-text editorials and columns on North Korea are also included from the two Korean newspapers ("KOREAN DATA ON DPRK"). Similarly, U.S. news data on North Korea are examined ("US DATA ON DPRK").

Despite its utility, content analysis of newspaper articles can be controversial because of its potentially subjective nature. Therefore, in what follows, the coding scheme and data-collection process are described in detail. Subsequently, the validity and reliability of the collected data are assessed.

Data on the United States, Korea, and U.S.-Korea Relations

SAMPLING CRITERIA

For the U.S. data, articles published in the *New York Times* and the *Washington Post* were obtained from the Lexis database, from which all articles published in the two newspapers during the study period were available. *Wall Street Journal* articles were gathered through the Historical Wall Street Journal Archive. Although two different databases were used, identical selection criteria were applied, and therefore, articles selected from the three newspapers are comparable. South Korean news articles were obtained from the KINDS database, the most extensive newspaper archiving database in South Korea.

In selecting relevant news articles, a census of articles was included, rather than a sample. Sampling texts by date or within subject categories makes it more practical to study broader issues over longer time frames than would be possible with a census of news coverage.[25] Yet even with random sampling, it may be difficult to explain how a single, critical story can dramatically alter the shape of coverage.[26] If that article is not captured in the sample, the symptoms may be apparent but the cause may be missed. For example, suppose that the news tone about the U.S.-ROK relationship shifted several times during the study period. A census of articles can better reveal the causes for such shifts.

For the U.S. data, all articles that mentioned "Korea," "Seoul," and/or "Pyongyang" were examined. The rationale for using "Korea" as a key word is obvious, and it is important to note that using it captures stories about both Koreas. Additionally, it is conventional to refer to the governments of the two Koreas as "Seoul" and "Pyongyang." These three keywords seem to have been sufficient to capture nearly all relevant articles.

For the Korean data, parallel key words were used when searching for news articles pertaining to issues involving the United States: "미국," "미" ("America") and "워싱턴" ("Washington"). When examining South Korean newspapers, however, it was necessary to use a few additional key words. First, the Chinese characters corresponding to "미국" (i.e., "美國") and "미" (i.e., "美") had to be used, because they were quite commonly used in South Korean newspapers' headlines. Additionally, it was not uncommon for many headlines with U.S.-related content to indicate this only through inclusion of the U.S. president's last name. This is a discrepancy between the United States and South Korea: Only a small fraction of U.S. newspaper readers would likely recognize the name of the South Korean president, whereas a majority of South Koreans would recognize the name of the U.S. president (especially among newspaper readers, who are typically considered better educated and informed). Accordingly, "클린턴" ("Clinton") and "부쉬/부시" ("Bush") were used as additional key words. Table 2.3 provides a full list of the key words used in database searches for relevant articles.

For newspapers of both countries, additional restrictions were imposed when choosing articles to be included in the study sample. First, if simply searching for these key words, the sample size would have become unmanageable. Accordingly, only the key words listed in Table 2.3 were searched for in the article's *headline*. (That is, articles were screened out that mentioned one or more key words *only* in their texts and *not* in their headlines.) At the practical level, this decision allowed for the sample to remain a reasonable size. More importantly, a vast majority of such articles lacked relevance to the current study. For instance, a large number of these news items appeared in sports sections and simply reported scores from athletic events. However, stories about sporting events in which one of the two Koreas was the main focus did contain at least one of the key words in their headlines and thus were included in the sample.

With these criteria and restrictions, the U.S. data consist of 5,122 valid articles: 2,109 were published in the *New York Times*; 1,219 in the *Washington Post*; and 1,794 in the *Wall Street Journal*. News stories were the most represented article type, comprising 73.5 percent of the U.S. news sample. Special features were the second most represented at 12.3 percent of the sample, and editorials comprised a meager 3 percent of the entire U.S. news sample. The *New York Times* published many more special features than either of the other newspapers, both in absolute and proportional terms. The *Washington Post* carried more regular and guest columns that the other newspapers (see Table 2.4). Overall, the vast majority of stories were original articles (88.6%), and only a minor portion were newswire stories fed by the Associated Press

TABLE 2.3
Key words in U.S. and Korean newspapers

U.S. newspapers	South Korean newspapers
"Korea"	"미", "미국", "美國", "美"
"Seoul"	"워싱턴", "클린턴", "부쉬/부시"
"Pyongyang"	

TABLE 2.4
U.S. news data

Type	New York Times	Washington Post	Wall Street Journal	Total
News story	1,386	941	1,437	3,764
	(65.7)	(77.2)	(80)	(73.5)
News analysis	19	32	5	56
	(0.9)	(2.6)	(.3)	(1.1)
Special feature	432	52	145	629
	(20.5)	(4.3)	(8.1)	(12.3)
Regular column	6	52	3	61
	(0.3)	(4.3)	(0.2)	(1.2)
Guest column	17	49	24	90
	(0.8)	(4)	(1.3)	(1.8)
Unsigned editorial	84	56	34	174
	(4)	(4.6)	(2)	(3.4)
Letters	101	27	19	147
	(4.8)	(2.2)	(1.1)	(2.9)
Other	64	10	127	201
	(3)	(0.8)	(7.1)	(3.9)
TOTAL	2,109	1,219	1,794	5,122
	(100)	(100)	(100)	(100)

NOTE: Parentheses contain percentages.

(AP) or Reuters. The *New York Times* relied more on these newswire services, although the bulk of its articles (79.4%) were original.

Table 2.5 examines the degree to which various article types contained descriptive and evaluative content. Nearly one-half of the sample's content was primarily descriptive (48.8%), more than one-fourth contained both descriptive and evaluative content (28.4%), and just over one-fifth had primarily evaluative content (22.8%).[27] Although there was not great variation among the newspapers, it should be noted that the *New York Times*'s content was slightly more descriptive (54.1%) than average when compared to the other newspapers, while the *Washington Post*'s content tended to be more evaluative (27.3%).

Certain article types tend to be primarily evaluative, while others are primarily descriptive. A slight majority of news analysis articles are primarily evaluative, while just under half are both descriptive and evaluative. Three-quarters of special features are primarily descriptive. Meanwhile, large majorities of regular columns, guest columns, and unsigned editorials and let-

TABLE 2.5
Article type

Type	Descriptive	Evaluative	Both	Total
News story	1,926	636	1,202	3,764
	(77.1)	(54.4)	(82.7)	(73.5)
News analysis	3	29	24	56
	(0.1)	(2.5)	(1.7)	(1.1)
Special feature	475	67	87	629
	(19)	(5.7)	(6)	(12.3)
Regular column	1	43	17	61
	(0.1)	(3.7)	(1.2)	(1.2)
Guest column	5	63	22	90
	(0.2)	(5.4)	(1.5)	(1.8)
Unsigned editorial	0	161	13	174
	(0)	(13.8)	(0.9)	(3.4)
Letters	3	127	17	147
	(0.1)	(10.9)	(1.2)	(2.9)
Other	85	44	72	201
	(3.4)	(3.8)	(5)	(3.9)
TOTAL	2,498	1,170	1,454	5,122
	(100)	(100)	(100)	(100)

NOTE: Parentheses contain percentages.

ters are primarily evaluative. Articles of these types are much more likely to express an opinion or offer an evaluation, and this may or may not occur in tandem with events. (Editorial agendas may play a role apart from events.) In contrast, news stories and special features tend to focus on describing events, and therefore, their publication tracks more closely with events.

For South Korean newspapers, further conditions were stipulated in searching for news articles to be included in the data of this study. Most significantly, *only unsigned editorials and opinion columns were examined.* This was done simply because too many articles would have been selected if the same restrictions applied to U.S. news media had been used. The United States is the most important foreign relations partner for South Korea, and the Korean press devotes a significant amount of coverage to alliance-related issues. Also, editorials and columns are likely to be representative of other articles in important aspects, including news volume and tone. In short, 573 editorials and 1,151 columns were collected from the two newspapers (see Table 2.6). Given that the main task of this research is to gauge the two dailies' views of the United States and U.S.-ROK relations, this data set is sufficiently large.

TABLE 2.6
South Korean data on the United States

	Chosun Ilbo	*Hankyoreh Shinmoon*	All
Editorials	259	314	573
	(27.6)	(39.9)	(33.2)
Columns	678	473	1,151
	(72.4)	(60.1)	(66.8)
TOTAL	937	787	1,724
	(100)	(100)	(100)

NOTE: Parentheses contain percentages.

CODING PROCEDURE

The study of media content can be challenging, because the process of converting the information and views contained in text into numerical data inevitably induces some amount of ambiguity and subjectivity. Therefore, various measures were stringently employed to limit these factors and increase both the validity and reliability of the data.

In content analysis, the norm is for multiple coders to collect data. This is primarily to prevent one coder's idiosyncratic views from dominating the coded data. Throughout this project, eight coders were employed for coding U.S. headlines and articles. All the coders were native English speakers and graduate or mature undergraduate students at Stanford University. In addition, coders were recruited who had at least some background knowledge of issues in East Asia. Arguably, these procedures reduced measurement errors that could have resulted from a coder's inadequate language skills or inability to understand the context of various topics featured in the articles.

Likewise, five coders examined South Korean news about the United States and North Korea, and a majority of these coders were graduate or mature undergraduate students at a major university in South Korea. All were native Korean speakers and had good knowledge of U.S.-related issues. These individuals were trained in Korea before commencing the news data coding.

A key challenge in using multiple coders is ensuring a high degree of so-called intercoder reliability. *Intercoder reliability*, also known as *reproducibility*, refers to the extent to which content classification produces the same results when the same text is coded by more than one coder. Conflicting coding can result from cognitive differences among the coders and/or ambiguous coding instructions. High reproducibility is necessary to ensure the consistency of shared understanding (or meaning) held by two or more coders. Unless there is significant agreement among coders, the collected data cannot be viewed as reliable.

To reach the level of intercoder reliability generally accepted by the research community, a well-defined code book was used. (See the Appendix for an example of a code book used for the U.S. data.) All coders from both countries went through extensive training and were subject to the same training procedures. They were given detailed explanations of each variable and provided numerous examples in initial training sessions. Once all the coders fully understood the definitions of all the variables, they quantified a substantial number of the same articles, from which intercoder reliability was assessed. Sources of disagreement or inconsistency were identified and remedied in subsequent sessions. Testing and revision of the coding scheme continued until between-coder agreement was satisfactory, reaching a level of intercoder reliability considered acceptable by the research community.

Initially, all articles were listed according to their publication dates. Subsequently, the articles were randomly assigned to coders. This practice prevented coder-specific attributes from confounding temporal trends. For instance, suppose that one coder, A, examined all the articles from one year, and a second coder, B, examined all the articles from another year. This approach would introduce an unnecessary confounding variable. To illustrate this point, further suppose that A tends to code the article's tone somewhat more *negatively* than other coders, whereas B tends to evaluate the same series of events more *positively* than others. Presume that the news tone is found to have changed between the two years. Because coder-specific features may interfere with the findings, nothing can necessarily be said about temporal shifts in news tone from one year to another. In this scenario, the observed news tone between the two years could not be attributed to true change, because it could simply reflect differences between the two *coders*. Thus, by the logic of randomization, coder-specific differences were neutralized and do not affect temporal shifts observed in the data.

KEY VARIABLES

For brevity, this discussion focuses on the two principal variables of this study: (1) article focus and (2) article tone.[28]

Article Focus

According to the established coding scheme, first an article's main focus was determined. In the case of U.S. news, the possible categories were "ROK," "DPRK," "U.S.-ROK relations," "U.S.-DPRK relations," and "inter-Korea relations." Most articles fell clearly into only one of these five categories. For example, a majority of stories featuring the recent nuclear standoff between the United States and the DPRK were classified as stories about "U.S.-DPRK relations" (not "DPRK"). Likewise, most articles concerning U.S. troops stationed in the ROK were classified as stories about "U.S.-ROK relations." It should be noted that the article's main topic and focus were not necessarily synonymous, however. To illustrate this point, not all articles concerning the current nuclear crisis concentrated, or *focused*, on interactions (or conflict) between the DPRK and the United States. For example, if the article primarily addressed the alignment of ROK and U.S. interests within the context of the current nuclear crisis, it was coded as focusing on "U.S.-ROK relations."

In the case of South Korean news about the United States, three parallel categories were used: "U.S.," "U.S.-ROK relations," and "U.S.-DPRK relations." Again, nearly all news articles fell conclusively into one of these three categories. To illustrate the meanings of these categories, news articles about the status of the U.S. economy were classified as stories focusing on internal matters of the United States. On the other hand, a majority of stories about trade between the United States and South Korea were classified as focusing on "U.S.-ROK relations." Likewise, many stories concerning U.S. troops in South Korea were viewed as topics pertaining to "U.S.-ROK relations," while stories about U.S.-North Korea tension related to the current nuclear crisis were coded as "U.S.-DPRK relations."

In examining news attention (or volume), this study evaluates the number of articles that were published within each *focus* category, in addition to the number of articles published within each *issue* category (e.g., security, economy) and each *subject matter* category (e.g., DPRK WMD, U.S.-ROK trade). (The Appendix provides a more detailed description of these content variables.)

Article Tone

After an article's focus was determined, its tone was coded. It is important to note that an article's tone was *not* coded on the basis of whether its author was critical of the parties involved in a given event. Rather, in an article focusing on the ROK, tone measurement was related to the description or evaluation of conditions in the ROK. For example, suppose that an article discussed the status of an economic indicator for the ROK economy. The article's news tone would measure whether it portrayed this issue in a positive or negative light. For an article focusing on U.S.-ROK or U.S.-DPRK relations, tone would measure the extent of accord or conflict between the relevant parties featured in the story. Admittedly, this coding scheme may not fully capture some subtle aspects of certain articles, but it offers important advantages over a more nuanced approach. Most importantly, it assures the highest possible level of reliability (i.e., reproducibility).[29]

Mimicking the conventions of the analysis of political news, each article's descriptive and evaluative news tone was coded separately for U.S. news articles. An article's *descriptive* tone refers to the tone of factual information featured in the article. Factual information simply *describes* when, where, and how the featured events occurred. *Evaluative* tone measures an author's interpretation and assessment of factual information or his or her prediction of future developments.[30]

Article tone was determined as mechanically as possible. First, each paragraph in an article was determined to be either descriptive or evaluative. Subsequently, each paragraph was coded "positive," "negative," or "neutral" in accordance with the principles described earlier. In computing an article's descriptive news tone, the numbers of positive and negative descriptive paragraphs were tallied. If the proportion of positive (or negative) descriptive paragraphs exceeded 75 percent of all descriptive paragraphs, the article's descriptive tone was determined as "primarily positive" (or "negative"), and it was assigned a score of 2 (or -2). If the proportion of positive (or negative) paragraphs fell between 60 percent and 75 percent, an article's descriptive tone was coded "somewhat positive" (or "negative"), and it was assigned a score of 1 (or -1). Other articles were determined to be "mixed/neutral" and assigned a score of 0. To avoid determining an article's tone based on inadequate information, the descriptive tone was not coded if fewer than three descriptive paragraphs were present. Evaluative tone was assessed in the same fashion.

For the South Korean data, the same five-point scale (-2 to 2) was used in coding news tone. However, because the Korean data set is composed of editorials and columns only, or predominantly evaluative content, no differentiation was made between descriptive and evaluative tone, as in the U.S. data.

This section assesses the reliability and validity of the news media data. In particular, two disparate aspects of data quality are examined: (1) intercoder reliability and (2) correlational validity. *Intercoder reliability* refers to the degree of agreement among coders, as explained earlier. This is an important criterion in all content analysis; insufficient intercoder agreement often indicates subjective coding. *Correlational validity* refers to the extent to which the data are consistent with intuitive expectations based on mundane observations. This is also an important yardstick by which the utility of the data can be judged. The data should show the most obvious trends researchers would expect from that which they already know.

Intercoder reliability was very high. In the United States, all eight coders examined roughly 200 of the same articles, from which intercoder reliability was assessed. They agreed roughly 80 percent of the time when coding articles' descriptive news tone. For articles' evaluative tone, the agreement level was roughly 75 percent. In most social science research, these numbers are certainly considered acceptable. When the kappa statistics are computed, the descriptive news tone shows that kappa equals 0.80, whereas 0.40 is typically considered "fair" and 0.50 is considered "good."[31] Comparable intercoder reliability was also obtained with the South Korean data (kappa equals 0.76). Thus, intercoder reliability was satisfactory by any standards.

Another important criterion in assessing the utility of the data is correlational validity (i.e., whether the coding scheme measured what it was intended to measure). In other words, is the variance in the data meaningful? In the most extreme case, all coders could perfectly agree on every article yet fail to capture a particular trend. One way of assessing this dimension of the data is to examine whether the variance is consistent with the most obvious knowledge of well-known events. In other words, the data must be consistent with intuitive knowledge of major events.

For U.S. news, expectations are clear with respect to news volume around the time of three major Korea-related events: (1) the first North Korean nuclear crisis, (2) the Asian financial crisis, and (3) the current North Korean nuclear crisis. In terms of news volume, it can generally be expected that at least one of the two Koreas attracted relatively high news attention in the

United States during these major events. In other words, it can be expected that the volume of news about Korea-related issues substantially increased while these major events were unfolding.

It is perhaps more difficult to generate a list of major events about the United States from the South Korean point of view. Although various U.S.-related topics consistently attract a high level of news attention in South Korea, it is still possible to generate a similar list. In general, news volume should have increased in 2002 and 2003, as the United States certainly became a central topic of media attention in South Korea. In particular, two events should have contributed to this trend: (1) the 2002 "schoolgirl incident" and the following tide of anti-American protests, and (2) the U.S. war on terrorism and the military conflict in Iraq. In addition, *Hankyoreh*, the progressive paper, which is critical of the United States and the alliance, should have led the coverage.

Figure 2.1 shows the yearly count of articles for each newspaper during the study period, and major events do appear to be well represented in the data. To begin, the volume of Korea-related news peaked in 1994 in all three U.S. newspapers, as the first nuclear standoff with North Korea captured U.S. media attention. There was another noticeable peak around 2002 and 2003 during the second nuclear standoff. Finally, there are fairly noticeable

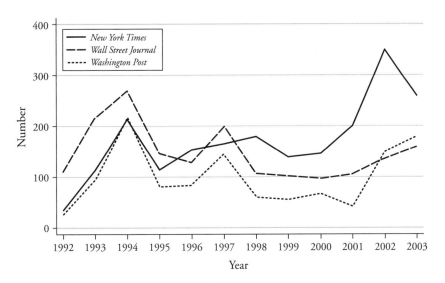

FIGURE 2.1 Number of articles on Korea in U.S. newspapers.

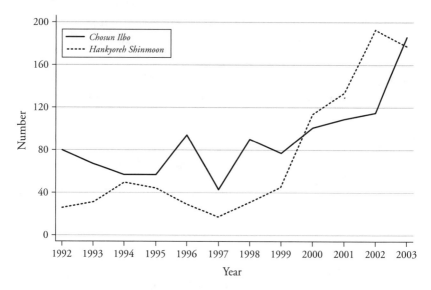

FIGURE 2.2 Number of articles on the United States in Korean newspapers.

local peaks around 1997 and 1998, indicating that news volume substantially increased during the Asian financial crisis. All these findings suggest that the current data set is fairly representative of major events pertaining to the two Koreas.

Likewise, the Korean data show a comparable level of correlational validity. Figure 2.2 confirms expectations well. There was a big increase in coverage of the United States in Korean newspapers, especially in the progressive *Hankyoreh*, from 2001 to 2002. News volume remained high in 2003 in both newspapers, when the United States became heavily engaged in its so-called war on terrorism.

In summary, the data show excellent intercoder reliability. No less importantly, the trends in the data are consistent with intuitive knowledge of major events in both countries, showing a high level of correlational validity. Therefore, the news media data obtained from full-text articles in the United States and Korea can be considered valid and reliable.

Data on North Korea

In addition to the two South Korean newspapers' coverage of the United States, the full texts of their editorials and columns on North Korea were

TABLE 2.7
Data on North Korea

Key words
북한/北韓, 평양, 북/北, 김일성, 김정일

Chosun Ilbo	597
Hankyoreh Shinmoon	487
TOTAL	1,084

coded. This set of data is used principally in analyzing South Korean press coverage of North Korea and its implications for U.S.-ROK relations, a major theme that will be addressed in Chapter 3. The data cover the same period of July 1992 through July 2003.

The search was also based on a Boolean search string, using the KINDS database. For searching articles on North Korea, the following key words were used: "북한" ("North Korea"), "북" ("the North"), "평양" ("Pyong-yang"), "김일성" ("Kim Il Sung"), and "김정일" ("Kim Jong Il"). The Chinese characters corresponding to "North Korea" ("北韓") and "the North" ("北") were also used, because they are quite commonly used in the headlines of South Korean newspapers. To maintain the sample size at a manageable level, these key words were searched for only in article headlines. This process produced a total of 1,084 editorials and columns: 597 in *Chosun Ilbo* and 487 in *Hankyoreh* (see Table 2.7). The North Korean data were coded applying the same procedure used for the U.S. data.[32]

Headline Data

As a supplement to the full-text data, headline data were also used in this study.

U.S. HEADLINE DATA

While it is not feasible to examine U.S. news coverage of all foreign countries, 26 other countries were selected for comparison with the two Koreas. A full list of these countries and their basic attributes is provided in Table 2.8. This list encompasses many countries that could serve as meaningful comparisons to the two Koreas, including East Asian neighbors Japan and China. Important U.S. allies, such as Great Britain and Australia, are also included. Furthermore, the list includes both developed (e.g., Great Britain,

TABLE 2.8

Basic attributes of selected countries

Country	Geographical Location					International Organization		Military Alliance		Demographic Attributes	
	Northeast Asia	Other Asia	Europe	Oceania/Other	Central/South America	OECD	EU	NATO	Bilateral Alliance with US	Population (millions)	GDP (billions, PPP)
Argentina					▲					40.0	$ 518.1
Australia				▲		▲			▲	20.0	640.1
Austria			▲			▲	▲			8.2	267.6
Brazil					▲					188.0	1,556.0
Chile					▲					16.0	187.1
China	▲									1,314.0	8,859.0
Czech Republic			▲			▲	▲	▲		10.0	199.4
France			▲			▲	▲	▲		61.0	1,816.0
Germany			▲			▲	▲	▲		82.0	2,504.0
India		▲								1,095.0	3,611.0
Indonesia		▲								245.0	865.6
Israel				▲						6.4	154.5
Italy			▲			▲	▲	▲		58.0	1,698.0
Japan	▲					▲			▲	127.0	4,018.0
South Korea (ROK)	▲					▲			▲	49.0	965.3
North Korea (DPRK)	▲									23.0	40.0
Malaysia		▲								24.0	290.2
Mexico					▲					107.0	1,067.0
Pakistan		▲								166.0	393.4
Philippines		▲								90.0	451.3
Portugal			▲			▲	▲	▲		11.0	204.4
Russia			▲							143.0	1,589.0
Singapore		▲								4.5	124.3
Spain			▲			▲	▲	▲		40.0	1,029.0
Switzerland			▲			▲	▲			7.5	241.8
Taiwan	▲									23.0	631.2
Thailand		▲								65.0	560.7
United Kingdom			▲			▲	▲	▲		61.0	1,830.0

SOURCES: NATO data: www.nato.org; OECD data: www.oecd.org, *2006 CIA World Factbook*.

Germany) and developing countries (e.g., Indonesia, Malaysia). Although no African or Arab nations are included in the list, a good mixture of countries is represented in terms of geographical location, economic strength, and relationship with the United States.

Primarily, these headline data are used as reference groups for the two Koreas (Chapter 5). Accordingly, as a basic principle, all important features of the sampling and coding schemes remained unaltered. The U.S. headline data come from the three U.S. newspapers mentioned earlier and cover the period from July 1992 to July 2003, except for the U.S. headline data on Korea, which reach as far back as 1982.

KOREAN HEADLINE DATA

Additionally, headlines were examined of the articles published in the two South Korean newspapers about the United States and North Korea. As with the U.S. headline data, the headlines of all editorials, columns, and front-page articles were selected. The headline data are used in measuring media attention to U.S.-DPRK relations and U.S.-ROK relations in Chapter 7.

All in all, comprehensive news content data were collected from both the United States and South Korea. In addition, the reliability and validity of the data were demonstrated. The news content data are used extensively in subsequent chapters to assess various aspects of U.S.-ROK relations.

THREE

North Korea and Contending South Korean Identities

After North Korea's nuclear test on October 9, 2006, the fate of South Korea's engagement policy with the North seemed to hang in the balance. To many, the nuclear test stood as a clear indictment of the Sunshine Policy and its successor, the Peace and Prosperity Policy of President Roh. After years of investing in and providing aid to the North under these policies, South Korea appeared to have received little in return. Conservative lawmakers charged that the nuclear test amounted to a "death penalty" for the Sunshine Policy,[1] and former President Kim Young Sam proclaimed that the policy "should be thrown into a trash can."[2] Roh's unification minister apologized to the National Assembly.[3]

Others, however, did not see the nuclear test as a verdict on South Korea's engagement of the North. To more progressive forces, including the Roh administration, this was not a story of inter-Korean cause and effect. Rather, from this view, the test occurred because the Bush administration had taken a hard line with North Korea. In doing so, the administration had created an environment characterized by regime change rhetoric and a preemptive strike doctrine that spurred the North to pursue weapons, considered the ultimate guarantee of security. For Korean progressives, the Sunshine Policy cannot be held to account for ruinous United States–Democratic People's Republic of Korea (U.S.-DPRK) relations, although such a circumstance does hinder inter-Korean engagement. While President Roh offered a careful, politically calibrated suggestion to the public in the wake of the nuclear test, saying he "would like to suggest that we take time to figure out the causal relationship between the engagement policy and the nuclear test,"[4] former President Kim Dae Jung pressed the progressive perspective in no uncertain terms, offering a direct, unequivocal answer: "North Korea has never said it would develop nuclear weapons because of South Korea's Sunshine Policy. It said that it was developing nuclear weapons as a last resort to survive, because the United States was hard on the country."[5]

In the face of such bold North Korean action, President Roh was under immense pressure to reconcile his government's progressive policies with U.S. appeals to suspend economic engagement and join the Proliferation Security Initiative (PSI),[6] a U.S.-led effort to interdict shipments of weapons of mass destruction (WMD) through improved intelligence cooperation and more robust enforcement of existing national regulations. Immediately after the North's test, Roh called for a full review of the engagement policy. But just days later, the South Korean president decided that, apart from a temporary suspension of aid and limited support for a UN Security Council resolution,[7] his government's policies would remain the same. Economic projects would continue at Kaesong and Mt. Kumgang, which many in the United States and the conservative Grand National Party (GNP) believed to be a significant source of cash for the DPRK (possibly channeled toward weapons programs), and Seoul would not join the PSI. Roh and his advisers had reached the conclusion that there was no viable alternative to engagement. They argued that suspension of inter-Korean relations would leave South Korea worse off in the long run and that a military accident might result in war if South Korea participated in the PSI. Policy makers in the United States were forced to face the stark reality that even a North Korean nuclear test could not lead South Korea to utilize its leverage to press its northern neighbor.[8]

As discussed in the introductory chapter, an important body of work has explained recent strains in the alliance as a consequence of increasingly disparate American and Korean perceptions and policies toward North Korea. A wave of anti-Americanism, continued inter-Korean engagement during the nuclear standoff, and the perception that the United States is a greater threat to peace on the peninsula than North Korea—all facets of an emergent, progressive perspective in South Korea—have captured the attention of experts seeking to chart a viable way forward for the alliance.[9] Indeed, over recent years, these progressive views, institutionalized through the establishment of two consecutive progressive governments, have become a durable feature of the political landscape in South Korea.

However, these perceptions of the North and the alliance—too often simply termed "South Korean views"—represent only half the story. As illustrated by reactions to the DPRK's nuclear test, South Korea has been deeply divided, and incongruous perceptions of North Korea and the United States held by conservative and progressive factions are central to these divisions. For South Koreans, the North Korean question is not simply a matter of policy; it is intimately related to the issue of national identity. While significant attention has been paid to differing American and Korean perceptions of the North, less is known about how these issues have been discussed, debated, and contested *within* South Korea, as well as why this fractious, seemingly intractable national debate is laden with such intensity and emotion. This chapter seeks to fill that research gap.

Using editorials and columns from *Chosun Ilbo* and *Hankyoreh Shinmoon*, this chapter examines South Korean conservative and progressive views of the North and assesses how these views have evolved from the pre-Sunshine period to more recent years. The central argument is that while U.S. officials approach the DPRK as a matter of security policy (as detailed in Chapter 6), North Korea and the relationship between the Koreas are fundamental to the evolution of South Korean national identity in the post–cold war, post-authoritarian era. This is because South Koreans, led by progressives, have been seeking to redefine their national identity in the newly forged and evolving regional and global orders of the post–cold war era, and the DPRK lies at the heart of that process. The deeply rooted divide over North Korea, which extends beyond domestic politics and is grounded in bitter disputes over South Korean national identity, presents a unique challenge for the United States as it seeks to cooperate with its alliance partner on this issue. Even with the new conservative Lee administration, there has not been a dramatic change in the political landscape; political division on the question of identity continues. This chapter examines the nature of identity politics in South Korea, as it relates to the North, and will discuss implications for United States–Republic of Korea (U.S.-ROK) relations.

In the Korean context, identity politics involving inter-Korean issues takes on a special meaning because of the peculiar circumstance of a nation with a strong sense of ethnic homogeneity being divided into two political entities. Throughout Korea's history of division, this shared sense of ethnic identity within discrete political systems has caused the governments of the two Koreas to contest rightful political leadership of the conceived national community. At present, the same agreement exists over ethnic unity but disagreement over the political notion of a nation *within* South Korea. Ethnic nationalism and the unique bitterness associated with ingroup disagreement over identity must be given proper consideration in understanding identity politics in South Korea.

The North in South Korean Politics of Identity

The North is undoubtedly an indispensable factor in South Korea's politics of national identity.[10] As discussed elsewhere, Koreans have long shared a strong sense of ethnic homogeneity, and that remains intact today. According to a survey conducted in late 2000, 95 percent of South Korean respondents believed that "North Korean people are of the same Korean ethnic-nation (*minjok*)."[11] However, the post-1945 territorial division violated the "nationalist principle of congruence of state and nation," to use Ernest Gellner's well-known phrase,[12] creating the unnatural situation of a single Korean family being divided into two parts.

Put differently, territorial partition, coupled with a strong sense of ethnic homogeneity, set in motion a contest for national representation between the two Koreas. Both sides claimed the legitimate right to represent the entire ethnic Korean community, appropriating a particular ideology—anticolonialism/anti-imperialism in the North and liberalism/anticommunism in the South—and linking these respective ideologies to national identity. Contention over national representation was framed as a struggle between patriots and traitors to the true nation, with "the "other" portrayed as the "black sheep" that contaminated the purity of the Korean national community by catering to the interests of foreign imperialists (either Americans or Russians). Within this process, both the North and the South distinguished between the traitor regime and its people—Korean brethren believed to be innocent victims and waiting to be liberated.

In the course of processes associated with the politics of national representation, anticommunism—a major focus of the capitalist bloc during the cold war—became powerful in the South and was often used as a construct to legitimize authoritarian politics. In the face of contention over national representation and both sides' strong desire to restore national unity, the two Koreas' respective identities hardened. This was especially true after the Korean War, by which time anti-imperialism and anticommunism were perceived to be more firmly established as indisputable ideologies on respective sides of the border. In South Korea, the authoritarian state monopolized discourse and policy toward the North, leaving little room for opposing views. Anticommunism, including intense anti–North Korea rhetoric and thought, became an indispensable element of the South Korean national identity.

In later years, contention over national identity expanded beyond the inter-Korean state level and moved into the realm of a state-society conflict within the South. Most notably, during the democracy movement of the 1980s, the authoritarian state's notion of national identity based on anticommunism faced serious challenges from the democratizing civil society. Although the protest movement began with antiauthoritarian (*yusin*) populism in the 1970s (called the *minjung* movement), it evolved into a nationalist struggle for democracy and eventual unification in the 1980s.

In challenging the state-sponsored ideology of anticommunism in pursuit of democracy, the allegedly close association between the United States and authoritarian regimes in the South led to questioning of the U.S. role, and the movement came to incorporate a vehement anti-Americanism, as featured in protest rhetoric and tactics. Not only was the United States the foreign other seen to be obstructing national unification, but it was also believed to have been involved in injustices and violations of the people's human rights, in collusion with authoritarian governments.

In this struggle for political democracy, the question of national identity came to the fore, provoking an intense and emotional contest between the authoritarian state and the democratizing civil society. Here, once again, the previously described dynamic of identity politics is obvious (i.e., the struggle to represent the true Korean national community).

The late 1980s brought important structural changes to South Korea. Internally, the ROK underwent democratization, and externally, it witnessed the collapse of the Soviet empire. In the post–cold war context, the power of anticommunism was weakened, and the Korean government pursued a Northern policy, normalizing relations with former enemies (Russia and China). However, the cold war structure did not immediately disappear from the peninsula, and South Korean views of the North were still largely negative (with the exception of a minority of activists who were sympathetic to the North). With democratization, anti-American nationalism gradually declined in the 1990s, although events such as the 1997 financial crisis occasionally sparked resurgence of this sentiment. More broadly, a rich civil society developed, expanding and diversifying national discourse on a number of issues, ranging from the North to unification to the U.S.-ROK alliance.

A turning point in South Korea's policy toward the North occurred with Kim Dae Jung's Sunshine Policy. South Koreans had witnessed the effects of a terrible famine and starvation in North Korea, which now lacked its state sponsors: the collapsed Soviet Union and a more market-oriented China. Motivated by progressive ideology and nationalism, President Kim instituted an engagement policy to assist North Korea and ensure peace on the peninsula. His policy also separated business from politics and advocated economic aid for the North to help its efforts at reform. This aggressive engagement policy led to the historic inter-Korean summit in the summer of 2000 in Pyongyang. While its tangible outcomes were modest, as discussed in the introductory chapter, the summit was instrumental in changing many South Koreans' views of the North from that of an enemy to a partner.

The Sunshine Policy, however, provoked a strong reaction from conservatives in the South. While not necessarily in opposition to engagement, conservative forces were skeptical that the North would change, and they demanded greater reciprocity. In their view, the North Korean threat had not diminished, and thus, the apparent unilateral pursuit of rapprochement seemed disconcerting, at best. As discussed in the introductory chapter, contrary to its founders' intentions, the Sunshine Policy produced bitter contention between progressives and conservatives regarding the North Korea issue.[13]

Spurred by ethnic nationalism and intensified debate over how to approach North Korea, the politics of identity reemerged in the South. This time, the actors locked in dispute over the politics of national identity were forces within civil society, with the leading advocates of leftist-nationalist ideology standing at the head of government, instead of protesting in the streets. The engagement policy, furthered by the Roh government, also clashed with the Bush administration's tough line on DPRK policy, straining U.S.-ROK relations.

This new iteration of the politics of national identity should be understood within the larger framework of Korean progressives actively seeking to redefine their position vis-à-vis their Northern half and foreign powers such as the United States. This new outlook is closely related to a self-assessment in the context of a changing regional order featuring the rise of China and

South Korea's discontent with U.S. unilateralism, especially the handling of the North Korean nuclear issue. But ultimately, it is the North that lies at the heart of the current politics of national identity.

The North in South Korean News

This chapter examines the new politics of national identity in South Korea by analyzing editorials and columns on North Korea published in two major daily newspapers (dailies)—the conservative *Chosun Ilbo* and the progressive *Hankyoreh Shinmoon*—between July 1, 1992, and July 30, 2003. Analysis of relevant articles from these newspapers reveals the principal and often contending views in the South regarding North Korea and inter-Korean relations.

More specifically, this chapter addresses a number of questions: How do Korean conservatives and progressives view the North? Has there been any meaningful change in their respective views? Are inter-Korean relations framed primarily in terms of economics or security? Are there, as is often argued, some unique features in the inter-Korean relations because of a sense of ethnic homogeneity widely held among Koreans (both North and South)? How has the conservative-progressive gap in perceptions of the North changed over time? How do tensions between the United States and the DPRK affect inter-Korean relations?

PRIMACY OF INTER-KOREAN RELATIONS

Both the conservative and progressive media's interests lie not so much in the North itself as in its relations with other nations, especially the South. As Figure 3.1 shows, the majority (60%) of editorials and columns in both newspapers focused on inter-Korean relations, and nearly 20 percent covered U.S.-DPRK relations.[14] In contrast with the significant interest in the North's relationships with other nations, foremost the ROK, there was comparatively little interest in the DPRK itself, as only 8 percent of *Chosun* and *Hankyoreh* editorials and columns claimed such a focus. (As shown later, most coverage of the DPRK focused on DPRK politics.[15])

These data, composed of editorials and op-ed columns, illustrate that the primary question facing the South Korean people, both conservatives and progressives, generally has not concerned defining the nature or circumstances of the North but rather formulating an appropriate response to the

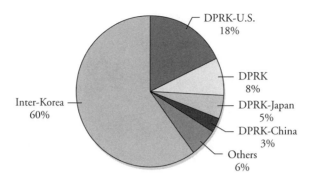

FIGURE 3.1 Article count by category.

precarious situation that lies at its border. In the post–cold war years, the nature of the Northern regime and the challenges it faces have become quite clear. Both conservatives and progressives see a government with an underdeveloped economy that is struggling to feed its people while channeling resources to nuclear and military programs to compensate for its weaknesses.

The period of the study included new developments, such as President Kim Dae Jung's engagement policy, the inter-Korean summit, and two nuclear crises. These topics spurred a great deal of discussion and debate within the South about inter-Korean relations and U.S.-DPRK relations, as these relations profoundly impact the future of the peninsula, and about whether the North's military capability poses a serious threat to the South.[16] In the second half of this chapter, an analysis of issue frames employed by the conservative and progressive newspapers reveals similar proportions of interest although often diametrically opposed attitudes regarding inter-Korean relations, threat perception, and the U.S. role on the peninsula.

SECURITY AND POLITICS OVERSHADOW ECONOMICS

Given the widely held perception among South Koreans that those living in the North are part of the same Korean ethnic nation and that Korea is artificially divided into two political entities,[17] the relationship between the two Koreas is of unique importance in South Korean society, meriting more in-depth attention here.[18] Figure 3.2 details the amount of attention, or coverage, the two newspapers devoted to issues within inter-Korean relations.

Naturally, peace and unification, or discussion of the future of the peninsula, captured a large share of the newspapers' attention to inter-Korean

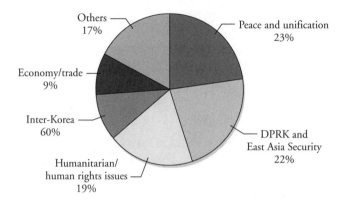

Others
17%

Peace and unification
23%

Economy/trade
9%

Inter-Korea
60%

DPRK and
East Asia Security
22%

Humanitarian/
human rights issues
19%

FIGURE 3.2 Article count by categories within inter-Korean relations.

relations (23%).[19] As one might expect, coverage of this issue spiked in 2000 in the wake of the historic inter-Korean summit and remained relatively high in 2001. Interestingly, the conservative *Chosun* devoted much more attention to this topic in 2000 (36 editorials and columns) than the progressive *Hankyoreh* (17).

The conservative newspaper's more extensive coverage of peace and unification issues may have stemmed from a sense of surprise at the summit and new prospects for improved inter-Korean relations. Greater coverage of peace and unification issues in 2000 was also likely due to the conservative newspaper's criticism of the *terms* by which its government should pursue further rapprochement. Such criticism of the terms of engagement came on the heels of the summit, as additional inter-Korean dialogue failed to meet expectations, diminishing the initial euphoria over prospects for reuniting the divided Korean nation. On September 4, 2000, the Yonhap News Agency reported that, out of all the Korean newspapers, *Chosun* had "lashed out the strongest at the government saying that it had failed to get any concrete results." One editorial charged, "It is certainly regrettable that the universal principle of mutuality was completely ignored." The conservative paper's concern with the lack of reciprocity in inter-Korean relations is clearly revealed in the frame analysis shown later in this chapter.

In addition to peace and unification issues, the conservative and progressive newspapers both published significant numbers of editorials and columns on the topic of the DPRK and East Asia security (22%) within their coverage of inter-Korean relations. This is understandable, as the study period covered two nuclear crises: the North's 1998 missile test over Japan and military conflict between the two Koreas in the Western Sea (Yellow Sea). As will be revealed in the issue-framing analysis later in this chapter, the threat represented by the DPRK is a point of fervent debate between conservative and progressive forces in South Korean society. Such differing views impact how these two groups define the possibilities for inter-Korean relations and, crucially, their own identity in relation to this "significant other." Consequently, intense societal debate must have spurred coverage in both newspapers.

Humanitarian and human rights issues rated as the third-largest coverage category, comprising 19 percent of inter-Korean relations news. Interestingly, approximately 70 percent of *Chosun* and 85 percent of *Hankyoreh* opinion pieces on DPRK humanitarian/human rights issues were published within the category of inter-Korean relations, not under the category of the DPRK itself. This indicates the terms on which conservative and progressive forces debate this issue. Family reunions, POW return, aid, suffering, and rights abuses—all of which fall into the category of humanitarian/human rights issues—are issues that confront both Seoul and Pyongyang. They are therefore embedded in South-North relations, not issues associated with another country, as is often the natural view of the United States, which does not share the same intimate ties. Both progressive and conservative South Korean newspapers have appealed (albeit sometimes to varying forces) for progress in inter-Korean ties based on humanitarian imperatives. In a September 4, 2000, editorial written in the wake of inter-Korean ministerial talks, the conservative *Dong-a Ilbo* passionately argued that "to enable [POWs and their families] to meet is a humanitarian call that neither the South nor the North can deny."[20]

As in many of the debates over inter-Korean policy, however, humanitarian and human rights issues are interpreted differently by Korean progressives and conservatives, and determining what role these kinds of issues should play in the pursuit of improved inter-Korean relations can be polarizing. From the progressive perspective, humanitarian aid is essential to saving the North's starving population and improving inter-Korean relations. However, conservatives are concerned that aid may not go to those in the greatest need and may also strengthen the autocratic regime. In addressing human rights issues, progressive ROK governments have suggested an approach of quiet diplomacy, believing that pressing these issues will not likely bring about any improvement but rather will likely retard progress in inter-Korean relations. But the opposing conservative forces have argued that Seoul must address the plight of brethren in the North and have even accused the government of appeasement for its silence on the issue.

Differences on human rights issues have arisen repeatedly in recent years, most conspicuously in accordance with annual votes on European Union–sponsored resolutions condemning the DPRK's human rights record in the United Nations and in disputes over the efficacy and appropriateness of a law that unanimously passed the U.S. Congress: the North Korean Human Rights Act of 2004.[21] Conservatives have hailed the importance of the UN resolution and the U.S. law, urging that their own nation should endorse these measures and be part of the international movement on human rights in the DPRK. However, progressive leaders have said that abstaining from the UN resolution was appropriate, as the ROK's top priority is to ensure peace and stability on the peninsula and that the U.S. law has only served to antagonize North Korea.

Despite the controversy over the role the human rights issue should play in Seoul's approach to inter-Korean relations, it is important to emphasize that, more broadly, South Koreans tend to view the issue in particular terms, focusing on the suffering of Korean people—*their* people. Both conservative and progressive newspapers use terms such as *compatriots, brethren, brothers,* and *miserable victims of national division*. In contrast, U.S. leaders tend to conceptualize the situation in the DPRK in more universal terms, focusing on violations of human rights by the *authoritarian* and *evil state*, or *regime*.

This difference in Korean and American perceptions of human rights and other issues has been translated into differing policies toward the DPRK. Included among them is the ROK approach of economic engagement and aid, which is intended to alleviate the suffering of brothers and sisters. This stands in contrast to the U.S. tendency to isolate and punish a regime engaged in the practices of torture, forced labor, and de facto prohibition of religious freedom.

It is important to note that even though the governments of Kim Dae Jung and Roh Moo Hyun emphasized economic cooperation and aid as key components of inter-Korean engagement, inter-Korean economic and trade issues received small coverage in *Chosun* and *Hankyoreh* (9%), especially when compared to coverage of peace and unification. As might be anticipated, coverage of economic issues rose in the wake of the 2000 summit, with the progressive newspaper giving more attention to these types of developments than the conservative newspaper. Yet despite the fact that economic engagement forms the backbone of the South Korean government's approach, the political and security aspects of inter-Korean relations (e.g., the summit, nuclear programs, etc.) are more visible and capable of eliciting greater public interest, emotion, and debate.

Figure 3.3 shows changes in media attention to security and economic issues over the course of the study period, allowing for a closer examination of the disparity in coverage between these two sets of issues. From 1992 through 1999, the data reveal a very low (nearly nonexistent) level of conservative and progressive interest in economic issues. Economic and trade coverage peaked in the summit year of 2000 (14 *Hankyoreh* and 9 *Chosun* editorials and columns over the course of this year) and remained higher than the presummit level for the rest of the study period. Yet the volume of coverage of economics paled in comparison to that of the DPRK's impact on regional security. Indeed, the disparity in DPRK-related economics and security coverage increased in postsummit years.[22]

While the surge in the security coverage in 2002 and 2003 reflects the second nuclear crisis, the general disparity in economics and security coverage

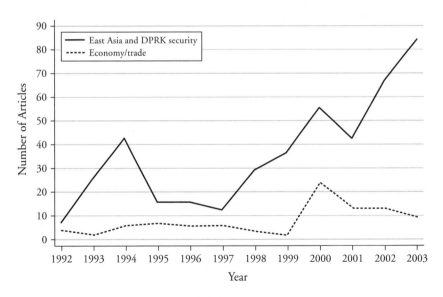

FIGURE 3.3 Media attention to issues of security versus economics.
NOTE: The figures for 1992 and 2003 are weighted.

has two primary implications. First, it may be the case that there was less disagreement between conservatives and progressives on economic and trade issues and therefore less coverage overall. In fact, as shown later in this chapter (see Table 3.2), the category of economic and trade issues was one of the least divisive. Second and more importantly, it is plausible to assume that despite the ROK government's attempts at focusing on economic engagement and cultural ties in its relations with North Korea, the profundity and primacy of the security situation were inescapable. Furthermore, this continues to dominate the opinion pages in both conservative and progressive publications, which take starkly different positions on the nature of the North's threat and the best policy approach for this matter. An inflamed security situation on the peninsula, especially in the face of a second nuclear crisis, constrains the ability of ROK governments to pursue improvements in inter-Korean relations, impeding any significant public attention to economic and cultural matters in the North.

Indeed, a second inter-Korean summit was deemed impossible until North Korea appeared to be making sincere progress on denuclearization. President Roh Moo Hyun was only able to travel to Pyongyang in late 2007, after North Korea had shut down the Yongbyon nuclear reactor, permitted inspections, and pledged complete denuclearization. Given the progressive governments' attempts to focus inter-Korean relations on economic engagement, it is not surprising that the progressive *Hankyoreh*, in particular, accorded more coverage to economic matters after the 2000 summit.

CONTENTION AND PERCEPTION GAP

The North Korean issue became more contentious and divisive in the later years of this study. As Figure 3.4 illustrates, South Korean coverage of the North increased considerably from the late 1990s.[23] The most dramatic increase was in 2000, the year of the first inter-Korean summit, when *Chosun* coverage more than doubled and *Hankyoreh* coverage increased by more than four times over the previous year. Even though this increased volume of opinion pieces was not sustained at the year 2000 level, for every year after the summit, coverage remained above the presummit level. The Kim Dae Jung government's efforts to establish inter-Korean political and economic ties and the ensuing societywide policy debate on how to handle sometimes burgeoning and stymied inter-Korean relations placed North Korean and inter-Korean matters on the editorial pages of the nation's newspapers far

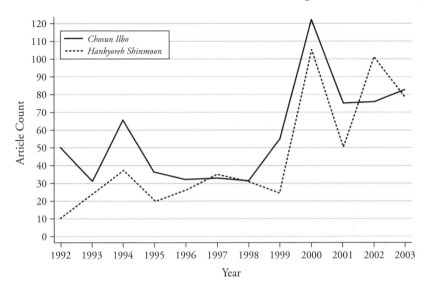

FIGURE 3.4 South Korean coverage of the North.

more often. These issues had gained a greater foothold in popular Korean consciousness.

Indeed, as shown by Figure 3.4, temporal changes in these two ideologically polarized newspapers track quite closely, suggesting that, in their contentious dispute about the North, conservatives and progressives generally gave similar levels of attention to these issues. The analysis of issue frames, which follows later in this chapter, examines this intense debate as it has played out regarding specific issues related to the North and inter-Korean relations.

As the North Korean issue became more contentious, South Korean views became more sharply divided. *Chosun* and *Hankyoreh* provided similar levels of attention to several DPRK-related focus categories, but as Table 3.1 illustrates, the two newspapers' average tones toward these categories were markedly different.[24] *Chosun* was clearly negative on inter-Korean relations (–0.62), while *Hankyoreh* was actually on the positive side (0.04), on average. This disparity demonstrates that during the study period, Korean conservatives remained skeptical of prospects for inter-Korean relations, despite aggressive engagement by the progressive administrations of Kim and Roh. There was a similarly notable difference in the newspapers' respective tones toward the DPRK (–0.69 for *Chosun* and 0.03 for *Hankyoreh*). While

TABLE 3.1
Average tone

Category	*Chosun Ilbo*	*Hankyoreh Shinmoon*	Overall
Inter-Korea	−0.62	0.04	−0.31
DPRK-U.S.	−0.71	−0.68	−0.70
DPRK	−0.69	0.03	−0.35
DPRK-Japan	0.25	−0.55	−0.31
DPRK-China	0.19	0.63	0.28
Average	−0.60	−0.14	−0.39

neither progressives nor conservatives may dispute the characterization of North Korea as a failing regime, as mentioned earlier, this finding demonstrates the presence of more sympathetic discourse from progressives and more critical rhetoric from conservatives.

Both newspapers revealed their most negative average tone ratings in the category of DPRK-U.S. relations, and unlike other categories, this one showed virtually no internewspaper difference (−0.71 for *Chosun* and −0.68 for *Hankyoreh*). While this result ostensibly indicates a similarity in perspectives, it needs to be interpreted with caution. As will be discussed in greater detail in the next chapter, both Korean conservatives and progressives seemed quite pessimistic about prospects for U.S.-DPRK relations. This is not too surprising, given that the study period included two nuclear crises. However, these opposing sides likely reached this shared pessimism through very different logic: The conservative newspaper blamed the Northern regime for U.S.-DPRK tension, while the progressive newspaper blamed the Bush administration's hard-line policies. (See also the frame analysis presented later in this chapter.) As for DPRK-Japan and DPRK-China relations, it is interesting to note the disparity in DPRK-Japan relations (wherein the progressive newspaper was negative and the conservative newspaper was positive), as well as the fact that both the newspapers seemed to harbor positive sentiment for DPRK-China relations. Regardless, these findings should be taken only as suggestive, due to the small number of cases.

Table 3.2 presents average tones on the five most frequently editorialized/opinionated issues *within* inter-Korean relations. As expected, *Chosun* was more negative than *Hankyoreh* on all five categories—with especially negative average tones toward security, ROK politics, and humanitarian issues—and there were significant disparities between the two newspapers in nearly all

TABLE 3.2

Average tone for inter-Korea relations by topic category

Category	Chosun Ilbo	Hankyoreh Shinmoon	Overall
Peace and unification	−0.31	0.41	0.03
DPRK and East Asian security	−1.09	−0.36	−0.81
Humanitarian/Human rights issues	−0.71	−0.04	−0.44
Economy/Trade	−0.16	0.38	0.16
ROK politics	−1.18	−0.61	−0.80

issue categories, reinforcing impressions of a highly contentious political environment. It is not surprising that the category of DPRK and East Asia Security received highly negative coverage in both newspapers, as the study period encompasses many critical security-related events, as mentioned earlier.

It is, however, noteworthy that both newspapers recorded quite negative ratings on ROK politics within the context of inter-Korean relations. In fact, *Hankyoreh's* most negative tone in any category was found here. As apparent, conservatives have long been critical of what they consider the Kim Dae Jung and Roh Moo Hyun administrations' manipulation of inter-Korean issues for political gain. Conservative forces accused President Roh of scheduling the second inter-Korean summit right before the presidential election in order to give a political boost to progressive forces.

Yet these negative tone ratings on national politics run deeper, as each side's politics and posturing, criticized by the other, is connected to its own identity. Each strongly believes that it has the correct prescription for how to pursue inter-Korean relations, and these beliefs do not yield easily to political compromise. It is likely that the conservative tone on ROK politics has been more negative than its progressive counterpart since 2000 because there have only been progressive governments during the study period. The opposition must always be louder and more strident to be heard. As is often the case in news coverage around the world (including in the United States), the categories that *Chosun* gave the most coverage, such as security, were also the categories that it rated most negatively (see Figure 3.2).

It is interesting to note that although significant disparity exists between conservative and progressive opinion pieces on peace and unification, *Chosun's* tone was only *mildly* negative at −0.31. As the next section on issue frames will explain in more detail, conservatives tend not to criticize the goals of peace and unification but rather the methods and priorities that progressive governments use to realize these aspirations. Even in the presence of starkly differentiated conservative and progressive identities, establishing a peace regime and eventually unifying the nation are general goals across Korean society. Indeed, in the lead-up to the June 2000 summit, the Kim Dae Jung government received much praise from the conservative press, with *Chosun Ilbo*, *Dong-a Ilbo*, and *Joong-Ang Ilbo* all lauding the government for its achievements in advancing the dialogue and producing a turning point in the history of the peninsula.[25]

In the years since the summit, which have been marked by anything but a linear progression in the development of inter-Korean relations, the establishment of a peace regime and eventual unification continue to be important, broadly held goals (one might even call them *values*), although across the ideological divide, they are not buttressed by the same levels of hope and optimism. Apart from having an opinion on an administration's specific engagement policy toward the North, adherence to these broader values has become politically correct, as agreement is nearly a societywide expectation or a marker of Korean patriotism.[26] Indeed, the fact that both newspapers accorded more positive (or less negative) tone ratings to peace and unification than to inter-Korean relations in general supports this point.

In addition to being quite positive on peace and unification, *Hankyoreh* was positive on inter-Korean economic and trade issues. (Even *Chosun* was only slightly negative.) This most likely indicates a progressive hope that economic relations with the North can serve as a basis for broader inter-Korean prospects. Framing data (presented below) affirm this progressive optimism or, at the very least, this effort to portray a healthy degree of optimism.

U.S.–DPRK RELATIONS AND INTER-KOREAN RELATIONS

Additionally, the research findings demonstrate that U.S.-DPRK relations significantly affect inter-Korean relations. Figure 3.5 depicts the two newspapers' tones toward inter-Korean relations during four combinations of U.S. and ROK administrations. The Clinton–Kim Dae Jung years recorded the most positive tone ratings in both dailies. These years not only included the inter-Korean summit but also featured significant improvements in U.S.-DPRK relations, evidenced by high-level dialogue and reciprocal visits.

In contrast, the Clinton–Kim Young Sam and the Bush–Roh Moo Hyun years recorded more negative tone ratings. These periods included two nuclear crises, which seem to have influenced both newspapers' views on prospects for inter-Korean relations. Indeed, during the first nuclear cri-

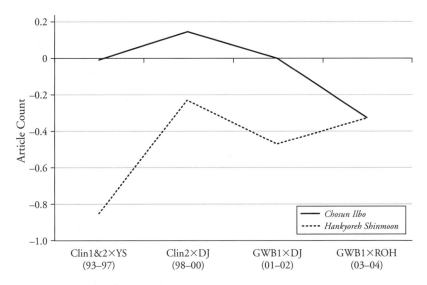

FIGURE 3.5 Average tone for inter-Korean relations during administration overlaps.

sis, *Chosun*'s tone toward inter-Korean relations was –0.31, and during the second nuclear crisis, its tone was –0.48. However, during years that were not characterized by nuclear crisis, this conservative publication's evaluative tone toward inter-Korean relations averaged –0.26. A similar dynamic can be seen in the progressive *Hankyoreh*; its tone toward inter-Korean relations was 0.05 during the first nuclear crisis, –0.01 during the second nuclear crisis, and 0.19 during years when there was no nuclear crisis. This is strong evidence that nuclear crises, or security tensions on the peninsula, dulled both progressive and conservative hopes for progress in inter-Korean relations. Both newspapers were most positive (or least negative) on inter-Korean relations in the absence of security crises.

Korean leaders such as President Roh have resented the constraints that nuclear crises put on inter-Korean relations, especially as progressive forces tend to view such crises as U.S.-DPRK problems. But these are acknowledged constraints, recognized by both conservatives and progressives. As mentioned earlier, the second Korea summit was held only after significant progress in U.S.-DPRK talks on nuclear issues. These findings clearly indicate that inter-Korean relations are bound by the security situation on the peninsula, especially major tensions from U.S.-DPRK relations.

The findings in Figure 3.5 provide the basis for several additional interesting observations. *Chosun* recorded its most negative tone rating during the Clinton–Kim Young Sam years. This very negative tone rating by the conservative newspaper most likely reflects President Kim's hard-line policy toward the North in response to its hostile actions. In the wake of a 1996 DPRK submarine incursion, for instance, Kim deliberated for months on whether to pursue a so-called soft-landing strategy but ultimately decided to take a firm approach with the North, suspending inter-Korean economic cooperation and withdrawing from Korean Peninsula Energy Development Organization (KEDO) activities. North Korea, in turn, responded by threatening possible military action against the South.

In contrast, after the first nuclear standoff with the DPRK, the Clinton administration took a more conciliatory approach toward the North, trying to keep the Agreed Framework on track. The Kim government and South Korean conservatives viewed the United States' soft approach toward the North as appeasement and were concerned that the South was being left out in the new U.S.-DPRK relationship. Thus, the North's hostile behavior— from announcing its withdrawal from the Nuclear Non-Proliferation Treaty (NPT) only 15 days into Kim's presidency to the submarine incursion—coupled with frustration over a soft Clinton administration response, led conservatives to evaluate prospects for inter-Korean relations in negative terms during the overlap of the Kim Young Sam and Clinton administrations.[27]

Under such circumstances, it seems curious that over the same time period, *Hankyoreh* recorded a neutral tone score. Yet *Hankyoreh* published fewer articles over this time period than *Chosun*, and the progressive newspaper's editorial coverage tended to focus more on achievements in inter-Korean relations (e.g., the establishment of an inter-Korean economic cooperation dialogue, the ROK role in KEDO) than on negative developments. Rather, the progressive newspaper's most negative tone toward inter-Korean relations occurred during the Bush-Roh years, a period in which there was remarkable inter-Korean activity compared to the 1990s but also a second nuclear crisis. During this period, the Roh government clashed with the Bush administration over North Korea's nuclear program, which not only strained U.S.-ROK relations but also hindered further progress in inter-Korean relations.

Identity Politics in the Sunshine Era: Frame Analysis

South Koreans' view of the North and inter-Korean relations can be further examined by considering how *Chosun and Hankyoreh* have framed issues within their coverage of North Korean–related issues. In this context, *issue framing* refers to definitions, constructions, and depictions of a policy issue.[28] Policy issues are multifaceted, and political elites define them for the public in the ways that cast the best possible light on their own preferred course of action. In doing so, political elites attempt to impose their own meaning on the issue and gain popular support.[29] The mass media serve as the conduit through which the messages flow, and the pervasiveness and cumulative effects of these messages over time means that the mass media may serve as a platform in forging, modifying, and reinforcing a nation's identity.

In particular, this section considers the frequency with which South Korean newspapers employed various issue frames over the study period (1992–2003). To evaluate how the discourse has evolved over time and to demonstrate the significant psychological impact of the Sunshine Policy, this section also considers the frequency of North Korea–related media frames before Kim Dae Jung's term in office (1992–1997) as compared to the period after his inauguration (1998–2003). Together, issue frames related to the North compose a political orientation that is largely rooted in identity, as will be demonstrated in both the conservative and progressive cases.

From the data, stark contrasts can be observed in conservative and progressive framing of issues related to North Korea. Observing and analyzing the difference in issue framing is important, since, as shown earlier, the two newspapers covered most relevant focus and topic categories with similar frequency. That is, although the two newspapers showed a similar frequency in focus and issue categories, they framed them in distinct ways. Therefore, the analysis of issue framing presented here can reveal the *extent* of disagreement between conservative and progressive views and how particular issue frames coalesce around distinct, opposing identities.

Figure 3.6 depicts the six most prevalent media frames in *Chosun Ilbo*'s North Korea coverage from 1992 to 2003.[30] These six media frames are congruous with conventional conservative rhetoric in South Korea, highlighting the need for greater reciprocity in Seoul's engagement of Pyongyang, disparaging the current state of inter-Korean relations, reaffirming the North's security threat, and emphasizing cooperation within the U.S.-ROK alliance. The relative incidence of these frames provides important insight into the terms of the DPRK-related debate that courses through Korean media.

By far, the most prevalent frame was the need for reciprocity between the two Koreas, which represents both a policy prescription and an indictment

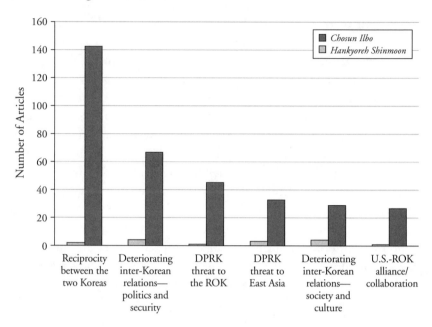

FIGURE 3.6 Most prevalent conservative frames in North Korea coverage.

of progressive administrations' engagement of the North, featuring front-loaded benefits. It is clear that the terms by which the ROK government pursues a relationship with Pyongyang elicited a more voluminous response than any other aspect of the so-called North Korean problem. This fervent suggestion of a basis on which to rectify the course of engagement policy is logically supported and made more pressing by the observation inherent in *Chosun's* second most frequently employed frame: that inter-Korean relations are deteriorating in the political and security arenas. In other words, these findings suggest that Korean conservatives would not have objected to the engagement policy per se, but they were clearly dissatisfied with the state of inter-Korean relations during these study years, especially the perceived asymmetry of gains and sincerity.

In large part, the other top media frames from *Chosun* spoke to basic interpretations of the political and strategic landscape, rather than recommend explicit policies. While the administrations of Kim Dae Jung and Roh Moo Hyun took conciliatory actions, such as removing references to North Korea as the "main enemy" from defense white papers (based on DPRK complaints, rather than in-kind actions), *Chosun's* body of editorials and columns affirmed that conservatives continued to view North Korea as a threat to the ROK and to the region. (As noted previously, the newspaper devoted more than 20 percent of its coverage to and records very negative tones on the DPRK and its impact on security in East Asia.) The prevalence of these threat frames (the third and fourth most frequent) indicates that the newspaper was concerned with a changing view in the South of the North from that of an enemy to a partner, largely due to progressive governments' engagement policy, and was thus motivated to highlight this concern.

The U.S.-ROK alliance was the sixth most prevalent frame within *Chosun*'s articles on North Korea. This indicated a significant role for the alliance in national security, especially vis-à-vis North Korea, from *Chosun*'s perspective. Although the conservative newspaper employed this frame with less than one-fifth the frequency of its primary frame (reciprocity between the Koreas), the relatively smaller number reflects the fact that this data set includes editorials and columns primarily about North Korea, not the United States or the U.S.-ROK alliance. Considering this, it can be said that the conservative daily clearly continued to equate the North Korean threat and the importance of the alliance.

In addition to featuring *Chosun*'s most prevalent media frames, Figure 3.6 also includes data on the frequency with which *Hankyoreh* employed these same frames. Conspicuously, the progressive paper almost never utilized any of the media frames that *Chosun* employed with relatively great frequency, clearly showing a sharp division in views of the North within South Korea. In other words, while both newspapers addressed similar issues areas with relatively proportional volumes of coverage, the ways in which they view or frame these issues were starkly different.

The differences between the two newspapers' coverage of North Korea become even more dramatic upon observation of Figure 3.7. It identifies *Hankyoreh*'s six most prevalent media frames, which addressed the same issue areas as *Chosun*'s frames but took an antithetical position in nearly each case, signaling the vehement, seemingly interminable debate over the DPRK in the South Korean media. Similar to the dynamic observed between the two newspapers in Figure 3.6, Figure 3.7 reveals that *Chosun* hardly utilized any of *Hankyoreh*'s most frequently employed media frames concerning North Korea. Thus, data on media rhetoric bear out the popular perception of diametrically opposed media outlets engaged in a belligerent debate, in which neither side yielded any ground. The *extent* of disagreement is truly striking.

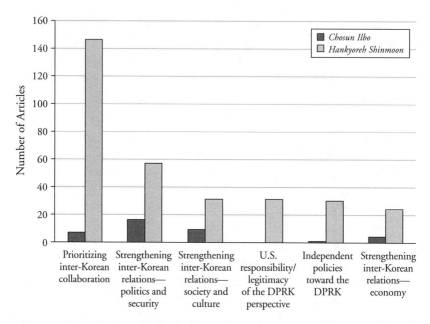

FIGURE 3.7 Most prevalent progressive frames in North Korea coverage.

Like *Chosun*, *Hankyoreh* most frequently used a frame that encapsulated its position toward engagement with North Korea. The persistent use of the conservative "achieve reciprocity in inter-Korean relations" and the progressive "prioritize inter-Korean collaboration" at a rate proportional to each other (and several times higher than any other preferred frame) demonstrates that the terms of engagement with North Korea was an issue of profound importance in this debate. Once again, this finding suggests that both sides recognized the need for engagement, which was hard to reject, given a strong sense of ethnic identity. Even so, their policy approaches were fundamentally different, reflecting their respective political identities.

The frame regarding U.S. responsibility/legitimacy of the DPRK perspective spoke to the perception among progressives that the United States fostered a security environment in which Pyongyang had few options but to develop nuclear weapons. This perception came to prominence more recently, in connection with the Bush administration's "axis of evil"/regime change rhetoric and preemptive strike doctrine. Former President Kim Dae Jung echoed variations of this reasoning in the wake of North Korea's nuclear test.

The frame regarding independent policies toward the DPRK was linked to such a view and underpinned by the ideas, popularized by the 1980s protest movement, that the U.S.-ROK alliance had been grossly inequitable and that the ROK had to extricate itself from U.S. dominance. This nationalistic, essentially anti-American component was largely dormant during the 1990s (with the exception of the financial crisis) but was reawakened by a new generation of policy elites—former activists who had been integrated into electoral politics and the bureaucracy—and in conjunction with recent U.S. policies perceived to be heavy handed and counter to South Korean interests.

Additional prevalent *Hankyoreh* frames included the strengthening of inter-Korean relations across a number of areas: politics and security, society and culture, and the economy. Interestingly but not surprisingly, the newspaper put the most emphasis on political and security issues in inter-Korean relations. Once again, although economic projects actually formed the backbone of the progressive administrations' engagement policy, political and security relations may have had the biggest psychological impact on South Koreans and were also a subject of contentious debate between conservatives and progressives (being the second most important frame for both newspapers).

The filtering of current events through these ideological, opposing media frames at once catered to two political expressions of nationalism—two *identities*—and reinforced the views of each camp. In the wake of President Kim Dae Jung's implementation of the Sunshine Policy, it could have been expected that the two identities developing in South Korea, related to the North and the United States, would have hardened, thus creating a more contentious political atmosphere.

To examine this proposition, the media frame data were divided into two distinct time periods within the study period: before Kim Dae Jung's presidency and after his inauguration. These analyses would shed light on how disparate identities evolved over time and in response to events. President Kim's policies toward North Korea represented a departure from the approach of previous administrations, and the Sunshine Policy's implementation signified a profound, normative statement on the shape and priorities of the country's nationalism. It could be expected that the prevalence of certain media frames (demonstrating a polarized, national debate on North Korea) increased after Kim took office. Even though this would likely be the case in both newspapers, the increase would be greater in *Hankyoreh*, as the introduction of the Sunshine Policy created more political room for the expression of progressive views on North Korea.

The Sunshine Policy proceeded in fits and starts, with gestures of unity during Olympic ceremonies, aid shipments, naval clashes, economic agreements, and promised meetings scrapped along the way. Its successor, President Roh's Peace and Prosperity Policy, weathered the peninsula's second nuclear crisis, including a nuclear test, but not without great debate over its efficacy. Given how issues related to North Korea were tied to these two senses of identity, each side experienced these events in different ways. The media frames and their frequencies provide insight into these experiences, revealing the filters through which new information was often assimilated in line with these respective identity-based political views.

Figures 3.8 and 3.9 demonstrate that both newspapers increased their use of the media frames, as discussed earlier, after Kim Dae Jung took office.[31] The frequency of the top six frames in both newspapers increased in the Sunshine era. This indicates that Korean society became more polarized in its view of the North after the launch of the Sunshine Policy, hardening two competing identities.

More specifically, Figure 3.8 shows that *Chosun*'s frequency of the reciprocity frame more than doubled, reflecting conservatives' dissatisfaction with the Sunshine Policy.[32] The number of editorials and columns using the two frames of deteriorating inter-Korean relations also increased. However, their increase was rather marginal, especially compared with the increase in the reciprocity frame. Once again, this suggests that conservatives did not oppose engagement in itself. Rather, their concern was with the specific terms of the engagement policy and the perceived lack of reciprocity.

It is also interesting to note that the frame concerning the DPRK's threat to East Asia and that on the U.S.-ROK alliance more than doubled in prevalence after Kim became president. Although the frame concerning the DPRK's threat to the ROK did not double, it also increased. This indicates that conservatives were increasingly concerned with the danger the North posed to regional stability. It was during the Sunshine era that the North test-fired a two-stage ballistic missile over Japan (1998) and became embroiled in a nuclear crisis (2002), certainly raising concerns about regional security. This may also indicate that Korean conservatives came to agree with U.S. concern over the North as a regional proliferation threat. Finally, that *Chosun* coverage utilizing the frame of DPRK's threat to East

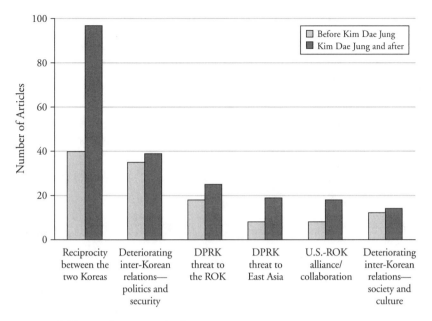

FIGURE 3.8 Changes in conservative frames.

Asia seemed to increase in tandem with the alliance frame is logical. That is, if one was increasingly concerned that North Korea was a threat, then one would be more willing to accept the U.S. troop presence and more likely to value the alliance's contribution to national security and regional stability.

In *Hankyoreh*'s coverage, the prevalence of the previously discussed top six media frames also increased significantly from before Kim's presidency to after his inauguration. In fact, as Figure 3.9 shows, the prevalence of each frame increased by at least an astonishing 100 percent. Besides stressing the importance of inter-Korean collaboration, the progressive newspaper came to more strongly emphasize the U.S. responsibility and the value of ROK's independent policy toward the North. This is in stark contrast to the conservative newspaper's increased stress on the U.S.-ROK alliance and collaboration in dealing with the Northern regime. A progressive administration in office and early gains made by the Sunshine Policy created a different political environment,[33] one in which there was more political space for advocacy of progressive views on North Korea. The environment also featured strong criticism of the government's engagement policy from conservative media, which created the perceived necessity of a strong response

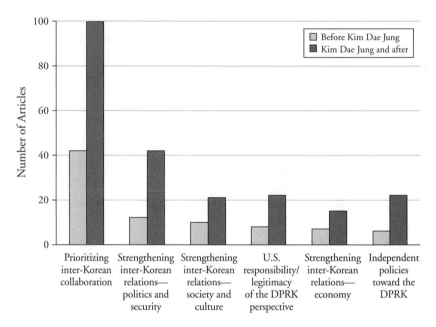

FIGURE 3.9 Changes in progressive frames.

from the progressive media. The finding that not a single frame category from either newspaper decreased in prevalence strongly suggests the hardening of both the conservative and progressive identities following institution of the Sunshine Policy.

The most conspicuous trend in Figures 3.8 and 3.9 is the increased prevalence of the reciprocity (*Chosun*) and prioritizing inter-Korean collaboration (*Hankyoreh*) frames from the earlier to the latter period. Once again, these findings indicate that Kim's Sunshine Policy provoked intense debate over the proper policy approach toward the North—that is, the terms of engagement, rather than the concept of engagement itself. Among progressive forces, it altered the threat perception[34] and therefore devalued the alliance in some respects. Especially after the Bush administration took office, many Koreans of this orientation questioned the compatibility of Korean and U.S. interests and priorities.[35] Much like the student movements of the mid and late 1980s, these individuals were eager to liberate a proud, successful, prosperous Korea from foreign (i.e., American) influence and to pursue independence in their foreign policy. Korean conservatives responded fiercely to this progressive challenge by demanding more reciprocity from the North and stressing the continued importance of the military alliance with the United States. It is noteworthy to reiterate that the most important conservative argument against engagement had to do with reciprocity, not threats or the effects on the alliance.

The Persistence of Contentious Politics of Identity

Whereas North Korea is principally a policy matter for the United States, it is fundamentally an identity issue for South Korea. As presented in this chapter, South Koreans see the North as a Korean issue, and they perceive DPRK-related events to be in the realm of inter-Korean relations; this is in accordance with a broadly held vision that someday, the peninsula will be unified.

Both newspapers, *Chosun* and *Hankyoreh*, devoted approximately 60 percent of all North Korea–related editorials and columns to coverage of inter-Korean relations, while only 8 percent of editorials and columns were primarily about the DPRK itself. In the post–cold war years, conservative-progressive disagreement over the North has not focused on the nature or circumstance of the regime or its people. Rather, a key question, one that is hotly debated and deeply immersed in identity politics, is what approach to take to this problem—to the suffering of Northern brethren struggling to survive in a hostile and aggressive country. Both sides recognize the need for engagement, which is hard to reject, given a strong sense of ethnic identity, but their policy approaches are fundamentally different. One emphasizes inter-Korean relations above competing priorities, while the other demands more reciprocity from the North. Each side strongly believes it has the correct prescription for the terms on which inter-Korean relations should be pursued, and these beliefs—featured in domestic politics but grounded in identity—do not yield easily to political compromise.

This contention over the North needs to be understood in the larger context of the politics of national identity. With the collapse of the Soviet empire, the democratization of the ROK, and the implementation of the Sunshine Policy, many in the South have sought to redefine their conception of national identity, and the North, as part of the same ethnic Korean nation, is a central factor in this process. However, this process of redefining or reformulating national identity can be contentious and conflict ridden, and this is exactly what has happened in the South with respect to views of the North: One group has firmly retained the established identity, and the other group has reinterpreted relationships and events, forging a progressive identity. As revealed by the framing data presented earlier, these two identities, in complete opposition, have hardened over time, especially since implementation of the Sunshine Policy.

The politics of national identity take on special meaning in the Korean context. While both conservatives and progressives agree on a shared sense of ethnic unity, they debate the political notion of nation. Counterintuitively, agreement on ethnic unity makes the political debate especially bitter, because it creates normative expectations and prescriptions for the behavior of *all* the members (i.e., one group expects the other group to behave just as it would). When the groups articulate disparate political conceptions of nation, they define conflicting terms for true patriotism and loyalty to the Korean race. Therefore, the conflict is highly charged and does not lend itself to political compromise. Each group views its position as part of an essential state of order, not conducive to concessions. Each is wedded to a vision of ethnic unity in which the greatest threat to identity is not external actors but internal challenges and corrosion.[36]

The divided political landscape is not likely to change in the near term. Although the Lee Myung Bak administration does not deny the importance of engagement with the North (indeed, Lee's Vision 3000 North Korea policy would catapult inter-Korean interaction and investment to new levels), the question still remains: What should be the new terms of engagement? Moreover, what will the South do if the North refuses to accept those terms?

Lee has emphasized greater conditionality in dealing with the North (e.g., denuclearization before deepened economic engagement), but this has already provoked furious reaction from the Northern regime, and inter-Korea relations have been practically frozen. The new policy also drew strong criticism from progressive forces as they criticized the new administration's policy of not giving food aid to the North unless it makes a formal request, even as a major food shortage looms there.[37] Deep and bitter division over North Korea has important implications for the U.S.-ROK relations as South Koreans' views of the North, as shown earlier, are closely intertwined with their views of the United States.

The following chapter turns to a fuller examination of South Korean conservative and progressive views toward the United States and U.S.-ROK relations.

FOUR

Alliance Politics in South Korea

In late 2004, South Korean President Roh Moo Hyun told a World Affairs Council luncheon in Los Angeles that he had been "blunt and direct" in pressing for an *exclusively* diplomatic approach to the North Korean nuclear issue, denouncing alternative coercive means, such as economic sanctions. In a warning unmistakably directed at the Bush administration, President Roh stressed that "a hard-line policy [toward North Korea] will have very grave repercussions and implications for the Korean peninsula." While expressing apprehension over the direction of U.S. policy, he added that, in his judgment, the claim by the Democratic People's Republic of Korea (DPRK) that nuclear weapons and missiles are necessary to safeguard the regime is "understandable considering the environment they live in."[1]

Roh's comments may well have been an attempt to exert influence in an opportune political moment, as U.S. foreign policy was being reassessed in the wake of President Bush's reelection victory. Prominent neoconservatives with connections to the administration had mounted a visible campaign for an increasingly hard-line policy toward the DPRK.[2] Apparently, as part of this effort to influence a reconfigured Bush foreign policy team, American Enterprise Institute scholar Nicholas Eberstadt published an article in the *Weekly Standard* entitled "Tear Down This Tyranny: A Korea Strategy for Bush's Second Term." Eberstadt argued that diplomacy with the current North Korean regime was futile and advocated a tougher U.S. policy that would work "around the pro-appeasement crowd in the South Korean government" and at the U.S. State Department. Referring to Roh's Los Angeles remarks, Eberstadt maintained that South Korea was a "runaway ally." He went so far as to posit that Seoul's behavior constituted the second crisis on the Korean peninsula from the U.S. perspective.[3]

Roh's remarks were perhaps timed to the reassessment of U.S. foreign policy. Nonetheless, the fact that he delivered them on U.S. soil en route to an Asia-Pacific Economic Cooperation (APEC) summit at which he would meet with President Bush revealed the persistence of DPRK policy discord between the two allies. The conservative *Chosun Ilbo* had diagnosed the problematic, discernible "big gap" on North Korea policy at the outset of the nuclear crisis,[4] and Roh's Los Angeles comments demonstrated that two years into the crisis, Washington and Seoul were still out of sync on the most significant challenge facing the alliance.

Roh's speech received scant attention in the U.S. media and little, if any, response from Washington officials, but it spurred a serious and intense debate in South Korean newspapers, with prominent conservative and progressive publications taking starkly different positions on the president's remarks. The conservative *Chosun Ilbo* published an editorial titled "A Miscalculated Attempt to Show Off Roh's Confidence in Diplomatic Relations," in which it argued that international pressure had been an effective tool in changing Libya's strategic calculus on its nuclear program. The editorial maintained that "President Roh's publicly-stated opposition to an embargo against North Korea, therefore, is tantamount to an abandonment of negotiating tools with the North" and thus promoted unnecessary discord within the alliance.[5]

In contrast, the progressive *Hankyoreh Shinmoon*'s reaction to the same speech rationalized United States–Republic of Korea (U.S.-ROK) policy differences, arguing that "the Korean and American views can always differ, and indeed they must, because the U.S. sees the peninsula as one part of its global strategy." Furthermore, the newspaper strongly disagreed with the charge levied by conservative forces that Roh's comments amounted to a "big mistake for sounding like he was siding with the North when instead he should be working on U.S.-Korea [ROK] cooperation." Instead, the progressive newspaper bitterly contended that "at the root of such criticism appears to be the deeply engrained belief that Korea should not in any way offend a recently reelected Bush."[6]

This heated debate over when, how, and to what extent the ROK should seek common cause with the United States, most notably on the vital issue of North Korea, indicates a particular depth of disagreement, one that goes beyond normal domestic policy disputes. Rather, it is a symptom of a larger phenomenon, or rather a *process*, at work in South Korean society: an intense debate over national identity that has come to prominence as significant changes have occurred on the peninsula, in the region, and in the world.

As discussed in the previous chapter, democratization provided an environment conducive to this identity debate—something not possible during authoritarian years (and indeed, in many ways, a reaction to this time). Due to the particular ethnic and historic features, respectively, of South Korea's relationships with the North and the United States, these two nations loom large in South Koreans' conception of their place and identity in the world. During the cold war, South Koreans retained an anticommunist identity, binding themselves to this U.S. ideology and contrasting their nation with the regime in the North. However, in the wake of the cold war, democratization, and implementation of engagement with the North, the way in which South Koreans define their position vis-à-vis North Korea and the United States has become more passionately debated.

As Daniel Sneider has argued, it is a myth that there ever was a golden age of U.S.-ROK relations.[7] Rather, the alliance has been marked by periods of serious stress. In the 1970s, tension was caused by the so-called Koreagate scandal and the Carter administration's plan to withdraw U.S. troops, and during the 1980s, there were anti-American movements. These periods, as well as others, were characterized by doubt, disappointment, and mistrust. Yet recent discord in U.S.-ROK relations has been portrayed in the Korean media in a much bigger and more contentious way, as democratization has created the political space for debate and the fever pitch of criticism of the alliance has moved from examining the *terms* of the alliance to a fundamental, broader questioning of the *rationale* of the alliance. In this sense, what has been witnessed in the Korean media during this study period is really quite new, and this chapter will argue, as did the previous chapter, that this phenomenon is inextricably linked to societywide contention over identity.

Whereas Chapter 3 examined how the South Korean identity has evolved in accordance with perceptions of North Korea, this chapter evaluates how it has developed in accordance with changing perceptions of both the United States and the U.S.-ROK relationship (of which the military alliance is a significant part). The dissimilarity of the *Chosun* and *Hankyoreh* editorials on Roh's remarks in Los Angeles provides a glimpse into the deep division over how South Koreans see themselves in relation to the United States and the alliance, and it illustrates that two variables are at work in conceptualizing that identity in relational terms.

To understand the Korean politics of national identity, one must examine how Koreans define themselves in relation to the "significant other"—in this case, the United States (and North Korea in the previous chapter). Before doing so, however, it is important to consider how Koreans define the other. In recent years, Korean—and indeed, global—perceptions of the United States have changed in accordance with criticism of President Bush's war on terror. Thus, changes in perception of the nature of the other (combined with new dynamics at play within the South Korean self-definition) have stimulated changes in how Koreans define themselves vis-à-vis the other. It is critical to consider both the essential and relational elements of identity in reference to the other—in this case, the United States and U.S.-ROK relations.

Key Arguments

Based on analyses of the Korean media data collected on the United States and the U.S.-ROK relationship, this chapter will advance four principal arguments. First, the U.S.-ROK relationship receives significant coverage in the Korean media—*much* more coverage than in the U.S. media—and security issues predominate in this coverage, defining the bilateral relationship (despite the importance of the economic and trade relationship).

Second, the U.S.-ROK relationship has indeed become increasingly contentious over time—a phenomenon that is evident in both the conservative and the progressive newspapers' increases in attention. The progressive media are clearly setting the agenda through their challenges to conventional wisdom, putting the conservative media on the defensive.

Third, anti-American and anti-alliance sentiment must be distinguished to better understand the shape of South Korean attitudes and their implications for U.S. policy. The two are often conflated in the general public perception of events in Korea but should be separated both conceptually and empirically. This study shows that although the progressive and conservative newspapers have both become more critical of the U.S. since 2000, only the progressive newspaper has become more critical of the U.S.-ROK relationship.

Finally, reflecting intensified contention between progressives and conservatives, the disparity in the overall picture the two newspapers present has widened in recent years, and this is true for both the United States and U.S.-ROK relations. Because the ROK is a democratic country, public opinion is now more important than ever in the formulation of foreign policy, and thus, this societal division and perception gap have serious policy implications for Washington.

Before presenting these findings, it is important to note that in this study, South Korean views of the United States have been conceptually separated from those of the relationship between the two allies, since, as will be revealed, the two views are not necessarily the same. As discussed in the introductory chapter, there is a tendency to conflate anti-Americanism and anti-alliance sentiment (per the anti-Americanism thesis), but as demonstrated later, they need to be treated as distinct.

In addition, care has been taken in the study to distinguish between attention and attitudes toward the broader U.S.-ROK bilateral relationship and the military alliance. While the military alliance forms a significant (some argue crucial[8]) part of the bilateral relationship, it is not synonymous with the U.S.-ROK relationship, as the latter also encompass financial, trade, and cultural interactions. Indeed, as will be discussed in greater detail in the next chapter, U.S. newspapers give most of their coverage to economic aspects of the U.S.-ROK relationship.

In a similar vein, it is also important not to equate the U.S.-ROK alliance with the presence of U.S. forces in the ROK. Although the latter may be the most visible, immediately relevant part of the alliance in the eyes of many Koreans, the presence of U.S. forces in Korea is only one of many important features of the alliance. Figure 4.1 depicts the relationship among these aspects. Careful delineation of these aspects may lead to greater, more refined understanding of the current tension in the alliance.

Korean Views of the United States and the U.S.-ROK Relationship

As did the previous chapter, this chapter analyzes editorials and columns published in *Chosun Ilbo* and *Hankyoreh Shinmoon* from July 1992 to July 2003. (See Chapter 2 for a detailed description of the data set.) Once again, news media coverage reflects public debate, and news media messages are a good proxy of contending views on ROK foreign policy.

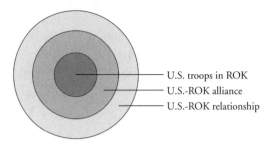

U.S. troops in ROK
U.S.-ROK alliance
U.S.-ROK relationship

FIGURE 4.1 Multiple aspects of the U.S.-ROK relationship.

The following sections present descriptive views of South Korean media coverage of the United States and the U.S.-ROK relationship. The specific focus on the types of issues that elicit the most coverage reflects the goal of uncovering the mix of attention to U.S.-related security and economic issues, including which is the primary driver of ROK interest in its relationship with the United States. Further, the analysis seeks to identify key problem areas by examining issue-specific news attention and tone in coverage of U.S.-related matters. Here, the goal is to assess the extent of anti-American and anti-alliance sentiment expressed in the Korean media. This discussion is followed by an evaluation of the temporal changes in media attention and tone to see whether the U.S.-ROK relationship has become an increasingly contentious issue in Korea. The goal here is to assess whether the gap between conservatives and progressives in their views of the United States and U.S.-ROK relations has grown over these years. Although data were collected on the U.S.-DPRK relationship, they will be referenced only where they relate to the U.S.-ROK relationship.

KEEN ATTENTION TO SECURITY AND THE ALLIANCE

This section looks at Korean media coverage of U.S.-related topics. When data from *Chosun* and *Hankyoreh* are averaged, as shown in Table 4.1, almost half (44.7%) of all editorials and columns focused on issues pertaining to the U.S. itself. The U.S.-ROK relationship received approximately one-third of all U.S.-related coverage (32.2%).

These statistics indicate that the Korean media's interest in the United States extends beyond the bilateral relationship. Still, compared with U.S. media coverage of ROK-related matters, the Korean media devoted far more coverage to the relationship.[9] It is interesting to point out that the progres-

TABLE 4.1
Article count by focus category

Category	*Chosun Ilbo*	*Hankyoreh Shinmoon*	Total
U.S.	467	304	771
	(49.8)	(38.6)	(44.7)
U.S.-ROK	263	295	558
	(28.1)	(37.5)	(32.3)
U.S.-DPRK	171	169	340
	(18.3)	(21.5)	(19.7)
Other	36	19	55
	(3.8)	(2.4)	(3.2)
TOTAL	937	787	1,724
	(100)	(100)	(100)

NOTE: Parentheses contain percentages.

sive newspaper accorded nearly equal attention to the United States and U.S.-South Korea relations (38.6% and 37.5%, respectively) over the course of this study. These findings suggest two things. First, the bilateral relationship is seen as a more critical issue to Koreans than to Americans.[10] Second, Korean progressives have been more active in making the current status of the U.S.-South Korea relationship a major policy issue in accordance with their ideology, an issue that will be explored more later in this chapter.

As shown in Table 4.2, within this sample, *Hankyoreh* and *Chosun* both accorded significant percentages of their coverage to security issues, especially in their coverage of the U.S.-ROK relationship. (Security aspects of the bilateral relationship are tantamount to the alliance.) Alliance issues composed nearly half (48.62%) of the conservative daily's coverage of the

TABLE 4.2
Most prevalent issues by focus category (percent)

Category/issue	*Chosun Ilbo*	*Hankyoreh Shinmoon*	Total
United States			
Security	28.15	47.38	35.74
U.S. politics	34.12	17.97	27.74
Economy/Trade	18.34	18.95	18.58
U.S.-ROK			
Security	48.62	68.27	59.09
Economy/Trade	18.43	13.45	15.78
Foreign affairs	18.82	8.97	13.58

bilateral relationship over the study period, and for *Hankyoreh*, alliance issues composed more than two-thirds (68.27%) of U.S.-ROK relations coverage.

These statistics provide insight into how the Korean media—and by extension, the Korean people—perceive the role of the alliance within the larger realm of U.S.-ROK relations. The alliance seems to dominate the media's conception of the bilateral relationship. In this vein, it is noteworthy that the progressive newspaper devoted a higher percentage of its coverage to security issues, within both U.S.-ROK and U.S. coverage, than the conservative newspaper did. Subsequent sections of this chapter will investigate how, in leading the challenge to the conventional wisdom about the alliance, progressive forces, including *Hankyoreh*, had an agenda-setting effect. They provoked a debate that increased both progressive and conservative newspapers' coverage of alliance issues, as ideologically opposed media outlets sought to refute each other and advance their own positions.

Chosun and *Hankyoreh* devoted rather similar levels of coverage to economic and trade issues within the U.S. focus category, while *Chosun* accorded slightly more coverage to these issues than its progressive counterpart within the U.S.-ROK relations focus category. As will be discussed in the following chapter, economic and trade issues were much more prominently featured in U.S. newspapers' coverage of the ROK. This is an interesting disparity in perception, given that for the duration of the study period, the United States was the ROK's largest trading partner. This finding shows that despite the importance of the United States to the ROK economy, it is still security that defines the U.S.-ROK relationship in the minds of the Korean people.

Moving from general issues to the more specific level of subjects covered in *Chosun* and *Hankyoreh* editorials and columns (see Table 4.3), it is apparent that the presence of U.S. troops in South Korea was the leading topic within coverage of U.S.-ROK relations, again demonstrating that in terms of Korean interest and perception, the military alliance is the core of the U.S.-ROK relationship. (The topic of U.S.-ROK trade was a distant second at 13.95%.) Table 4.3 reveals that *Hankyoreh* devoted half of its coverage of the U.S.-ROK relationship to the subject of troops, while *Chosun* devoted less than one-quarter of its coverage to this subject—a noteworthy disparity. Korean progressives led the questioning of the U.S. military presence on ROK soil by focusing on and consistently expressing outrage over negative

TABLE 4.3
Most prevalent subjects by focus category (percent)

Category/subject	*Chosun Ilbo*	*Hankyoreh Shinmoon*	Total
United States			
Domestic politics	22.29	7.84	16.60
Economy/Industry	15.92	14.71	15.44
Security	9.98	18.95	13.51
Election	11.46	9.48	10.68
Security of Iraq	4.25	10.13	6.56
U.S.-ROK			
U.S. troops in ROK	23.95	50.34	37.92
Trade	15.97	12.16	13.95
Other diplomacy	10.65	4.73	7.51
DPRK WMD	11.03	3.72	7.16
Anti-Americanism in ROK	8.37	4.05	6.08

aspects, including the attitudes conveyed through large and small crimes committed by American GIs.

A second noteworthy disparity in coverage of U.S.-ROK relations is evident in *Chosun*'s higher level of attention to DPRK weapons of mass destruction (WMD) (11.03% versus 3.72% in *Hankyoreh*). This indicates conservative concern over the threat posed by North Korea and is in line with findings from the previous chapter. Still, the North's WMD received much less attention, even in the conservative newspaper, than in the U.S. press, as shown in the next chapter, suggesting a big perception gap between Koreans and Americans as to the threat from the Northern regime and the role this threat plays in U.S.-ROK relations. In other words, Koreans, even conservatives, are less concerned with the DPRK threat than Americans, who see it in the larger context of nuclear proliferation and the war against terrorism.

Additionally, Table 4.3 shows that *Chosun* accorded more coverage to anti-Americanism in the ROK, which suggests concern over and/or criticism of this phenomenon, especially its impact on the alliance. Indeed, throughout the study years, *Chosun* urged progressive forces harboring anti-U.S. sentiment to "examine the big picture and consider the national interest."[11] For example, just before the presidential election of 2002, the conservative daily lamented, "A poisonous atmosphere has been spreading like a fad throughout the basis of this country's society,"[12] pointing out that many Koreans believed protestors had gone too far. In 2004, when the United States announced its plan to reduce its level of troops on the peninsula, conservatives were similarly critical of anti-American elements, arguing that it was persistent and showy demonstrations of anti-Americanism that precipitated this "natural reaction" from Washington.[13]

In addition to the high rate of security-related coverage within U.S.-ROK editorials and columns, *Hankyoreh* also devoted more coverage to U.S. security (18.95%) than to any other subject within its U.S. news sections. This likely reflects more recent developments, including opposition to the U.S. war in Iraq and to Korean troop deployments to that conflict. Indeed, the progressive paper cast U.S. foreign policy as hard lined and unilateral, a perception that became increasingly prevalent after the inauguration of President Bush—one that made more pressing its case for an "independent way," apart from the United States.

It can also be inferred that this type of reasoning has remained prominent in the progressive press, up to and even beyond the study years. In an October 22, 2007, editorial, *Hankyoreh* railed against President Roh's decision to renew the ROK's Iraq troop deployment, calling it a "bad precedent, in which Korea gets put into a position where it has to pay a big price because of being caught up in American interests."[14] In contrast, as Table 4.3 shows, *Chosun* devoted most of its U.S. coverage to nonsecurity subjects, led by domestic politics (22.29%), a topic in which its progressive counterpart takes comparatively little interest (7.84%).

Together, these findings clearly show that the U.S.-ROK relationship yields significant coverage in the Korean media (more so than in the U.S. media). Moreover, security—and to a large extent, the U.S. troop presence—is what defines the bilateral relationship, despite the importance of economic ties.

INTENSIFICATION OF THE IDENTITY DEBATE

Is media attention toward the U.S.-ROK relationship and alliance-related issues event specific, or has there been a general trend in news volume over time? In other words, has the U.S.-ROK relationship become increasingly newsworthy in the South Korean press, as many experts on Korean affairs argue? The findings of the study reveal that the U.S.-ROK relationship has become more contentious over time in relation to the intensification of the identity debate.[15]

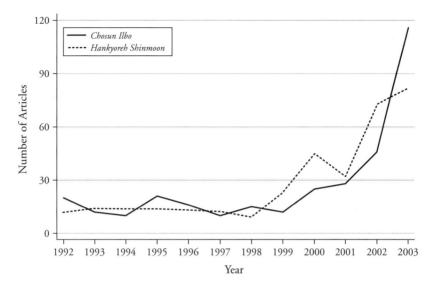

FIGURE 4.2 Media attention to the U.S.-ROK relationship.

As Figure 4.2 shows, prior to 1999, *Hankyoreh*'s interest in the relationship appeared rather flat, and the progressive newspaper accorded a roughly similar level of coverage as its conservative counterpart. Yet after 1999, attention levels substantially increased and internewspaper disparities became apparent, indicating a very different environment—one in which the U.S.-ROK relationship was a topic of heated debate. It appears that *Hankyoreh* led this debate, challenging the conventional wisdom (e.g., the conservative position) on the relationship through a significant increase in critical editorials and columns. *Chosun* followed suit, increasing the number of editorials and columns it published on the relationship, refuting progressive criticism, defending its positions, and persistently criticizing the attitudes and actions of the progressive administrations that had come to power.

This pattern of dramatic increases in Korean media coverage of the United States and U.S.-ROK relations after 1999 pervades the data set. Two additional cases can also be provided to illustrate this pattern. In each case, *Hankyoreh*'s initial increase in coverage and *Chosun*'s subsequent response is significant, as increased coverage on a topic—especially on the scale seen here—can foster and/or perpetuate societywide scrutiny.

In this regard, the progressive "shot across the bow" (fired by *Hankyoreh* and other progressive forces) has significant implications. In an attempt to promote the progressive perspective on U.S.-ROK relations, these forces framed the debate, setting the terms to which the conservative side had to respond—namely, that it is in South Korea's interests to wholehcartedly pursue a new relationship with North Korea and to make changes to its unequal alliance with the United States. *Hankyoreh* has accused conservative forces of being "trapped in the Cold War-era concept," arguing that conservative notions of South Korea's security interests vis-à-vis the North and the United States are sadly outdated[16] and that when it comes to brethren in the North, *Chosun* can be "cold-hearted."[17]

Figure 4.3 depicts the volume of editorials and columns the two newspapers published on the issue of East Asia security within all U.S.-ROK and U.S.-related news (i.e., the United States and the U.S.-ROK alliance's role in East Asia security). Again, it can be observed that coverage before 1999 was relatively low in both newspapers (i.e., each published less than 35 articles per year, or less than one per week on average), with *Chosun* generally providing a higher level of attention. After 1999, however, *Hankyoreh*'s attention to the United States and East Asia security grew dramatically, and the progressive newspaper published increasingly more articles than its conservative counterpart. *Chosun*'s increase in attention after 1999, although slightly less dramatic, followed *Hankyoreh*'s lead, seemingly in an attempt to respond to progressive criticism of security arrangements. By 2003, both newspapers were publishing almost two editorials and/or columns per week on this topic.

There were certainly many important events between 1999 and 2003 that contributed to increased coverage of the role of the United States and the alliance in East Asia security, from the U.S.-DPRK's high-level reciprocal visits during the Clinton administration to the inception of a second nuclear crisis. For example, coverage of the two nuclear crises was several times greater in 2002 than in 1994. One of the principal differences between the two crises, for the purpose of this analysis, is that the second crisis took place in an environment in which the nature of the nuclear threat and the U.S. role vis-à-vis that threat were both contested, due to the bitter battle over South Korean national identity.

It is also likely that the policies of the Bush administration (including fear over the policies' potentially destabilizing effects on the peninsula) have contributed to the dramatic increase in coverage. Just as the Korean media frames about the North, analyzed in the previous chapter, illustrated a dra-

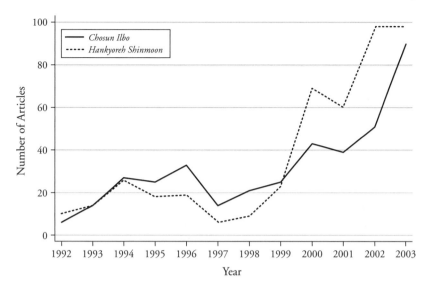

FIGURE 4.3 Media attention to East Asia security.

matic increase in debate since implementation of the Sunshine Policy, the increase in both newspapers' attention to the U.S. role in East Asia security was born of the intensification of the politics of identity and compounded by events. Indeed, events such as the 2002 U.S. military training accident that killed two South Korean schoolgirls and spurred dramatic candlelight protests can be termed *identity-invoking events*. This term will be used in the remainder of this book to describe events that may not be directly related to identity upon cursory examination but that are interpreted through the larger scaled lens of national identity. Such events capture headlines for prolonged periods of time, often feature social movements in response to them, and become embedded in larger narratives about collective identity.

Figure 4.4 charts the number of editorials and columns each newspaper published on U.S. troops in the ROK. As has already been observed from the aggregate data, *Hankyoreh* exhibited a very negative tone toward this subject and published many more articles on it than its conservative counterpart. In fact, this was the only topic on which *Hankyoreh* consistently published more editorials and columns than *Chosun* throughout the study period. While both newspapers published less than 10 editorials and/or columns per year on the presence of U.S. troops in the ROK before 1999, coverage levels increased fourfold by 2003. Once again, *Hankyoreh* initiated the

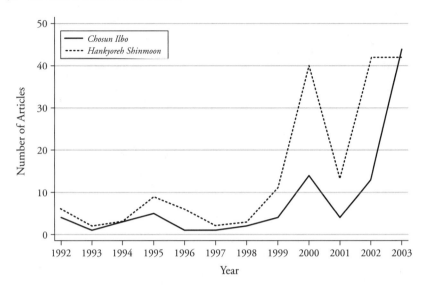

FIGURE 4.4 Media attention to U.S. troops in the ROK.

dramatic increase in coverage, and *Chosun* mirrored the increase, although to a lesser degree.

The extraordinary increase in *Hankyoreh*'s editorials and columns from 1999 to 2000 likely reflected an environment in which progress in inter-Korean relations, including the landmark summit, spurred a broader re-examination of the alliance, especially in the wake of unfortunate and even accidental incidents involving U.S. soldiers. In these years, nationwide outrage was incited by the Nogun-ri controversy, the Maehyang-ri bombing range accident, the discharging of formaldehyde into the Han River, and the negotiations of the Status of Forces Agreement—all identity-invoking events that were focused on heavily by the progressive media (and much less so by the conservative mainstream). According to a senior U.S. diplomat in Seoul at that time, the standard story line in the media was that U.S. Forces Korea (USFK) was on a rampage, showing no respect for the lives of Koreans.[18] Additionally, according to former Foreign Minister Han Sung Joo, "[The] perception of a thaw between North and South Korea in the wake of the June summit . . . provided a convenient platform for those who have always opposed the U.S. troop presence to promote their cause among the broader spectrum of the South Korean public."[19] Ardent progressives' crusade on this issue and a new spirit of inter-Korean cooperation persuaded additional elements of the political spectrum that it was no longer necessary to endure the inconveniences associated with U.S. troops stationed on the peninsula, despite President Kim Dae Jung's strong argument that the alliance remained relevant in the Sunshine era, if only for regional security.

The precipitous drop in coverage of the troop issue in 2001 was most likely due to the effects of the September 11 terrorist attacks on the United States. At that time, there was a palpable sense in Korea that, given the international outpouring of sympathy for the United States, it was not appropriate to criticize this alliance partner or other developments related to the September 11 attacks (i.e., the initiation of the war on terror). In this vein, Soh Chang Rok, an international relations specialist at Korea University, described Koreans' recognized need for discretion to the *Washington Post*: "There's enormous international pressure to help out the U.S., so we [Koreans] have to keep our lips sealed [at this critical time.]" This attitude held even as the United States discussed plans to expand its alliance with Japan in connection with war on terror-related operations in Afghanistan.[20]

Yet this effect was only temporary, as the tragic 2002 schoolgirl incident—an identity-invoking event that provoked a reaction greater than the sum of its parts—led to reinstatement of higher levels of coverage of U.S. troops in Korea. This was especially true of *Hankyoreh*, whose volume of editorials and columns remained nearly four times greater than that of *Chosun*. By 2003, a dramatic increase in the number of articles that *Chosun* published illustrated that the debate had reached a new level of aggravation, as the United States and the ROK initiated Future of the Alliance consultations on the relocation of Yongsan Garrison along with a variety of other troop presence issues.

Together, temporal assessments of attention to U.S.-ROK relations, East Asian security, and U.S. troops in Korea demonstrate that Korean media coverage of the United States and the U.S.-ROK relationship has increased substantially since the late 1990s. These assessments also show that this rise has been spurred by progressives challenging conventional wisdom and the status quo and that it has been noticed by the conservative media, leading to intense debates between the opposing camps.

ANTI-AMERICAN VERSUS ANTI-ALLIANCE SENTIMENTS

This study argues for the necessity of separating anti-alliance and anti-American sentiment in the context of examining Korean attitudes. According to the

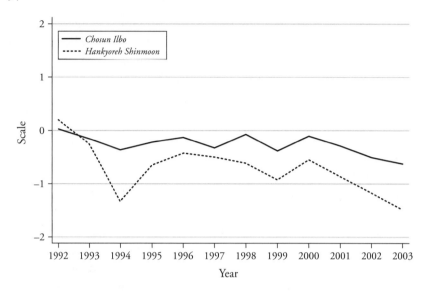

FIGURE 4.5 Average news tone on the United States.

data, after 2000, there was a steady downward trend in both newspapers' tones toward the United States, with *Hankyoreh*'s tone declining at a slightly steeper rate (see Figure 4.5).[21] Predating the second nuclear crisis, this decline in tone seems most likely connected to the Bush administration's rhetoric on preemption, regime change, and the axis of evil, which elicited resounding criticism from South Koreans, in general, and especially from the progressive camp.

For instance, an early 2002 survey showed that 62 percent of South Koreans viewed the Bush "axis of evil" statement as "escalating tensions in the Korean peninsula," while only 31 percent regarded it as a measured description of the North Korean threat.[22] However, a Pew Research Center commentary from August 2003 pointed out that while increasing anti-American sentiment in many other countries was driven primarily by fervent opposition to the Bush administration, in the ROK, only 20 percent of those critical of the United States believed that Bush was the main problem, while 72 believed that "America in general" was the problem.[23] That is, even though anti-Americanism was a worldwide trend over these years and Korea could certainly be said to be part of this trend, Korean anti-American sentiment was of a different flavor. Koreans experienced anti-Americanism in the context of the politics of national identity, whereas people of other nations expressed a general protest to Bush administration policy worldwide. Although the policies of the Bush administration surely stoked similar sentiment, it appears naïve to attribute broader Korean notions of their position related to the United States primarily to a single U.S. administration.[24]

Figure 4.6 illustrates the two newspapers' tones toward the U.S.-ROK relationship over time, revealing a rather different pattern in tone fluctuations than that observed in reference to the United States. Most importantly, the tone toward U.S.-ROK relations did not exhibit a steady decline after 2000, as was the case with both newspapers' tones toward the United States. As expected, *Chosun* was consistently less negative in its tone toward U.S.-ROK relations than *Hankyoreh*, which maintained a tone close to the very critical –1 for most of the years covered in this study.[25]

As shown in Figure 4.6, in several of the years in which the progressive newspaper became increasingly critical of the relationship, the conservative newspaper's tone remained unchanged or actually became slightly more positive. This is especially noteworthy for the changes between 1999 and 2000 and between 2001 and 2002. For instance, the June 2000 inter-Korean summit may have reinforced conservatives' beliefs that U.S.-ROK relations allow the ROK to deal with the DPRK from a position of strength and that the alliance remains necessary and relevant. Yet the summit may also have simul-

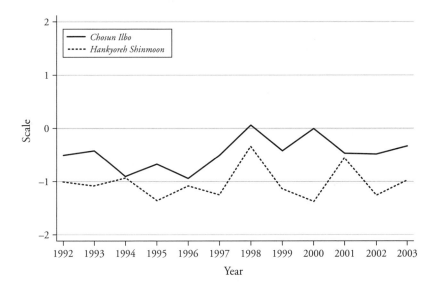

FIGURE 4.6 Average news tone on the U.S.-ROK relationship.

taneously reinforced progressives' views that in the post–cold war era, new rapprochement was possible in inter-Korean relations and the ROK's subordinate relationship to the United States merely hindered such possibility. Indeed, in the immediate aftermath of the historic summit, *Hankyoreh* argued that the leaders' meeting meant that the "U.S. military presence and mutual arms reduction [could now] become agenda items," while a *Chosun* editorial sought to reassert the importance of the alliance, maintaining that "Seoul should not dare think about having U.S. troops withdraw from Korea."[26]

Similarly, it is important to note the change (or lack of change) in tone from 2001 to 2002 in the two newspapers. The year 2002 included two pivotal, identity-defining moments: the death of the two schoolgirls, which ignited severe demonstrations as well as propelled demands for revision of the U.S.-ROK Status of Forces Agreement (SOFA), and the initiation of the current nuclear standoff. As expected, the progressive newspaper turned much more negative in its tone toward U.S.-ROK relations, while the conservative newspaper showed no discernible change in tone. Again, these data, paired with the framing data from Chapter 3 (recall that both newspapers included U.S./alliance frames in their North Korea-related arguments), provide compelling evidence of an increasingly apparent debate between progressives and conservatives. As progressives became more critical of the U.S.-ROK relationship, conservatives became more concerned with the deteriorating relationship and reacted by stressing the importance of the alliance.

For 2001, changes in tone toward United States and U.S.-ROK relations are somewhat difficult to interpret. This was the year of the unsuccessful Bush-Kim Dae Jung summit but also that of sympathy in the aftermath of September 11. In a sense, 2001 was a year that produced mixed feelings of disappointment and sympathy among many South Koreans. Naturally, one might expect more critical views of U.S.-ROK relations but more sympathetic views toward the United States itself. In fact, U.S. newspapers (as will be discussed in Chapter 5) became very critical of U.S.-ROK relations beginning in 2001, reflecting policy disputes between the two countries' administrations.

However, as demonstrated by Figures 4.5 and 4.6, while *Chosun* became more critical in its views of both the United States and U.S.-ROK relations, *Hankyoreh* became more critical only of the United States. The progressive newspaper's tone toward U.S.-ROK relations actually became more positive in 2001 over 2000, contrary to expectation. These findings seem to suggest that conservatives and progressives in Korea both blamed the Bush administration for the unsuccessful summit (anti-U.S.), but they had different views of its implications for U.S.-ROK relations. The conservative newspaper was greatly concerned over what this summit and this policy discord would mean for the bilateral relationship, while the progressive newspaper did not appear to be as concerned or perhaps simply did not pay as much attention to U.S.-ROK relations in the aftermath of September 11. In fact, closer examination of distribution of tone scores reveals that the year 2001 did not necessarily demonstrate positive tones in the progressive newspaper but rather a lack of very negative tones.[27]

In sum, these findings demonstrate that there has been an anti-American trend in the Korean media in recent years (both progressive and conservative), but that trend has *not* seamlessly translated into opposition to or negative views about the U.S.-ROK relationship. Notably, both the progressive and conservative newspapers became more critical of the United States in the Kim Dae Jung era. However, over the same period, *Chosun* showed a decline in tone toward the United States and assessed U.S.-ROK relations more positively. This was most likely due to the conservative concern that a progressive government and increasingly strident progressive voice in Korean society might undermine the alliance.

The more positive *Chosun* reflected conservatives' fear of "strategic abandonment" by the United States due to their displeasure with arguments advanced by progressive critics.[28] Driven by such concern over the U.S. perception of Korean (progressive) ingratitude and hostility, then, *Chosun* increased its number of editorials and columns stressing the importance of the relationship, which were significantly more positive than those published by *Hankyoreh*. Korean conservatives might not have been pleased with U.S. policy toward the North or, for that matter, with U.S. foreign policy on the world stage. (The Pew survey shows this was the case for a number of U.S. allies at this time.) Regardless, that did not preclude them from arguing the merits of the alliance.

Chosun's record demonstrates that a critical distinction must be made between shades of anti-American sentiment and anti-alliance views, as they do not necessarily go hand in hand. Most discourse on this topic, including the anti-Americanism thesis presented in the introductory chapter, tends to conflate the two, obscuring valuable insight into the state of Korean sentiment and how changes in these two areas have stimulated changes in Korean identity vis-à-vis the United States and U.S.-ROK relations. This finding also implies that the return to power of Korean conservatives does not preclude serious questions about the United States' approach to the world and to Asia. American policy makers and analysts tend to overlook the complexities of Korean sentiments, which can have important policy implications.

GROWING DISPARITIES AND THE POLITICS OF IDENTITY

The previous section clearly suggests that Korean progressives and conservatives have different views or attitudes toward the United States and/or the U.S.-ROK relationship. This section probes this disparity in perception by identifying the main areas of difference and assessing whether disparities have increased over time.

In no uncertain terms, *Hankyoreh* exhibited more negative tones than *Chosun*—toward the United States, U.S.-ROK relations, and every U.S.-related issue. Table 4.4 introduces aggregate data on both papers' average news tones toward the United States and U.S.-ROK relations, as well as relevant issues and subjects. The greatest disparity in tone between the two newspapers is observed for the subject of U.S. forces in the ROK (–1.34 for *Hankyoreh* versus –0.23 for *Chosun*). As shown in Table 4.3, the progressive newspaper devoted the highest proportion of its U.S.-ROK coverage to this

TABLE 4.4
Average news tone by focus category, issue, and subject

	Chosun Ilbo Average Tone	*Hankyoreh Shinmoon* Average Tone	All Average Tone
Focus Category			
United States	–0.23	–0.90	–0.57
U.S.-ROK relations	–0.42	–1.11	–0.77
Issue			
Security	–0.52	–0.85	–0.69
Economics/Trade	–0.37	–0.90	–0.64
U.S. politics	–0.01	–0.51	–0.26
Subject			
DPRK WMD	–0.61	–0.40	–0.51
U.S. troops in ROK	–0.23	–1.34	–0.79

subject, and this coverage was clearly quite negative. Thus, these sizeable disparities in views confirm not only that Korean progressives are very critical of the U.S.-ROK alliance but also that the alliance, including the U.S. troop presence in Korea, has become a point of significant contention between progressives and conservatives.

The only topic for which *Chosun* recorded a more negative tone than *Hankyoreh* was that of DPRK WMD. Again, as shown in Table 4.3, the conservative newspaper devoted much more coverage to this topic than its progressive counterpart. In accordance with the findings of Chapter 3, this confirms conservative criticism of and concern over the threat posed by North Korea. Contrasting progressive and conservative views on U.S. troops in South Korea and DPRK WMD attest to the crucial differences in how each side perceives security issues vis-à-vis the nation's significant others (the United States and North Korea), revealing some of the most crucial points of contested politics of national identity. An examination of Korean media data shows that the papers gave not only *more* coverage but also *more negative* coverage to topics about which they were critical (i.e., U.S. troops and DPRK WMD), confirming the negativity bias of the media.

Overall, the Korean media's tone toward the bilateral relationship (–0.77) was much more negative than the U.S. media's coverage of the relationship (–0.18). This was also the case in their respective coverage of economic and trade issues (–0.64 in the Korean media versus –0.38 in the U.S. media). However, the U.S. media were more critical on the topic of DPRK WMD (–1.05 in the U.S. media versus –0.51 in the Korean media). In a general sense and not surprisingly, Korean conservative views of the U.S.-ROK relationship and the DPRK are closer to U.S. views, while Korean progressive views appear quite distinct. Later chapters will return to these perception gaps—within Korea and between the United States and the ROK—as they have important policy implications for officials in Washington and Seoul, who face the challenge of repairing recent strains and charting a mutually agreed on strategic course.

To assess the magnitude of disparities in perception and its changes over time, a composite index was created by combining news attention and tone, one in which tone scores are multiplied by number of words. Using this index allowed for creating an overall picture of that which is conveyed to the newspaper-reading public in Korea. Most critically, this measure reveals that as attention to the United States and issues related to the U.S.-ROK

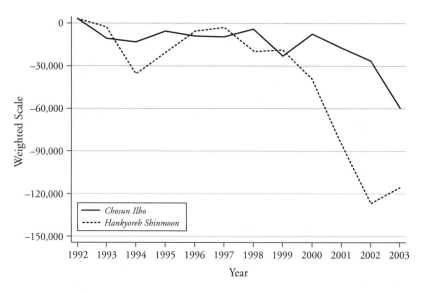

FIGURE 4.7 Weighted news tones on the United States.

relationship increased in recent years, the progressive-conservative perception gap grew significantly, thus illustrating growing disparities in views of the United States and the relationship—views with critical implications for the meaning of Korean identity in a new era.

Figure 4.7 reveals in stark terms that while progressive and conservative views of the United States fluctuated within a relatively narrow range through 1999, the year 2000 marked a point of departure, after which a significant divergence can be observed in progressive and conservative views on the United States, even though both deteriorated. The precipitous decline in *Hankyoreh*'s weighted tone between 2000 and 2002 is especially noteworthy. This trend gives an important indication as to the volume of very negative stories about the United States that appeared in the Korean media even *before* the inception of the peninsula's second nuclear crisis.

Another observation is that, considering the *Hankyoreh* data from 1999, 2000, and 2001, it should have been expected that a progressive candidate would run for president in 2002, utilizing anti-American themes to his advantage and advocating independence for South Korea. Although Roh's ultimate electoral success may have been influenced, to some degree, by the national outpouring of emotion in the wake of the schoolgirl incident, his politics were certainly built on a broader foundation of public sentiment that gained new relevance after 2000.[29] In other words, Roh came to represent a redefined Korean identity in relation to the United States; his candidacy, coming two years after this process of redefinition (and associated sentiment toward the United States and U.S.-ROK relationship), had gained traction and significant visibility in South Korean society.

Figure 4.8 depicts trends in the Korean media's views of the U.S.-ROK relationship, measured in weighted tone, once again, to convey the overall extent to which the public was exposed to a particular view of U.S.-ROK relations. Here, a dramatic increase can be observed since 1999 in the perception gap between the progressive and conservative newspapers concerning the bilateral relationship. Thus, while both progressive and conservative sentiment toward the United States became more critical, the progressive tone toward U.S.-ROK relations sharply declined whereas the conservative tone remained only slightly negative and within a reasonable range. Moreover, by comparing Figure 4.6 with Figure 4.8, it becomes apparent that an editorial or column that was more critical of the relationship tended to be longer in length (for both newspapers).

Finally, it is noteworthy that the progressive newspaper exhibited very critical views toward the U.S.-ROK relationship after 1999 (except in 2001, for the reasons specified earlier), but the U.S. media, as will be shown in

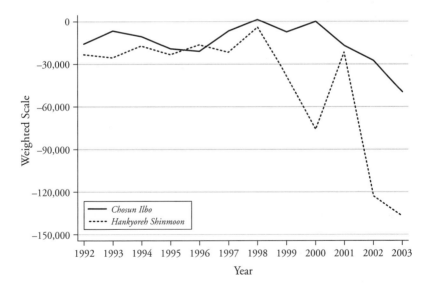

FIGURE 4.8 Weighted news tones on the U.S.-ROK relationship.

subsequent chapters, did not become critical of the relationship until 2001. This difference can be interpreted as reflecting the disparate frameworks that Koreans and Americans employ in conceptualizing the bilateral relationship. (That is, for Koreans, it is a question of identity, while for Americans, it is a matter of policy.) This theme will be explored more fully in Chapter 7.

In addition, it is worthwhile to examine how the Korean media have evaluated U.S.-DPRK relations over time, especially because the study period covers two nuclear standoffs between the United States and the DPRK, both of which have been critical challenges for U.S.-ROK relations. As shown clearly in Figure 4.9, *Hankyoreh* has traditionally recorded more positive tone ratings on prospects for U.S.-DPRK relations. This is in accordance with the progressive identity's priority for rapprochement between the North and each of the alliance partners and its emphasis on an evolved role for the ROK vis-à-vis the United States (and therefore a more mature relationship between the ROK and the United States). However, in recent years, both the progressive and conservative tones toward U.S.-DPRK relations have plummeted. In fact, as shown in Figure 4.9, these two newspapers have very similar trend lines on tone toward U.S.-DPRK relations, including in 2002 and 2003, when the second nuclear crisis occurred on the peninsula.

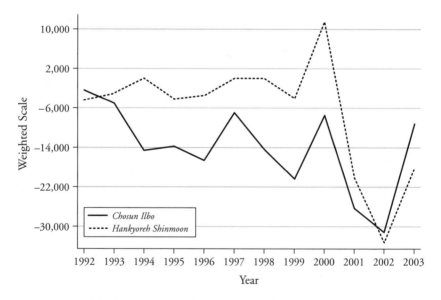

FIGURE 4.9 Weighted news tones on the U.S.-DPRK relationship.

In contrast to the general trend of a growing perception gap between conservatives and progressives, these groups' views of the U.S.-DPRK relationship have actually narrowed in recent years. In this instance, however, it is important to recognize that being similarly pessimistic on the prospect of U.S.-DPRK relations does not indicate a uniformity of opinion between progressives and conservatives on the matter. Rather, as discussed in the previous chapter, whereas conservatives predominantly blame the DPRK, its WMD programs, and its crisis diplomacy for impeding progress in U.S.-DPRK relations, progressives tend to blame the United States for its hard-line policies. (Recall President Roh's strong warning to the United States in his 2004 speech from Los Angeles.) So, interestingly enough, both sides have arrived at similarly pessimistic views of U.S.-DPRK relations but through very different logic.

Challenges and Tasks for the Alliance

In the post–cold war, postauthoritarian era, South Korean society, led by progressives, has been seeking to redefine its national identity vis-à-vis two significant others: North Korea and the United States. As shown by the frame analysis in Chapter 3, South Koreans' views of the United States are closely intertwined with their views of the North. Conservatives see the North as a continuing threat and therefore advocate strong ties to the United States as being in the national interest. Progressives, on the other hand, see the North more as a potential partner and thus advocate improved inter-Korean collaboration while blaming the United States for impeding improvement. The findings throughout this chapter that show increasing media coverage to be coincident with an increasing progressive-conservative perception gap illustrate that the debate over national identity has intensified in recent years. This nationwide debate will continue to be divisive and bitter, as contention over fundamental notions of identity are, by nature, difficult to resolve.

As demonstrated earlier, *Hankyoreh* has taken issue with the U.S.-ROK relationship—most notably, its security dimension—in the context of new political openness in a democratic society. Conservative newspapers have responded, and an intense debate related to identity politics has ensued. As was observed from the North Korea frame data, opposing conservative and progressive identities have hardened over time, especially since implementation of the Sunshine Policy. Disparate political conceptions of the nation and its roles vis-à-vis North Korea and the United States have developed into a highly charged and very volatile conflict. Views of South Korea's relationship with the United States are especially difficult and embittered, since part of the traditional Korean ethos—for conservatives and progressives, for Northerners and Southerners—includes an aversion to contamination by a foreign other in the interest of preserving a unique Korean identity.

While the findings clearly show an anti-U.S. trend in the Korean media during the latter years of this study, that trend did not translate directly into an intensification of criticism toward U.S.-ROK relations. Over the same period that *Chosun* showed a more negative tone toward the United States, for instance, it showed a more positive stance toward U.S.-ROK relations. This was likely due to conservatives' concern that the progressive governments' engagement policy toward the North (and consequent reduction in threat perception) might undermine the alliance. Propelled by such concern, the conservative newspaper increased its number of editorials and columns stressing the importance of the relationship. While Korean conservatives might not have been pleased with U.S. policy in the region or in the war on terror, that did not dissuade them from arguing the continued merits of the alliance. This finding demonstrates the need for making a careful distinction between shades of anti-American sentiment and anti-alliance views, as they may not always be congruent. The tendency to conflate the two is mistaken, as it obscures valuable insight into the state of Korean sentiment and how changes in popular sentiment have stimulated evolution in notions of Korean identity vis-à-vis the United States and U.S.-ROK relations.

Both sides of the alliance have expectations that President Lee's election represents an opportunity to improve the U.S.-ROK relationship. The Lee administration has repeatedly stressed the importance of the U.S.-ROK alliance and sought to restore trilateral collaboration among South Korea, the United States, and Japan. Still, as South Korea remains deeply divided, the new administration faces the daunting task of building consensus for its policy toward the North and the alliance. Thus, the United States must consider the interests associated with both identities and acknowledge the constraints that a divided polity imposes on the Korean government.

In addition, the establishment of a conservative administration in South Korea may galvanize the progressives in challenging its policy agenda, including (perhaps foremost) its approach toward the North and the alliance. In a sense, the administrations of Kim Dae Jung and Roh Moo Hyun compelled progressives to reluctantly agree on certain policies that ran counter to their ideological stance, as mentioned above. In the face of a conservative administration, however, they could become more aggressive in advancing their progressive agenda. This would mean further intensification of identity politics, and the United States could easily be caught between a conservative ROK president and progressive activists. Even under a conservative president, an identity-invoking event could ignite a tinderbox of national emotion. The candlelight protests over the reimportation of the American beef that swept the country in the summer of 2008 has proven that.

In managing the alliance in the face of such enduring identity politics within South Korea, the United States must strive to look for bases for cooperation that appeal to both progressive and conservative constituencies. This will no doubt be a complicated exercise. However, careful alliance management and creative thinking on alliance revitalization are in all parties' interests—those of the United States, the Republic of Korea, and the region.

FIVE

American Views of South Korea and the Alliance

In December 2005, North Korea's official media took aim at the new U.S. ambassador in Seoul, calling him a tyrant and proclaiming that his statements about the Democratic People's Republic of Korea (DPRK) amounted to a declaration of war. Although this type of rhetoric is not necessarily unusual for Pyongyang, that same month, South Korea's leading journalists' organization demanded an apology for what it dubbed the ambassador's "problematic remarks" concerning North Korea. The consternation was caused by Ambassador Alexander Vershbow's references to North Korea as a "criminal regime" and his blunt statements about Pyongyang's counterfeiting and drug-trafficking activities. Fervent South Korean criticism of the ambassador's remarks did not dispute their substance but rather focused on their ineffectiveness in encouraging North Korea to return to the negotiating table.

Ambassador Vershbow, a seasoned diplomat, had arrived in Seoul in October 2005. From November 1, 2005, to July 31, 2006, he made 24 official speeches: 12 focusing on United States–Republic of Korea (U.S.-ROK) relations and cooperation, 9 on economic matters (predominantly extolling the potential benefits of a free trade agreement [FTA]), and 1 each on the future of the Korean peninsula, North Korea, and nonproliferation efforts. Although the vast majority of Vershbow's official speeches were about U.S.-ROK relations and economic issues, most of the coverage in the U.S. news media focused on his remarks about North Korea. From the beginning of Vershbow's tenure in Seoul, 16 stories mainly about or featuring multiple quotes from him had appeared in the *New York Times*, *Washington Post*, and Associated Press. However, only 2 of these articles discussed his efforts to promote a free trade agreement. The other 14 articles—nearly 90 percent of the total—covered the ambassador's calls for North Korea to return to talks, stop its counterfeiting activities, and improve its human rights record.

It is somewhat curious that the U.S. representative in Seoul was most often quoted on issues regarding North Korea, rather than significant and timely U.S.-ROK issues, such as the FTA. But as this study explores in depth, North Korea and disparate U.S.-ROK approaches to North Korea are major and often divisive issues within the alliance. South Korean reaction to the "criminal regime" comments illustrates how the U.S. position on North Korea can be challenging for the alliance, as well as how such contention increases newsworthiness from the perspective of the U.S. media. That is, the U.S. position on North Korea warrants coverage on its own, but when it creates division within the U.S.-ROK alliance, it becomes an even more conflict-ridden, and thus appealing, news story.

In some ways, and as data analyses in this chapter will show, this example might be viewed as a proxy for general U.S. media coverage of the Korean peninsula. That is, in terms of news attention, even when major policy issues in the U.S.-ROK relationship (such as the proposed FTA) are being discussed, they are often overshadowed by DPRK-related disputes, which strike at the foundation of the alliance.

This chapter and the subsequent chapter examine U.S. media coverage of the Korean peninsula from a comparative perspective. The main task in these two chapters is to identify key issues in U.S. press coverage of the two Koreas, examining the relevance of these nations to various U.S. interests and across contexts. For instance, what types of issues evoke the highest concentration of U.S. interest? Do primarily security or economic interests drive the U.S. relationship with the two Koreas? What issues and subjects are most prominent in ROK coverage versus DPRK coverage? For example, how much attention is devoted to the ostensibly troubled alliance with the ROK versus the DPRK's development of nuclear weapons? Has the U.S. press portrayed the two Koreas differently over time? If so, were the changes event specific or can a trend be identified? And in light of anecdotal evidence of a troubled alliance, can these data isolate decided shifts in news tone toward U.S.-ROK relations?

This chapter focuses on U.S. media coverage of South Korea and that nation's relationship with the United States. In examining this coverage, the argument will be made that South Korea does not function as a "significant other" for the United States against which its identity is defined, while the United States does serve this role for South Korea. The U.S. media are not engaged in any sort of bitter or emotional debate over the ROK, the bilateral relationship, or the alliance; rather, the differences in coverage stem from varied interests in particular issue areas, such as trade and finance, instead of ideology. Further, Korean news may be said to be underrepresented in the U.S. media, compared to the economic and security importance of the country. Understanding the roots of the asymmetry of news attention and how the United States and the ROK view each other is critical to comprehending the evolution of this important bilateral relationship.

Before a full analysis of U.S. media coverage of South Korea, the relationship, and specific issues is presented, a comparative context will be established. Thus, the chapter begins by comparing the frequency of news on the United States appearing in the Korean media with that of Korean news appearing in the U.S. media. Then, the chapter compares the extent of U.S. media attention to Korean news with that given to other nations.

Korean News in Comparative Context

Chapter 4 established that the United States is a significant other against which South Koreans define their identity and that the converse is not true. That is, even though the United States plays an important role in ROK security and U.S. troops being stationed on the peninsula is a feature of daily life for many Koreans, the ROK does not guarantee U.S. security and the alliance rarely touches the lives of average Americans. Koreans have not influenced U.S. politics in the same way Americans are perceived to have influenced Korean politics, and Americans certainly do not believe that Koreans have perpetrated great injustices on their fellow citizens. These differing national perceptions on the practical and the political, which are rooted in historical and structural factors, mean that American perceptions of Korea can only be compared to ROK perceptions of the United States within consideration of this context of asymmetry.

Figures 5.1 and 5.2 illustrate the extent of Korean news attention to the United States and that of U.S. news attention to the ROK, respectively, over the course of this study. The disparity in coverage is stark, especially with regard to the U.S.-ROK relationship. On average, the Korean newspapers published about 1.6 times as many articles on the United States (1,012) as the

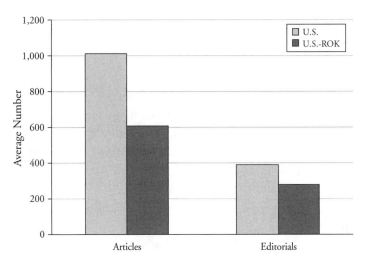

FIGURE 5.1 The United States and the U.S.-ROK relationship in Korean news.

U.S. newspapers published on the ROK (630). However, the Korean newspapers published 4 times as many articles about U.S.-ROK relations (610) as the U.S. newspapers did (151) over the study years. Even more dramatically, on average, the Korean newspapers published 56 times the number of editorials and columns on U.S.-ROK relations as the U.S. newspapers did.

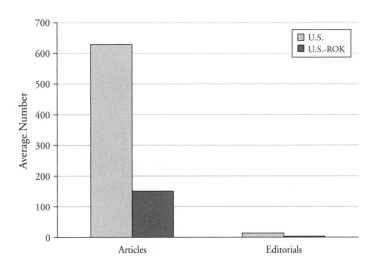

FIGURE 5.2 The ROK and the U.S.-ROK relationship in U.S. news.

Indeed, it is important to highlight that, on average, each U.S. newspaper published a mere 13 editorials and columns on the ROK and only 5 editorials and columns on U.S.-ROK relations over the 12-year study period.

Thus, Figures 5.1 and 5.2 illustrate the extent to which the Korean press takes a much greater interest in the United States and the bilateral relationship than the U.S. press takes in the ROK and the relationship. Clearly, there exists an unmistakable asymmetry in media attention, one that is the inverse image of the asymmetry in power that exists between these two allies.

Figure 5.3 shows how U.S. media attention to Korea compares to that paid to other countries. When the number of words and number of articles devoted to South Korea over the study period is calibrated to be equal to 1, the figure allows for easy comparison of other nations' rates of coverage compared to that of South Korea. (For example, in terms of both number of words and number of articles, France received just over three times the coverage of South Korea.) Here, the *New York Times*'s foreign coverage is used as a proxy for that of U.S. news, as its coverage rates of South Korea and other nations fell between that of the *Wall Street Journal* and the *Washington Post* (see Table 5.1).

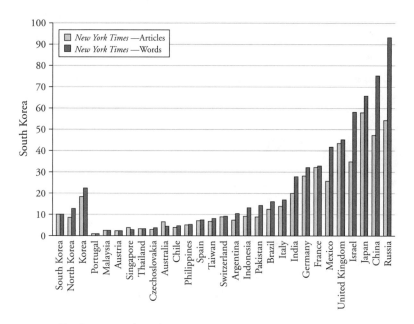

FIGURE 5.3 Foreign news volume by country.
Note: South Korea = 1.

TABLE 5.1
ROK visibility in U.S. newspapers

Category	New York Times	Washington Post	Wall Street Journal	All
ROK	742	149	999	1,890
	(81.71)	(60.6)	(83.95)	(80.63)
U.S.-ROK relationship	166	97	191	454
	(18.28)	(39.43)	(16.05)	(19.37)
Total/All ROK	908	246	1,190	2,344
	(100)	(100)	(100)	(100)
All ROK as share of all Korean peninsula news	(43.1)	(20.2)	(68.3)	(45.8)

NOTE: Parentheses contain percentages.

Figure 5.3 reveals that the ROK received a level of coverage comparable to the levels for Switzerland, Argentina, Indonesia, Pakistan, and even North Korea, which was accorded slightly more words but fewer articles. Over a dozen countries received higher levels of coverage than the ROK, with some of these countries receiving several times the amount of coverage: Germany received three times, the United Kingdom four times, and Japan six times the level of news attention. In terms of number of words, China received seven-and-one-half times and Russia over nine times the amount of U.S. media attention accorded to the ROK. (Note that the countries that received the highest levels of coverage—Israel, Japan, Russia, and China—all had lengthy articles written about them.) Although the United States is the country that received the most coverage in the ROK media (only North Korea received comparable coverage), this figure clearly illustrates that in the U.S. media, many countries received several times the level of coverage accorded to the ROK and even that of the two Koreas together (i.e., see "Korea," the third entry from the left in Figure 5.3).

Just how much U.S. news coverage *should* the ROK receive? Consider the following factors: The U.S.-ROK alliance is one of a handful of military arrangements to remain robust in the post–cold war era, as U.S. forces continue to be stationed in the peninsula. Moreover, the ROK, which has seen dramatic economic swings in the last dozen years, is currently the seventh-largest trading partner of the United States. Cultural influences have also increased in recent years, along with the population of Korean Americans and the number of Korean students who go to the United States to attend colleges and universities.

Deciding how much coverage to give the ROK is difficult and highly subjective. The daily decisions of U.S. newspaper editors can have as much (if not more) to do with day-to-day events, foreign correspondents' locations and talents, and the size of the "news hole" (i.e., the amount of space available for stories) as with the type of relationship that the United States maintains with a given country.

While acknowledging these myriad factors, trade volume is one context in which a systematic analysis can address the question of what level of news coverage a given country should receive. (The preponderance of U.S. news coverage of the ROK is related to economics and trade, as will be explained later in this chapter.) Figure 5.4 illustrates the average percentage of foreign news articles devoted to a given country in the *New York Times*, *Washington Post*, and *Wall Street Journal* and juxtaposes that average with the country's trade volume (average of 2002 and 2003) with the United States, as measured in billions of U.S. dollars.[1] Using trade volume as a measure reveals which countries are relatively overrepresented and underrepresented in terms of news coverage. The trend line illustrates that beyond a certain baseline of news volume, there is generally a linear relationship between increased trade and increased news coverage.

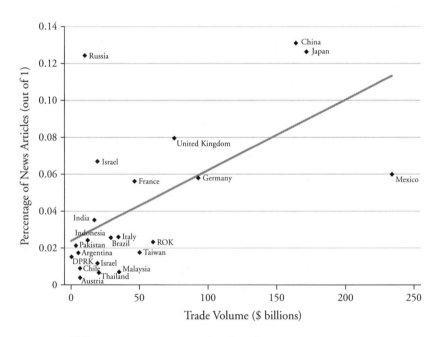

FIGURE 5.4 U.S. news coverage versus trade volume by country.
Note: Each country's trade volume is the average for 2002 and 2003.

In these terms, the ROK is underrepresented in U.S. news coverage, given its relative economic importance to the United States. Russia, Israel, and France all traded less with the United States but received significantly more news coverage than the ROK. In fact, according to business journalist Martin Fackler of the *New York Times*, "Unlike China or India, South Korea is not large enough (or potentially large enough) in economic terms to command readers' interest just by its name alone. No matter how fast South Korea grows, it will not get big enough to reshape the global economy, or place the entire planet at environmental risk, as China stands to do."[2]

It is interesting to note that the three countries that received more than 12 percent of foreign news coverage—Russia, Japan, and China[3]—had widely varying trade volumes with the United States. Moreover, all three have been perceived as competitors (at least at one time) of the United States. Indeed, even if there is only one superpower (a circumstance and label that some hold to be increasingly dubious), then each of these three nations is a major power in its own right. That is, each has the ability to affect the international system and the status of threats to the system.

This relationship is intimately tied to the American national identity, according to noted American ethicist William May. May argues that after World War II, Americans conceived of a grand struggle between the West, with the United States as its leader, and tyranny. However, after September 11, that perception shifted to a grand struggle between the West and anarchy. May posits that how the United States exercises its power in defense of itself and the international system against the twin threats of tyranny and anarchy—which is intimately related to the nation's self-conception as either an exceptional republic or empire—is the basis of the internal struggle over American national identity.[4] In other words, the domestic debate over national identity is more closely tied to the ways in which the United States exercises power in the world, rather than the United States' relationship with any one particular country, especially in the post–cold war era. (Thus, controversy over the war in Iraq is less about the particulars of that country than the merits of or justifications for intervention.) It is in this context that it becomes logical for the U.S. press, in the absence of any clear significant other, to accord its highest levels of news coverage to powerful countries that have the ability to help or hinder the United States in its struggle to maintain the status quo of the international system and to defend against threats to it.

In sum, the Korean press published substantially higher numbers of articles and opinion pieces on the U.S.-ROK relationship than the U.S. press did. Additionally, Korean newspapers published many more articles and opinion pieces on the United States than U.S. newspapers published on the ROK. Indeed, the U.S. press accorded more news coverage to over a dozen other countries. Given the strategic, military, and economic/trade importance of the ROK to the United States, the ROK can be said to be underrepresented in the U.S. news. Whereas the United States is an important significant other against which South Koreans define their identity (and over which there is significant societal contention), South Korea simply does not play this role in definitions of and debates over American national identity. Indeed, it may be argued that no single country plays this role in the formation of the American national identity in any way analogous to the U.S. role in the ROK, owing to structural factors in international relations. It is within this context that this chapter proceeds in describing U.S. news coverage of South Korea and the U.S.-ROK relationship.

South Korea in U.S. News

As presented in Figure 5.5, the U.S. data show that of all the Korean peninsula news featured in the three U.S. daily newspapers (dailies), 36.9 percent covered the ROK and 8.9 percent covered the U.S.-ROK relationship.[5] In addition, 28.2 percent of articles covered the U.S.-DPRK relationship, and

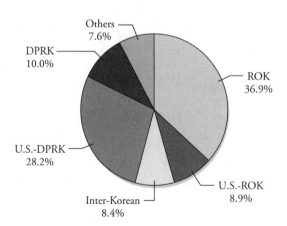

FIGURE 5.5 U.S. news on Korea by focus category.

10 percent dealt with the DPRK itself. Another 8.4 percent of U.S. media articles covered developments in inter-Korean relations.[6]

Using this data set, this chapter will focus on U.S. news about South Korea and the U.S.-ROK relationship in seeking to explain the terms and character of U.S. interest in South Korea in the post–cold war era. Subsequently, Chapter 6 will examine U.S. news about the DPRK and the U.S.-DPRK relationship.

GREATER ATTENTION TO THE ROK OVER BILATERAL RELATIONS

Chapter 4 revealed that the progressive *Hankyoreh Shinmoon* covered the United States and the U.S.-ROK relationship in nearly equal proportion, while the conservative *Chosun Ilbo* devoted much more coverage—roughly twice as much—to the United States (showing a keen interest in U.S. domestic politics) than to the bilateral relationship. In Table 5.1, the data show that within ROK-related coverage, all three U.S. newspapers devoted significantly more attention to the ROK than to the U.S.-ROK relationship.

This is especially true in the cases of the *New York Times* and *Wall Street Journal*, which both allocated more than 80 percent of ROK-related coverage to the country itself and less than 20 percent to the U.S.-ROK relationship. The *Washington Post* also provided relatively greater attention to the ROK than to bilateral relations, although to less of an extreme; approximately 60 percent of its articles addressed the ROK, while nearly 40 percent addressed issues within the bilateral relationship.[7] In fact, the *Washington Post* devoted only 20 percent of its coverage of the Korean peninsula to ROK-related issues, which may be understood in terms of this newspaper's relative lack of interest in economic issues in favor of diplomatic and security interests. Given the location of its audience and reporters inside the Washington Beltway, the *Post* tends to contextualize foreign events in terms of U.S. interests to a greater degree (e.g., discussing an event in terms of U.S.-ROK relations). Overall, however, these data demonstrate that the ROK is of relatively greater interest to the American public than the alliance relationship. The ROK is a dynamic nation, and its recent post–cold war history has featured dramatic turns.

Figure 5.6 illustrates the persistent disparity in media attention between the ROK and the U.S.-ROK relationship. In no single year did the relationship receive more coverage than the country. A major peak in news on the ROK occurred in 1997, reflecting the financial crisis. However, sharp rises

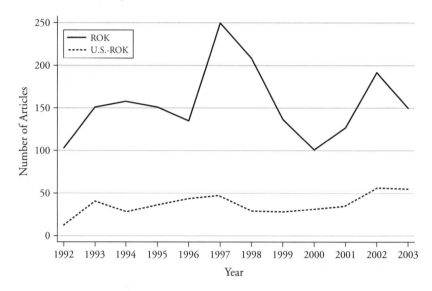

FIGURE 5.6 Media attention to the ROK and the U.S.-ROK relationship.

in coverage of ROK news during the financial crisis were not mirrored in coverage of U.S.-ROK relations. This suggests that the U.S. media focused on reporting phenomena associated with the crisis itself, rather than how the crisis might impact the U.S.-ROK relationship. Figure 5.6 also shows a small peak in news coverage of South Korea in 2002—the year of a South Korean presidential election in which anti-American themes played out and the peninsula's second nuclear crisis erupted. In that election, South Koreans elected a left-leaning, relatively unknown former human rights lawyer who, unlike his predecessors, did not have ties to the United States, and that may have been newsworthy.

It is interesting to note that for all the Korean peninsula focus categories (ROK, the U.S.-ROK relationship, DPRK, the U.S.-DPRK relationship, and inter-Korean relations), media attention to ROK news was the most dynamic. That is, there were greater differences among newspapers and more variation in coverage levels for this focus category than for any other. In the early 1990s, ostensibly owing to the ROK's rapid economic development, the *Wall Street Journal* showed high rates of coverage for ROK-related issues. The *Journal*'s level of coverage began to drop in 1995, dramatically increased during the 1997 financial crisis, but then embarked on a gradual, if relatively steady, downward trend. After 1997, the *New York Times* and *Wall*

Street Journal switched positions in terms of which newspaper published the most articles on the ROK, but the *Washington Post* always remained in third position. More recently, the *New York Times* has accorded the most attention to ROK issues.

While all three U.S. newspapers' ROK news reporting, taken together, has fluctuated widely over time and in accordance with events, reaching its peak during the financial crisis of 1997, U.S. coverage of the U.S.-ROK bilateral relationship has remained relatively consistent, showing a small increase in the numbers of articles in the last two years of this study. In Korean coverage of the bilateral relationship, both newspapers significantly increased their coverage of U.S.-ROK relations after 2000 (by 3 to 4 times 1999 attention levels, with *Hankyoreh* seeming to initiate this trend), as the alliance came under greater scrutiny and progressive and conservative forces debated its efficacy. But even in the face of significant discord over the alliance in South Korea—as seen through dramatic events such as candlelight vigils and anti-American protests in the wake of the schoolgirl incident—U.S. reporting on the bilateral relationship rose only slightly, with the U.S. newspapers' level of coverage (not reported here) providing little consensus on the importance of this topic. The three newspapers' coverage of U.S.-ROK matters fluctuated irregularly within the narrow margin of less than 30 articles per year.[8]

Overall, these patterns stand in contrast to the South Korean media data, which exhibited a steady increase in U.S.-related coverage over time and an especially dramatic increase in coverage of the bilateral relationship in the latter years of the study. This difference clearly indicates that the U.S.-ROK relationship is of much greater interest to Koreans than Americans.

ECONOMIC STORIES TOP COVERAGE

As shown in Table 5.2, economic issues dominated U.S. press coverage of the ROK, accounting for nearly 70 percent of articles. Not surprisingly, the *Wall Street Journal* devoted the highest percentage of articles on the ROK to economic issues, at 83.58 percent, while approximately 59 percent of *New York Times* articles covered such matters. In contrast to its counterparts, the *Washington Post* devoted only one-third of its attention to economic issues, while according significant attention to domestic politics in South Korea (35.57%), an issue to which the *Times* (18.83%) and especially the *Journal* (8.61%) paid proportionally less attention. The newspapers rarely published

TABLE 5.2
ROK-related issues in the U.S. media (percent)

Category/Issue	*New York Times*	*Washington Post*	*Wall Street Journal*	All
ROK				
Economic issues	58.54	32.21	83.58	69.72
Domestic politics	18.83	35.57	8.61	14.74
Security	3.52	3.36	2.20	2.815
General diplomacy	1.08	2.68	1.30	1.33
Humanitarian/Human rights issues	1.90	2.68	0.30	1.11
Others	16.12	23.49	4.00	10.29
Total	100.0	100.0	100.0	100.0
U.S.-ROK relationship				
Economic issues	34.34	15.46	70.53	45.47
Domestic politics	3.01	4.12	0.53	2.21
Security	38.55	46.39	23.16	33.77
General diplomacy	13.25	13.40	2.11	8.61
Humanitarian/Human rights issues	1.81	3.09	0.53	1.55
Others	9.04	17.53	3.16	8.395
Total	100.0	100.0	100.0	100.0

articles on security issues within their ROK news, as it is likely that they view ROK security in a contextualized way—that is, as a relevant topic in U.S.-ROK coverage or even in ROK-DPRK coverage.

Even within news on bilateral relations, economic issues drove much of the coverage, especially in the *Journal* (70.53%) and the *Times* (34.34%). To be sure, the *Times* (38.55%) and the *Post* (46.39%) both devoted more coverage of U.S.-ROK relations to security issues, but the U.S.-ROK coverage as a whole was relatively small. Thus, in a little over a decade, the *Times* published 63 articles, the *Post* 45 articles, and the *Journal* 43 articles on U.S.-ROK security relations. In comparison, over these same years, the *Times* published 434 articles, the *Post* 47 articles, and the *Journal* 834 articles on ROK economic issues.

This time period covers years of rapid economic development, as well as precipitous economic crisis, which makes this high proportion of economic coverage congruous with events. At the same time, despite policy elites' concern over strains in the alliance, issues of economy and trade seemed to persist as a central pillar of popular American interest in the ROK. Korean brands are increasingly successful in the U.S. market, and industries and companies that have built a significant presence in American consumer markets—such as Samsung, LG Electronics, and Hyundai Motors—are of great interest to Americans.[9] The governments of the United States and the ROK have also negotiated a free trade agreement, the KORUS FTA (pending legislative approval in both countries at the time of this writing), which has become a strategic initiative, as U.S. officials declare that the relationship has been artificially focused on security for too long. In this vein, it is interesting to note that neither alliance-related nor inter-Korean engagement-related topics occupy a central position in U.S. press coverage of South Korea. In other words, while these issues, which have spurred serious policy differences and proven divisive in recent years, occupy alliance managers in both governments, U.S. dailies published far fewer articles related to these (perhaps esoteric) matters. This is in clear contrast to Korean media coverage of the bilateral relationship, which focused primarily on security issues, as discussed in the previous chapter.

Figure 5.7 illustrates the volume of coverage by issue for all ROK-related news (ROK and U.S.-ROK together) in the three U.S. newspapers. It is immediately apparent that the fluctuations in economic coverage appear quite

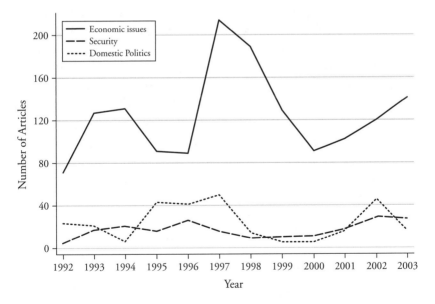

FIGURE 5.7 Number of articles for top issues (ROK and U.S.-ROK relationship).

similar to the fluctuations seen in ROK news in Figure 5.1. This should be expected, given the high percentage of ROK news that focuses on economic issues. Once again, the degree to which economic coverage drives news on South Korea is clear. In each year, economic issues were covered at least twice, and often three times, the rate of security or domestic political issues. All three newspapers dramatically increased their economic coverage during the 1997 financial crisis, contributing to the 1997 peak (over 200 articles that year), as seen in Figure 5.7.[10] Beyond such increases around 1997, however, there appears to be no unifying trend among the three newspapers' levels of attention to economic and trade issues. By comparison, as Figure 5.7 reveals, security issues revealed little fluctuation in coverage, and the three U.S. dailies' coverage tended to be consistent. The only exception to this was in 2002, when the *Times* placed more emphasis on how the events of that year—Roh's election, anti-American protests, the Washington-Pyongyang confrontation—affected the U.S.-ROK alliance.[11] A comparable peak in alliance coverage was not seen during the 1994 nuclear crisis.

Even though South Korean domestic politics were a major news item in the United States in the 1980s, coverage declined after democracy was established. All three newspapers recorded comparatively high coverage of domestic politics between 1995 and 1997, the period when South Korea began to confront its authoritarian past through the indictment of former presidents (Chun Doo Hwan and Roh Tae Woo), when the Kim Young Sam government was marred by political scandals, and when the economic miracle looked as though it was beginning to crumble. After this period of relatively high interest, coverage receded in all three dailies (less than five articles per year), with one exception: The *New York Times* increased its coverage of domestic politics significantly in 2002 (although that level of coverage was not sustained in 2003). Once again, this was the year of a presidential election featuring identity politics and anti-American themes. Provocative moves by the North and alliance tension exacerbated and reinforced political division during the Korean national election. In the face of such dramatic events, it is somewhat curious that the other two newspapers did not increase their attention to domestic politics.

SCANT ATTENTION TO THE ALLIANCE

Thus far, the discussion has shown that during the study years, the U.S. media provided far more coverage of the ROK than of the U.S.-ROK relationship, and within coverage of the ROK, economic issues dominated. Four of the five most prevalent subjects (not reported here) were related to economics and trade, and the only noneconomic topic was domestic politics; there was no security-related subject among the top five.

In sharp contrast, U.S. news on the DPRK focused primarily on security-related issues (see Chapter 6). The relatively low yield of articles on security-related subjects in U.S. press coverage of the ROK news may reflect (from the American perspective) the relative stability of the alliance over most of the study years, even in the face of North Korean missile and nuclear weapons development. Still, this lack of news attention to security issues is counterintuitive given that much of Korea experts' recent discourse on the alliance has focused on anti-Americanism and what it means for the continuing U.S. security commitment to Korea.

As discussed in the previous chapter, the progressive *Hankyoreh* devoted over half its coverage of bilateral relations to the U.S. troop presence. Even the conservative *Chosun* accorded a still significant, although comparably smaller, one-quarter of its coverage to this subject. In sharp contrast, U.S. newspapers were far less interested in the U.S. troop presence in Korea. Over the course of this study, the *Post* and the *Journal* published only 7 and 4 articles on this subject, respectively, although the *New York Times* took a greater interest, publishing 29 articles (but still only just over 2 articles per year, on average). Similarly, U.S. newspapers published a meager number of articles on anti-Americanism in South Korea—only 16 articles over the course of this study.

This lack of news attention—on U.S. troops stationed in South Korea and on anti-Americanism—may seem surprising, given the media's negativity bias and Korea experts' focus on anti-Americanism and what it means for the alliance.[12] While U.S. troops in the ROK have a visible presence and for some South Koreans are even a part of daily life, U.S. military personnel stationed halfway around the world are far removed from the concerns of average Americans, for whom the alliance is more of an abstract notion— one security commitment among many on a global scale. With actual military engagements in progress elsewhere throughout the length of this study (the first Gulf War and the conflicts in Somalia, the Balkans, Afghanistan, and Iraq), maintenance-level security commitments seemed to yield little coverage in the face of more pressing, pertinent military coverage priorities. Basing arrangements and troop-community relations, both specific manifestations of U.S. security commitments, seem even more obscure topics to the general American audience. While for South Koreans, the U.S. troop presence may function as a symbol of foreign influence or paternalistic relations between the United States and the ROK, from the American perspective, these heavy connotations are absent, and the troop presence is seen as a generous, if underpublicized, sacrifice on the part of Americans to protect Koreans.

In the wake of slowed progress in inter-Korean relations, Bush's "axis of evil" remark, vividly played out anti-American themes, and several identity-invoking events, U.S. soldiers came "to symbolize both an insensitivity to Korean nationalism and a heightened American arrogance in world affairs," as asserted by Doug Struck, the *Washington Post*'s East Asia correspondent from 1999 to 2003.[13] The events of December 2002—the glowing candle-light vigils and searing anti-American chants—did receive coverage in U.S. newspapers. Indeed, 2002 was the first year this issue provoked any significant level of attention in the U.S. media. Thus, it was a relatively new topic for the U.S. press in the context of South Korea, one that had not been examined in any concerted way since the democratization movements of the 1980s. Owing to the complex origins of this topic, it was esoteric and difficult to cover in the space of a newspaper article.

According to former diplomat David Straub, "The American media covered most of the major issues in U.S.-South Korean relations during the period 1999–2002, but was not able to present a complete picture to readers and viewers due largely to the complexity of the situation and the inherent limitations of media reporting for a general audience."[14] Struck echoed Straub's assertion that the complexity of and linkages among anti-Americanism, inter-Korean relations, and South Korean domestic politics and nationalism made for difficult reporting:

> We who covered the story often treated the various themes as separate and distinct subjects. We wrote the story of the Korean election as another episode in South Korea's still nascent democracy. We wrote the anti-Americanism story as though it was a discrete event. We wrote the North Korean story as though it was isolated from the other issues. In fact, these issues were all intertwined, and all reverberated on the others.[15]

Stepping back from the Korean case, anti-American sentiment abroad is not a topic generally covered in the U.S. press. From 1992 to 2003, the

Times published 60 articles (of which, as noted, 9 were on South Korea) that included the term *anti-American*, and the *Post* published 42 (7 on South Korea) such articles.[16] These articles spanned a wide range of topics, from Greek anti-Americanism in response to a trip by President Clinton to Chinese anti-Americanism in the wake of the accidental U.S. bombing of the People's Republic of China embassy in Belgrade. These articles discussed specific events or incidents that spurred anti-American sentiment in Germany, Canada, Russia, and the Middle East and even on American college campuses. Articles published after 2002 focused heavily on opposition to the U.S. war in Iraq and American conduct in the war on terror. That is, these articles largely reflected a spreading global anti-Americanism based on current U.S. policies, rather than the particular, interactive, or historical circumstances associated with any one country.

Returning to 2002 in Korea, according to Straub:

> Millions of South Koreans interpreted the [schoolgirl] accident through a prism of collective memory significantly shaped by their understanding of the U.S. role in 1979–1980. For almost all Americans, whose own collective memory tells them that the U.S. saved the Republic of Korea from a military invasion from the North in 1950 and then nurtured the South's near-miraculous economic and political development, the massive protests came out of the blue.[17]

Differences in collective memory have led to misperceptions and misinterpretations of American and South Korean calculations and motivations. Whereas Americans sometimes do not understand why Koreans react with such passion and emotion to seemingly insignificant events in the alliance, such as the schoolgirl accident, Koreans rarely acknowledge that the alliance does not hold the same prominence in American imagination. This misinterpretation could be seen both when Koreans assumed that former Secretary of Defense Donald Rumsfeld decided to reduce U.S. troop numbers in the ROK primarily as a punishment for anti-American protests and when Koreans worried that Americans might retaliate against them for a mass shooting at a Virginia university that was committed by a Korean American student.[18]

NEITHER ANTI-KOREAN NOR ANTI-ALLIANCE SENTIMENT

The discussion in Chapter 4 identified anti-American trends in both Korean newspapers but significant anti-alliance sentiment principally in the progressive newspaper, *Hankyoreh Shinmoon*. The argument was made in that chapter for the need to separate anti-American from anti-alliance sentiment. Now, the discussion turns to assessing whether anti-Korean and/or anti-alliance sentiment has appeared in the U.S. press.

Because the U.S. data feature many types of articles, from descriptive news stories to evaluative editorials, two types of tone can be derived: *descriptive tone*, which measures the sentiment found in descriptive content, and *evaluative tone*, which measures the sentiment found in evaluative content. This chapter considers both descriptive tone and evaluative tone, which tend to have a high rate of correlation (0.79). Points of divergence, where they exist, may provide insights into the U.S. media coverage of the Koreas.

When a category's evaluative tone is more negative than its descriptive tone, it indicates that the newspaper's *assessment* of the implications of events is more negative than the events themselves. For example, if there is a mildly negative domestic political event, the event may be described in several news articles, registering a mildly negative descriptive tone. For a variety of reasons—perhaps if the event is perceived to be part of larger, very negative trend—critical editorials and special features may yield a very negative tone. More negative evaluative than descriptive tones are often seen for particularly contentious categories, which carry strong connotations beyond specific events. When a category's evaluative tone is more positive than its descriptive tone, it indicates that a newspaper's assessment of events and their implications are less harsh than might be suggested by the events themselves.

As presented in Table 5.3, the U.S. media rated the U.S.-ROK relationship most positively out of all ROK-related focus categories. In contrast to the Korean media, which registered an average evaluate tone of –0.77 on the bilateral relationship, the U.S. media produced an average descriptive tone of –0.06 (effectively neutral) and an average evaluative tone of –0.18 (only slightly negative). Indeed, each U.S. newspaper's descriptive and evaluative tones toward the relationship were far less negative than even the conservative *Chosun Ilbo*'s tone (–0.42; the progressive *Hankyoreh*'s tone was a very negative –1.11).

The newspapers' average evaluative tone toward the ROK (–0.21) was only slightly more negative than its tone toward U.S.-ROK relations, and it is likely that a fair portion of what little negativity was recorded was due, in large part, to events surrounding the 1997 financial crisis. The U.S. media's average evaluative tone toward the ROK was similar to *Chosun*'s evaluative

TABLE 5.3
News tone by focus category, issue, and subject

	Tone	*New York Times*	*Washington Post*	*Wall Street Journal*	Average
Category					
ROK	Descriptive	−0.48	−0.50	−0.10	−0.36
	Evaluative	−0.21	−0.24	−0.19	−0.21
U.S.-ROK relationship	Descriptive	−0.12	−0.12	0.05	−0.06
	Evaluative	−0.17	−0.13	−0.24	−0.18
Issue					
Security	Descriptive	−0.69	−0.32	−0.64	−0.55
	Evaluative	−0.67	−0.33	−0.79	−0.59
Domestic politics	Descriptive	−0.92	−0.57	−0.94	−0.81
	Evaluative	−0.34	−0.26	−0.59	−0.39
Economy and trade	Descriptive	−0.28	−0.71	0.02	−0.32
	Evaluative	−0.43	−0.50	−0.21	−0.38
Subject					
ROK economy/industry	Descriptive	−0.08	0.17	0.22	0.10
	Evaluative	−0.18	0.20	0.04	0.02
ROK domestic politics	Descriptive	−1.24	−0.81	−1.14	−1.06
	Evaluative	−0.71	−0.48	−0.62	−0.61
ROK-U.S. trade	Descriptive	0.45	−0.88	0.17	−0.09
	Evaluative	0.30	−0.43	−0.09	−0.07

coverage of the United States (−0.23) while *Hankyoreh* recorded a very negative evaluative tone (−0.90). Once again, this indicates that the U.S. media did not see the U.S.-ROK relationship as troublesome as the Korean media did for most of the study period.

Within news about the ROK (both the ROK and U.S.-ROK relationship focus categories), economic and trade issues registered slightly negative descriptive and evaluative tone scores. It must be remembered, however, that the subject of the financial crisis captured a significant portion of coverage on this issue. An examination of the subjects related to the South Korean economy and industry, as well as U.S.-ROK trade, reveals neutral to positive tone scores.[19] Indeed, on the subject of bilateral trade, the *New York Times* recorded the most positive scores seen in any category (0.45 and 0.30).

More positive (and less negative) tones on issues other than security, such as economics, may imply that the United States and ROK have bases on which to build a more robust, strengthened relationship, apart from their partnership in countering the threat presented by the DPRK. As the nature and extent of this threat become increasingly contentious for Washington and Seoul and the two countries strive to coordinate diplomatic responses to the DPRK, diversifying the number of issues receiving attention might be a constructive way to manage this important relationship. In this regard, successful passage of the proposed KORUS FTA could potentially contribute to strengthening the predominantly security-based bilateral relationship.

The issue of domestic politics shows greater disparities between descriptive and evaluative tone scores, with descriptive scores being more negative in all three U.S. newspapers. That is, the average evaluative tone was –0.39, while the average descriptive tone was –0.81, and similar results were seen with reference to South Korean domestic political subjects (for which the average descriptive tone was especially negative at –1.06). Thus, the U.S. media evaluated ROK domestic politics less negatively than the actual events might suggest—something that may make sense in a democracy, where debate and dissent are expected. The results indicate that despite negative events in Korean politics (e.g., political corruption or scandals), the U.S. media showed some confidence in the durability of South Korean political institutions and democracy, as well as in the direction of domestic politics for most of the study years. Yet this may also indicate that over the course of the study years, U.S. newspapers were not concerned over and/or did not appreciate until much later the depth and fervor associated with the intensified politics of identity and its role in fostering an increasingly polarized South Korean society, as discussed in the previous chapter.[20]

The *Post*'s coverage of economic and trade issues (–0.71 descriptive, –0.50 evaluative) was more negative than that appearing in the *Times* (–0.28 descriptive, –0.43 evaluative) and the *Journal* (0.02 descriptive, –0.21 evaluative). Indeed, this issue exhibits an even greater degree of variation in tone—both descriptive and evaluative—among newspapers than was the case for domestic politics. However, the *Post* published very few articles on economics and trade, and most of the articles it did publish were about the 1997 financial crisis and its fallout. Not being predisposed to cover economic issues, the *Post* covered this topic only when the news was very dramatic and negative, rising to the level of affecting South Korean society, politics, and U.S.-ROK relations.

The significant variations in reporting and opinion among U.S. newspapers regarding these two prevalent issues demonstrate the diverse portrayals of the ROK in the U.S. media. Yet unlike the case of the Korean media, these differences among U.S. newspapers have little to do with ideology or the politics of identity. Indeed, the differences may be taken as a healthy sign that the U.S. media reports much more on the ROK itself than on the country seen only through the lens of its relationship with the United States.

The differences in tone among the U.S. newspapers on ROK-related security issues also appear not to be related to ideology or contention over American identity. Overall, the U.S. newspapers' average evaluative tone on security issues was –0.59, quite similar to *Chosun*'s average tone on security issues, which was –0.52. *Hankyoreh* was much more negative (–0.85) and is only comparable to the *Wall Street Journal*'s average evaluative tone on security (–0.79). The *Washington Post* was the most positive (or rather least negative, at –0.33) on security of any of the newspapers in this study, Korean or U.S. This is likely a result of the *Post*'s tendency to focus on policy, including officials' statements, diplomacy, and bilateral agreements concluded—all topics that tend to be relatively more positive (as governments spin them positively). The tight correlation between descriptive and evaluative tones on security indicates dispassionate, sober reporting on U.S.-ROK security issues.[21]

Figure 5.8 depicts the three newspapers' evaluative tones on coverage of ROK-related issues. From the data, it is clear that these tones tended to move in tandem, indicating that overall, U.S. newspapers evaluate ROK

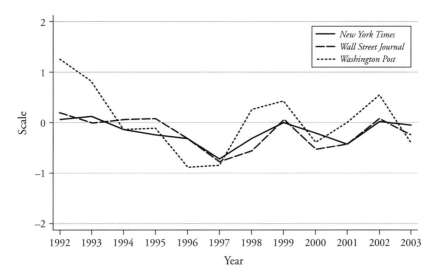

FIGURE 5.8 Average evaluative news tones toward the ROK.

news in relatively similar, fairly positive terms. In large part, the tones ebbed and flowed over time between being neutral and slightly negative, exhibiting only slight differences.

For example, the *Post*'s positive tone in 1992 and 1993 must have reflected Korea's election of a civilian government, the first in 30 years. Similarly, Kim Dae Jung's inauguration and introduction of new policies likely drove the *Post*'s positive tone in 1998 and 1999. As established previously, the *Post* devoted a greater percentage of its Korean coverage to domestic political issues. Evaluative tone data for 1998 and 1999 from the *Times* and the *Journal*, which saw similar, if more gradual, trends of improvement over these years, likely reflected a recuperating South Korean economy.

The U.S. newspapers' tight coordination in tone scores over the length of the study indicates similar assessments among newspapers, in contrast to the case of the Korean press, wherein a debate-oriented atmosphere produced coverage with discernible, consistent disparities in tone. Also, whereas both Korean dailies showed a marked deterioration in evaluative tone toward U.S.-related topics after 2000, the U.S. newspapers exhibited limited fluctuations in tone toward the ROK in the same period, recording neutral scores.

Figure 5.9 reveals a dynamic picture of U.S. media evaluative tone toward the U.S.-ROK relationship. While the three newspapers' coverage gener-

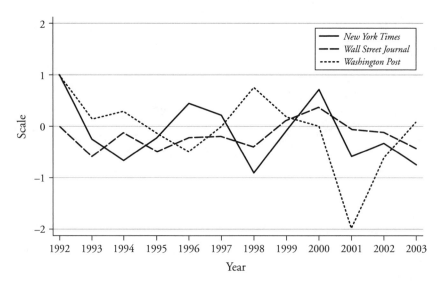

FIGURE 5.9 Average evaluative news tones toward the U.S.-ROK relationship.

ally followed the same tone trends in ROK coverage, U.S.-ROK coverage showed disparate trends among the three newspapers. That is, while one newspaper saw a vast improvement in evaluative tone, over the same years, a second experienced a stark drop in tone score (e.g., *Post* and *Times* coverage between 1996 and 1998). This divergence among newspapers indicates more complex views and varied opinion on the U.S.-ROK relationship versus South Korea itself.

It appears that 2001 was a critical year in the U.S. media's evaluation of the alliance. From 2000 to 2001, all three newspapers showed a decline in tone, although to starkly different degrees. The *Wall Street Journal*'s tone fell slightly to become neutral, the *New York Times*'s tone turned moderately negative, and the *Washington Post*'s tone dropped significantly, becoming highly negative (approximately –2.0, the most negative rating on this scale). It is likely that friction caused by differing policy views between the Kim Dae Jung administration and the newly elected Bush administration informed this downward turn in U.S.-ROK tone.

The fact that the *Post*'s score was most negative lends credence to this view, given this newspaper's relative focus on security matters. President Kim's visit to Washington, DC, was one of the Bush administration's first formal forays into foreign policy, and the *Post* paid special attention, as the summit was thought to be a marker of the administration's approach to international relations, especially compared to that of the Clinton administration. Indeed, the *Post* delivered a harsh rebuke to the White House shortly after the summit, calling it a "diplomatic debacle" and chiding Bush's "shabby treatment" of a "great man, in a class with Nelson Mandela."[22]

Taken together, U.S. press coverage fluctuated, reflecting particular events or issues within a relatively narrow band. Unlike in the Korean media, there is no identifiable trend in the U.S. media to show anti-Korean or anti-alliance sentiments during the study period.

The Republic of Korea: No Longer a Security Story

For much of the post-1945 period, South Korea was portrayed as "one battlefield in a much broader conflict" in American press coverage,[23] but this chapter shows that the nation is no longer primarily a "security story" for Americans. Newspapers in the United States accorded substantially more coverage to news about the ROK, rather than to news about the bilateral relationship, and American interest in Korean economic and trade issues was the primary driver of that coverage. This finding suggests that the ROK, as a major trading partner, has importance to the United States beyond the security alliance, which received much less coverage.

To many Americans today, South Korea is represented by well-known consumer technology products, while the alliance conjures vague, largely static notions of a distant military assignment, a sacrifice made for a foreign land threatened by a cagey, cold war–style communist dictator. Significant coverage of trade, financial, and economic issues and scant attention to the presence of U.S. troops in South Korea may reflect this mindset of the American public. Many Koreans, on the other hand, are confronted with the alliance on a daily basis, and this level of interaction and recent mainstream movements to reconcile the alliance with Korea's changing identity are evident through the most prevalent subject in the Korean press: U.S. troops in Korea.

From the analysis of U.S. news in this chapter, it is clear that security and the alliance are no longer the primary bases for interest in the ROK by the U.S. media and public. News coverage reveals that Americans value and show interest in the South Korean economy and industry, as well as in the U.S.-ROK trade relationship. More positive (and less negative) tones on economic issues may imply that the United States and the ROK have bases on which to build a more robust, stronger relationship, even apart from their partnership in countering the threat presented by the DPRK.

Within the U.S. data, there were few opinion-editorials on ROK-related matters, indicating that ROK issues are not major topics of debate in the United States. Unlike Korean newspapers, U.S. newspapers are not engaged in any sort of bitter or emotional dispute over the ROK, the bilateral relationship, or the alliance. Neutral and only slightly negative average evaluative tones on the ROK and U.S.-ROK relationship focus categories reinforce this point. Furthermore, the vast majority of U.S. coverage of the ROK was driven by particular issue areas, such as trade and economics, rather than ideology. Newspapers played to their comparative advantages in issue areas, with the *Post* covering security, diplomatic, and political events and the *Journal* focusing on economic issues. While the alliance and U.S.-ROK relations have produced fervent debates in South Korea, in the United States, the alliance is an esoteric topic, not one that elicits popular interest. This reflects the American perception of the "forgotten war" in Korea—a conflict overshadowed by the preceding World War II and the succeeding Vietnam War, both of which have distinct places in popular consciousness, as each defined an American generation and made an imprint on national identity.

In light of recent tension in the security alliance, it is important to note that the U.S.-ROK relationship was the most positively portrayed focus category in U.S. coverage of the Korean peninsula. Even though it received less attention, news about the relationship registered a neutral descriptive tone and only a very slightly negative evaluative tone. This indicates that the U.S. press saw the status of the alliance quite positively during most of the study period. In addition, the fact that both the ROK and the U.S.-ROK relationship exhibited small differences in their respective descriptive and evaluative tones may mean that American views are largely determined by events, rather than residual images compounded over time.

However, further analysis of the data shows that the year 2001 was a turning point in the U.S. media view of the bilateral relationship. In this critical year, all three newspapers showed a decline in tone toward the alliance. Friction caused by differing policy views between the Kim Dae Jung government and the newly elected Bush administration informed this downward turn in U.S.-ROK tone. The fact that the *Washington Post*'s score was most negative is logical, given its proportionally higher focus on security matters.

As *Washington Post* journalist Doug Struck noted at the "First Drafts of Korea" media conference,[24] it is not a newspaper's mission to detail the sweep of history but rather, in most cases, to report the events of the day. On a daily basis, connections between events and their consequences can be hard to see with clarity. The analysis in Chapter 4 provided some idea of the complexities associated with changing notions of national identity in South Korea, but this larger trend was difficult for the U.S. press to capture from daily events. It may well be the case that *New York Times* coverage in 2002, which showed a substantial increase in attention to South Korean domestic politics, was attempting to connect these kinds of larger trends—a new generation taking power, a progressive ideology that had become mainstream, new attitudes toward the North, the intensification of identity politics, a wave of anti-Americanism, and tension in the alliance—to that year's momentous ROK presidential election.

Still, overall U.S. media coverage of these events was rather episodic and disconnected, despite deep concerns expressed by Korea specialists and policy makers in the United States. Once again, this scant media attention and lack of deep understanding reflect the mind-set of Americans. Owing to different historical experiences and different places in the international system, South Korea is not a significant other that informs Americans' notion of their own identity in the world, and this is reflected in U.S. press coverage of Korea.

SIX

Dealing with the "Axis of Evil"

On January 29, 2002, in delivering the first State of the Union address following the terrorist attacks of September 11, President George W. Bush made these remarks about his administration's goals for national security:

> Our second goal is to prevent regimes that sponsor terror from threatening America or our friends and allies with weapons of mass destruction. Some of these regimes have been pretty quiet since September the 11th. But we know their true nature. North Korea is a regime arming with missiles and weapons of mass destruction, while starving its citizens. . . .
>
> States like these [North Korea, Iran, and Iraq], and their terrorist allies, constitute an *axis of evil*, arming to threaten the peace of the world. By seeking weapons of mass destruction, these regimes pose a grave and growing danger. They could provide these arms to terrorists, giving them the means to match their hatred. They could attack our allies or attempt to blackmail the United States. In any of these cases, the price of indifference would be catastrophic.[1]

With these remarks, President Bush articulated his view of the prime threats to the United States in this new era and offered a new, strongly worded rationale for U.S. action in the world. In addition to defining al-Qaeda and similar terrorist organizations as enemies, Bush highlighted the potential threat of a nexus of terrorists and states operating largely outside international norms while developing weapons of mass destruction (WMD). The threat from these so-called rogue states, which had garnered increased focus after the end of the cold war, was perceived to be magnified in accordance with the inception of the war on terror.

Although many of these states threatened U.S. allies and regional interests, their ability to reach U.S. shores had been considered years away.

However, the extent of terrorist intent and organization revealed by the events of September 11 meant that the United States had to consider more than traditional vehicles of delivery. Even if such U.S. enemies did not have missiles capable of reaching across the oceans, the marriage of terrorists and WMD-producing rogue states could lead to the use of a WMD device on American soil.

After the catastrophic events of September 11, when traditional concepts such as deterrence and containment suddenly seemed ineffective, the efforts of various nations to develop nuclear weapons looked far more dangerous in U.S. eyes. Speaking to this heightened threat perception, Bush infamously dubbed the nations of North Korea, Iran, and Iraq an "axis of evil."

In the State of the Union address, Bush carefully fused the imperatives of national defense and a values-based approach to foreign policy. In the case of each regime, the president articulated both the threat its weapons development presented and its atrocities against and repression of its own people—in his view, crimes against human dignity. Doing so made clear his visceral sense that these regimes were *evil*, not only because they threatened the United States but also by their very nature. By designating them as evil and highlighting their cruelty to their own people, the president sought to underline that WMD, by definition, pose a threat, but WMD in the hands of such regimes pose a special threat. The phrase *axis of evil* left an indelible impression on Bush's presidency and the world's view of U.S. action at his direction, including on the Korean peninsula.[2]

The inclusion of North Korea in the axis of evil contextualized the threat it presented in new ways and also indicated persistent, deep-rooted American skepticism about the regime's intentions. Even though little reliable information is available about North Korea's intentions, from the first to the second nuclear standoff on the peninsula and throughout the years of this study, one explanation for the regime's escalatory, provocative behavior has appeared repeatedly in U.S. media coverage: *blackmail.*

In a 1993 article entitled "North Korea's Game Looks a Lot Like Nuclear Blackmail," longtime Korea watcher and *New York Times* journalist David Sanger presented what has become a customary explanation for the behavior of the Democratic People's Republic of Korea (DPRK). Namely, Sanger asserted that North Korea "has suddenly found the formula for dealing with America as an equal. . . . Nothing makes Washington take you seriously faster than a pile of plutonium."[3]

President Bush built his initial approach to North Korea's uranium en-richment program (UEP) on a promise not to give into blackmail, and his logic was echoed in a *Wall Street Journal* essay by Dr. Mohamed ElBaradei, Director General of the IAEA, entitled "No Nuclear Blackmail."[4] In further descriptions of North Korea's behavior, *Washington Post* journalists Glenn Kessler and John Pomfret have referred to the DPRK's tactics as "nuclear gamesmanship,"[5] and Georgetown University professor Victor Cha, who would later serve on the National Security Council, has written that "for North Korea, blackmail is more than a tactical expedient; it is a long-term strategy." Cha has also asserted that the North's calculated "coercive bar-gaining . . . reinforces the popular impression [among Americans] that the North Korean regime is unpredictable at best, irrational at worst—an im-pression that is completely false"[6] and more prevalent in political cartoons than serious journalism. Such impressions, along with the commonly al-leged blackmail motive, strongly influence American perceptions of how the United States should approach these issues.

For the United States, the DPRK—particularly its nuclear development—presents a sobering policy dilemma. Having only risky military options and distasteful diplomatic and economic buy-out alternatives, successive U.S. administrations have had to wrestle with the complexity of the North Ko-rean nuclear dilemma, while also considering nonproliferation, professed U.S. foreign policy principles, long-term strategic interests, security impli-cations, and cooperation with North Korea's neighbors—most notably, ally South Korea. As General Shalikashvili, chairman of the joint chiefs of staff, commented in 1993, "There is a fine line between persuading North Korea to do what needs to be done, and provoking a terrible reaction."[7] Every policy approach attempted—and even every instance of inattention—has garnered significant criticism from across the political aisle, and some ap-proaches have even led to policy battles within administrations.

As will be demonstrated in this chapter, U.S. newspapers tend to portray the DPRK in fairly uniform terms, and contention over U.S. policy toward the DPRK is what captures much of the U.S. press coverage related to that country. The popular, persistent sense that North Korea's actions amount to a most dangerous and insidious form of blackmail cast doubt on the efficacy of any diplomatic approach. After all, how would offering any benefits or concessions to a nuclear blackmailer protect the overall safety and legiti-macy of U.S. diplomacy? Even if there were some sort of an agreement, how could cheating be prohibited? Finally, is an imperfect agreement better than no agreement at all?

From the popular American perspective, using the term *evil*, as President Bush did, to describe an entity perceived to be engaged in nuclear blackmail while starving its people may not be a rhetorical leap (if although it may be ill advised from a policy perspective). This characterization is rooted in the pervasive good versus evil theme in Western culture and the security environment after September 11, when Americans felt a sense of victimization and confusion. *Evil* is a label that masks the complex motivations of the other; it is a simplifying and galvanizing concept.[8] While North Korea's development of nuclear weapons cannot be considered the most high-profile policy dilemma faced by recent U.S. presidents, it has certainly proven one of the most intractable.

This chapter explores how the U.S. media have depicted and evaluated the DPRK and the U.S.-DPRK relationship over the study years. As previous chapters have done, this chapter examines U.S. press coverage of DPRK-related issues (i.e., the DPRK and U.S.-DPRK relations) in terms of news attention and news tone, charting how these variables changed over time in three major U.S. newspapers: the *New York Times*, *Washington Post*, and *Wall Street Journal*. This examination pays special attention to coverage of the North's WMD development (including missile development) and the country's human rights plight.

The WMD issue was the single most prominent topic within U.S. news coverage of North Korea. In fact, when all the articles about South and North Korea are considered together, the WMD issue remains the single most prominent topic, commanding just under one-third of all U.S. newspaper coverage (and fully half of all Korean peninsula coverage in the *Washington Post*). The North's human rights record is the (distant) second-most prevalent topic in the U.S. press coverage of the DPRK.

It is important to note that even though U.S. estimates of North Korea's drive for nuclear weapons began in the late 1970s, and the Reagan and Bush (George H. W.) administrations demonstrated concern over nuclear development (to be discussed later), this issue received scant coverage in the U.S. media until the first nuclear crisis of the early 1990s. Similarly, human rights in North Korea also received virtually no attention from the U.S. media until the famine of the mid to late 1990s, when dramatic images conveyed to an American audience the depth of the humanitarian crisis in the closed regime. Since the famine, increasing numbers of North Korean defectors have been the source of more in-depth reporting on the human rights situation inside the country.[9]

The central arguments in this chapter are threefold. First, the DPRK is regarded, above all, as a security problem and a policy challenge to the United States. As a result, news about the U.S.-DPRK relationship is featured much more frequently than news about the DPRK itself. This finding also speaks to North Korea's purposefully erected barriers to the outside world, which severely hinder journalists' ability to report on the DPRK as a country, rather than as a policy issue.

Second, American skepticism of North Korean intentions is deep rooted. Newspapers in the United States tend to present a fairly unified image of North Korea, first, as a threat to U.S. security, and second, as a closed communist regime in violation of basic human rights. News about the U.S.-DPRK relationship consistently recorded highly negative tone ratings, and U.S. news outlets were fairly unified in this portrayal of U.S.-DPRK relations.

Finally, data from U.S. newspapers demonstrate that U.S. discourse and debate on North Korea is quite different from that seen in South Korea, where issues regarding the North are strongly tied to the politics of identity. Many in South Korea regard their relationship with the North as defining the Korean nation in the twenty-first century. The same cannot be said for Americans, however, who instead focus on seeking a policy that is effective in stopping the North's nuclear development and proliferation, amid other (often overshadowing) national security imperatives.

In analyzing DPRK coverage from 1992 to 2003 in the three U.S. daily newspapers (dailies), it is critical to keep in mind the fundamental limitations that journalists face. Given the closed nature of DPRK society—restricted travel and government minders, along with a lack of North Korean sources, economic statistics, bases for comparison (due to the rarity of visits), and even lack of reliable intelligence on North Korea—some of the most crucial lines of normal reporting are glaringly absent in coverage of this country. It is a country that is often "reported second- and third-hand" and "in headline terms."[10] Prior to presenting the key data and findings, the discussion in this chapter addresses the historical context for the formation of U.S. views of the DPRK.

Historical Context

Virtually from the beginning of its existence, the DPRK has been an enemy of the United States, whether as a satellite of the Soviet Union and/or as a threat to South Korea. At the end of World War II, as Japan surrendered, Soviet troops marched across Manchuria and onto the northern part of the Korean peninsula. Faced with the possibility of Soviet occupation of the entire Korean peninsula, two young U.S. officers were charged with demarcating a U.S. zone of occupation at an all-night meeting in Washington on August 10, 1945. "Working in haste and under great pressure, and using a *National Geographic* map for reference," noting both the location of Seoul and the midpoint of the peninsula, distinguished journalist and Korea watcher Don Oberdorfer recounts, they chose the thirty-eighth parallel as the line to hold back Soviet occupation. The Soviets heeded this decision and stopped their advance. No Koreans or even experts on Korea were consulted.[11]

By the fall of 1948, both the Republic of Korea (ROK) and the DPRK had been established and their leaders had been installed by the two great cold war powers. Soon after, Soviet military forces withdrew from the peninsula, and in the summer of 1949, U.S. troops followed suit, pulling back from the ROK. Only one year later, the North, backed by the Soviet Union and the People's Republic of China, invaded the South. In this brutal war, all parties incurred tremendous loss of life, including the United States, and the peninsula was left in a state of devastation. Even after fighting ceased in July 1953, the two sides technically remained at war in the absence of a peace accord, and there was great fear that the North might try again to reunite the peninsula through military force. The U.S.-ROK alliance, forged in blood, became a strategic feature of the Asia-Pacific, a bulwark against Northern aggression and communist domination of the peninsula.

Rather than launch another all-out military attack, however, North Korea turned to terrorist tactics to undermine the South, attempting to assassinate President Park in 1968 (succeeding in killing his wife in 1974), bombing senior South Korean officials in Rangoon in a failed assassination attempt on President Chun Doo Hwan in 1983, and bombing a South Korean passenger flight (Korean Airlines [KAL] 858) returning home from the Middle East in 1987. Grave American mistrust of the DPRK also intensified through direct U.S.-DPRK confrontations, including the DPRK's 1968 capture of the USS *Pueblo*, a U.S. Navy intelligence ship, and its crew (whom North

Korea held hostage for nearly a year) and confrontations along the demilitarized zone (DMZ) that resulted in the deaths of U.S. soldiers. These and other instances of aggression against South Korea and the United States reinforced the American perception that North Korea was an irrational international outlaw bent on aggressive action—an extremely dangerous actor beyond even Moscow's control.[12] North Korea came to be considered "the poster child for rogue states."[13]

Even before the United States officially designated North Korea as a state sponsor of terrorism after the October 1987 downing of KAL flight 858, President Reagan had sought to put North Korea on notice for its dangerous tactics. In the aftermath of the Rangoon bombing, Washington was stunned by the killing of several top South Korean officials highly respected by the Reagan government. The U.S. administration appreciated Chun's restraint from military action and vowed to "lead a worldwide campaign to censure and isolate North Korea."[14] In a 1985 speech, Reagan stated his view of North Korea in the international order and his intolerance for state terrorism in no uncertain terms:

> So there we have it, Iran, Libya, North Korea, Cuba, Nicaragua—continents away, tens of thousands of miles apart—but with the same goals and objectives. . . . This is terrorism that is part of a pattern—the work of a *confederation of terrorist states.* . . . And we are especially not going to tolerate these attacks from *outlaw states* run by the strangest collection of misfits, looney tunes and squalid criminals since the advent of the Third Reich.[15]

At the same time the Reagan administration was publicly voicing concerns over North Korean terrorism, it was quietly monitoring ominous developments at Yongbyon via satellites, including high-explosives testing and the construction of nuclear reactors in a huge complex. In the 1960s and 1970s, North Korea had unsuccessfully requested Chinese assistance to acquire nuclear weapons and had also made clear to East German interlocutors its interest in nuclear development. In 1985, Moscow finally agreed to supply Pyongyang with four light water reactors to address DPRK power shortages. At U.S. urging, the Soviet Union made the deal conditional on North Korea's accession to the Nuclear Non-Proliferation Treaty (NPT).

The DPRK joined the NTP in December of that year, but it did not reach a safeguards agreement with the International Atomic Energy Agency (IAEA). By 1988, when the deadline for that agreement had passed, the

Soviet Union was no longer in a position to provide the reactors. Despite continuing concern over North Korea's nuclear development programs, the Reagan administration supported South Korean moves toward inter-Korean engagement. The U.S. administration unveiled its own modest initiative in 1988, calling for informal exchanges between U.S. and DPRK diplomats and allowing for purchases of U.S. food and other humanitarian supplies.[16]

By 1989, the newly installed administration of George H. W. Bush decided that the best way to impede North Korea's drive toward nuclear weaponry was to inform other influential actors of its intelligence on Yongbyon—information that had heretofore only been known to a small number of U.S. officials—in order to build international pressure against Pyongyang's efforts. State department officials briefed Moscow and Beijing and subsequently Tokyo and Seoul. The contents of the briefing in Seoul, including the U.S. estimate that North Korea could produce nuclear weapons by the mid-1990s, quickly leaked to the South Korean and then the international press.

At this time, the United States had to confront a strategic and diplomatic reality: American arguments that North Korea should not have nuclear weapons were substantially weakened by the fact that the United States had stationed nuclear warheads in the ROK. The United States began to consider removing these weapons but worried that South Korean officials might see such a step as a sign of lagging U.S. commitment to their nation. Finally, in 1991, the breakup of the Soviet Union convinced President Bush to formulate an initiative he hoped would spur reciprocal measures from Moscow. He called for the withdrawal of all U.S. tactical nuclear weapons stationed around the world, including those in South Korea.[17] Thereafter, the Bush administration pursued a strategy of comprehensive engagement, under which the United States offered normalization of relations if the DPRK would honor its international commitments not to build nuclear weapons.[18]

By 1992, after North Korea had entered into a non-nuclear agreement with South Korea and the first senior-level U.S.-DPRK meetings had been held, state department officials were optimistic that North Korea would indeed relinquish its nuclear programs and that the parties would open talks on reunification of the peninsula and U.S.-DPRK normalization.[19] However, in 1993, the Clinton administration became concerned over North Korea's continued intransigence toward IAEA inspections compliance and inter-Korean diplomacy. Highlighting the crisis, North Korea announced its intention to withdraw from the NPT on March 12, 1993. According to declassified U.S.

official documents, "Compounding Washington's problems was the fact that it was being whipsawed by the views of allies and domestic critics, with Japan and South Korea pressing for more diplomacy, while pundits in the [American] press argued for a 'get tough' approach."[20]

Diplomacy between the United States and DPRK, undertaken in close consultation with South Korea, eventually yielded the Agreed Framework, which involved the freeze and monitoring of North Korean nuclear facilities in exchange for energy and economic benefits, including the provision of two light water reactors, as well as moves toward normalization.[21] The Clinton administration had focused on suspending North Korean nuclear progress and the likely manufacturing of large quantities of weapons-grade plutonium. Although this was a hard-won agreement, critics (some of whom would receive high-level appointments in the George W. Bush administration) condemned it for not immediately disarming North Korea, which U.S. intelligence already suspected of having one or two nuclear weapons. These critics felt the situation remained open to further North Korean exploitation; nuclear blackmail had been rewarded, they suggested, teaching North Korea a dangerous lesson. According to Oberdorfer, "There is no evidence that Pyongyang saw the nuclear program as a bargaining chip at its inception, but the record is clear that by the 1990s it had learned the program's value in relations with the outside world."[22]

Most of the incidents mentioned thus far, up until the shock of the first open nuclear crisis in 1993, sparked only fleeting, low levels of coverage in the U.S. media. Figure 6.1 demonstrates this as it charts the three newspapers' levels of coverage (measured in number of words) devoted to U.S.-DPRK relations.[23] As the standoff with North Korea intensified in 1994, coverage spiked.

Later reports indicated that the United States had considered military means to eliminate nuclear facilities at Yongbyon, an action that U.S. government analysts anticipated could result in all-out war with a casualty count as high as 1 million people. Nonmilitary options also carried significant risks, as the Clinton administration weighed how they might be interpreted and what response they might spur from Pyongyang.[24] The DPRK had asserted that sanctions would be tantamount to a declaration of war and had threatened to turn Seoul into a "sea of fire."

Even after negotiations had dampened tensions and the Agreed Framework was signed, it was apparent throughout the 1990s that the threat from

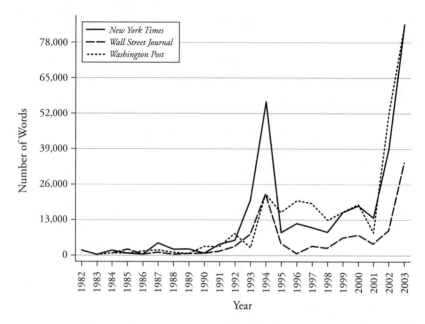

FIGURE 6.1 Number of words in U.S. newspapers on the U.S.-DPRK relationship.

North Korea had evolved. According to Joel Wit, a state department official working on North Korea issues under President Clinton, the dimensions of the DPRK threat had been transformed in three critical ways:

> First, in spite of the [George H. W.] Bush administration's efforts, North Korea was about to build a substantial nuclear weapons stockpile. . . . Second, by 1995, Pyongyang seemed to be teetering on the verge of collapse—the result of a declining economy, a worsening food crisis, and a slow-motion leadership succession after Kim Il Sung died in 1994—that could have destabilized the region. Third, North Korea's long-range missile test of August 1998 presented a possible threat to the continental United States, making it the first hostile country able to do so since the People's Republic of China began deploying long-range missiles in the early 1980s.[25]

In response to these threats, the Clinton administration intensified engagement, providing food aid and negotiating on the missile issue. The evolving nature of the threat and increased U.S.-DPRK interaction amplified U.S. news coverage from its 1982 to 1992 baseline, even after the 1993–1994 nuclear crisis had passed. By the end of the Clinton administration, Secretary of State Madeleine Albright had made a historic trip to Pyongyang to meet with Kim Jong Il, and there was cautious optimism that the diplomatic route had not only mitigated threat levels but had also laid a foundation for normalization of U.S.-DPRK relations.

Upon entering office in 2001, however, the administration of President George W. Bush reviewed North Korea policy and froze bilateral diplomacy. The new administration focused its energy initially on countering the North's missile threat through ballistic missile defense. Even before President Bush made his controversial "axis of evil" remark, he made clear that he did not trust North Korea and that he considered the Agreed Framework a highly problematic compact. Editorials criticized the administration for breaking with a diplomatic approach, damaging relations with South Korea, and giving the world the impression that the United States intended to address WMD and missile proliferation solely through new weapons systems, rather than diplomacy.

In June 2001, when the administration's policy review was completed, the United States signaled its willingness to talk to North Korea but added a host of additional issues for negotiation, including the DPRK military presence along the DMZ and the possible reopening of the 1994 agreement. Again, editorials in leading newspapers criticized the administration's approach, asserting that its policy of comprehensively addressing North Korea issues ignored gains made by the Clinton administration and risked piecemeal progress on the missile issue.[26] In the Bush administration's first official meeting with North Korean officials in Pyongyang in October 2002, state department officials charged that there was evidence that the DRPK was pursuing a uranium enrichment route to nuclear weapons. The U.S. officials said that it would not negotiate with the DPRK until it abandoned the uranium enrichment program. In the months that followed, North Korea expelled IAEA inspectors, withdrew from the NPT, and renewed plutonium production. The second nuclear crisis had begun, and news coverage of U.S.-DPRK relations reached new levels.

Although the Bush administration was reluctant to resume negotiations with North Korea and refused to call the standoff a "crisis," it had no shortage of harsh words for this charter member of the axis of evil. Condoleezza Rice called the North Korean regime an "outpost of tyranny" at the Senate confirmation hearing in January 2005 on her nomination as U.S. secretary of state,[27] and Vice President Dick Cheney, in a taped interview with U.S. media, called Kim Jong Il "one of the world's most irresponsible leaders." In

Bush at War, veteran Washington journalist Bob Woodward recounts an interview with the president in which Bush abruptly changed the topic from Iraq to North Korea: "The President sat forward in his chair. I thought he might jump up he became so emotional about the North Korean leader. 'I loathe Kim Jong Il!' Bush shouted, waving his finger in the air. 'I've got a visceral reaction to this guy, because he is starving his people.'"[28]

While there were many policy experts who did not agree with the Bush administration's approach, including the president's seeming personalization of the standoff, there was little, if any, American sympathy for North Korea—a country framed as a communist state with a record of terrorism that broke its word on nuclear development, remained closed off to the world, did not reciprocate South Korean efforts at peace, and tortured its own people in gulags. Moreover, journalists seemed under pressure to report to mainstream Americans on the pecularities of Kim Jong Il and his regime. There was a particular fascination with the North Korean leader's hair and attire, obsession with movies, and love of certain luxury goods. While many journalists considered these types of stories to be clichéd, there was a market for them in the popular press.[29] According to North Korea propaganda expert B. R. Meyers, "Improbably enough, the frequent characterization of North Korea as a Stalinist or hard-line communist nation appears to [have] a calming effect, perhaps because it evokes a happy time when all America's enemies were cold-hearted materialists who could therefore be reasoned with."[30] But apart from this "news of the weird," Figure 6.1 makes clear that U.S. media coverage of North Korea was defined by the nuclear issue.

North Korea in U.S. News

PRIMACY OF THE U.S.-DPRK RELATIONSHIP OVER THE DPRK

In contrast to U.S. interest in the ROK, which was more dynamic and spread over a range of issues, U.S. interest in the DPRK was much more monolithic, dominated by security concerns and the (often partisan) debate over how to approach this complex policy dilemma. Accordingly, while ROK-related stories were associated with newsworthy events covered in a primarily descriptive fashion, the U.S.-DPRK relationship commanded a high percentage of evaluative content, indicating a good amount of debate over policy options. In coverage of North Korea, both the Korean media (as detailed in Chapter 3) and the U.S. media gave primary focus not to the country itself but to their relations with the country—a matter for serious debate in both of these nations, although the factors informing these respective debates varied greatly.

Table 6.1 shows that approximately one-fourth of U.S. newspaper articles of DPRK-related matters focused on the country itself, while nearly three-fourths of articles focused on U.S.-DPRK relations. Certainly, part of this discrepancy is due to informational barriers that the North Korean regime imposed. As journalists have testified, it is very difficult to write anything new about North Korea, even if they are able to arrange trips into the "hermit kingdom."[31] At the same time, this finding suggests that the DPRK wins significant U.S. media attention only when its behavior—chiefly through its pursuit of nuclear weapons and missile proliferation—has led to circumstances in which the country is viewed as a security problem requiring U.S. attention and/or intervention. As recalled by Donald Macintyre, a former *Time* correspondent in Seoul who covered North Korean affairs, "Unless events in North Korea were going to have a direct impact on the United States there was often little interest."[32]

Table 6.1 also demonstrates that there was relatively little difference among U.S. newspapers in their distribution of DPRK versus U.S.-DPRK news. This is indicative of the overall remarkable agreement among newspapers on the newsworthiness of DPRK-related stories, something explored in more depth later in this chapter. Yet one clear area of difference involves newspapers' apportionment of DPRK-related news as a share of all Korean peninsula news. While the *New York Times* devoted 38 percent and the *Wall*

TABLE 6.1
U.S. media coverage of DPRK categories

Category	*New York Times*	*Washington Post*	*Wall Street Journal*	All
DPRK	193	190	129	512
	(24.09)	(25.27)	(32.09)	(26.19)
U.S.-DPRK relationship	608	562	273	1,443
	(75.91)	(74.73)	(67.92)	(73.81)
Total/All DPRK	801	752	402	1,955
	(100)	(100)	(100)	(100)
All DPRK as share of all Korean peninsula news	(38)	(61.7)	(22.4)	(38.2)

NOTE: Parentheses contain percentages.

Street Journal devoted 22.4 percent of their peninsular coverage to DPRK issues, the *Washington Post* gave significantly greater attention to DPRK-related matters, devoting 61.7 percent of its entire Korean coverage to such issues. These staggered levels of relative attention to the DPRK within news of the peninsula likely reflect the *Journal's* strong interest in the South Korean economy, given the orientation of the newspaper, as well as the *Post's* persistent preference for political, diplomatic, and security-related news. It should be noted that, even though the *Post* devoted a greater percentage of its Korean coverage to North Korea, in terms of actual number of articles, the *Times* gave slightly more coverage to DPRK-related matters (801 *Times* versus 752 *Post* articles).

Coverage of the U.S.-DPRK relationship plainly exhibited—more distinctly than any other Korean peninsula focus category—two clear peaks in 1994 and 2002. This is indicative, once again, of the high percentage of security-focused coverage within DPRK-related content. As demonstrated in Figure 6.2, it was U.S.-DPRK coverage that captured the increase in U.S. media attention during each nuclear crisis. The nuclear crises were clearly conceived as U.S.-DPRK issues, not simply developments in North Korea. That is, from the perspective of the U.S. media, they were problems that

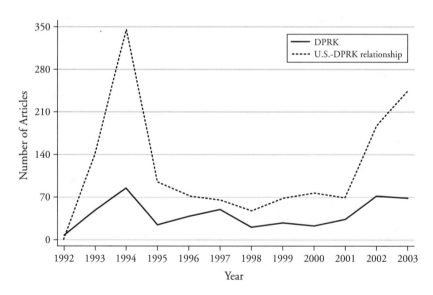

FIGURE 6.2 Number of articles in U.S. newspapers on DPRK and the U.S.-DPRK relationship.

involved the United States, that were seen through the prism of U.S. interests, and that the United States had a responsibility to address. However, as discussed in the introductory chapter, U.S. policy options had been politically controversial, especially since the early 1990s. This sense of policy controversy likely drove coverage to even higher levels. The U.S. treatment of partisan debate over this policy issue contributed to the crises' newsworthiness, which was similarly perceived among newspapers.

In contrast to the U.S. newspapers' ROK-related coverage of the two nuclear crises, this examination of U.S.-DPRK coverage illustrates that the total volume of coverage associated with the 1994 nuclear crisis was significantly greater than that for the second crisis in 2002 and 2003. This may be because the idea of a nuclear North Korea was not as new and perhaps not as shocking (although just as dangerous) during the second nuclear crisis. These are two qualities that tend to contribute to newsworthiness. Yet it is also likely that the competing story of the probable and then actual U.S. war with Iraq—an open military conflict in which U.S. soldiers were dying every day—had the effect of suppressing what might have been a higher level of coverage in the absence of the Iraq conflict.

According to *New York Times* journalist David Sanger, because President Bush was not talking publicly about the steps North Korea was taking at the time (including the transportation of fuel rods), the U.S. media's ability to focus on North Korea, "a distraction, [that was] taking attention away from the No. 1 priority at the time [Iraq]," was severely impeded. It even spurred a "journalistic conundrum" on how to handle the story, if the White House stayed virtually silent on North Korea while it emphasized Iraq.[33] In other words, greater U.S. media attention to U.S.-DPRK relations during the first nuclear crisis stemmed from a combination of factors, some of which had little or nothing to do with Korea but rather involved competing stories and the size of the so-called news hole.

It is interesting to note that from 1996 to 2001, a period not characterized by a nuclear crisis, DPRK and U.S.-DPRK coverage levels were much more comparable. Combined with headline data from the 1980s that show that North Korea did not receive any significant level of U.S. media attention before the first nuclear crisis (see Figure 6.1), this finding seems to reinforce the notion of "hot spot journalism,"[34] demonstrating that, in the absence of a nuclear crisis—indeed, even during a dramatic famine—U.S.-DPRK relations were accorded little attention in the mainstream U.S. media.

SALIENCE OF SECURITY AND HUMAN RIGHTS

The data presented in Table 6.2 leave little question that the U.S.-DPRK relationship is, for the United States, primarily a security issue. An overwhelming 86.69 percent of U.S. newspapers' coverage focused on security matters, and even the *Wall Street Journal* showed negligible deviation from the other two newspapers in this respect. This finding strongly suggests that there is a considerable degree of uniformity in U.S. media views toward U.S.-DPRK relations. It is primarily an issue of security, a finding that is not surprising, given that the vast majority of coverage was published during years of nuclear crisis.

Whereas security is primarily represented as a U.S.-DPRK issue, Table 6.2 illustrates that humanitarian and human rights issues are primarily conceptualized as a DPRK issue (comprising over 20 percent of DPRK coverage but only 4.85 percent of U.S.-DPRK news). Such coverage reflects bipartisan American concern over the human rights situation in North Korea—perhaps most concretely expressed in recent years through the U.S.

TABLE 6.2
U.S. media coverage of DPRK issues (percent)

Category/Issue	New York Times	Washington Post	Wall Street Journal	All
DPRK				
Security/military	26.56	50.26	42.64	39.41
Humanitarian/human rights issues	26.56	23.81	9.30	21.18
Economic issues	14.06	6.35	23.26	13.53
General diplomacy	13.02	4.23	3.88	7.45
Domestic politics	14.06	13.23	17.05	14.51
Other	5.73	2.12	3.88	3.92
Total	100.0	100.0	100.0	100.0
U.S.-DPRK Relationship				
Security/military	85.53	87.90	86.61	86.69
Humanitarian/human rights issues	5.43	4.98	3.30	4.85
Economic issues	1.97	1.25	7.33	2.70
General diplomacy	5.92	4.63	2.20	4.71
Domestic politics	0.16	0.18	0.00	0.14
Other	0.99	1.07	0.37	0.90
Total	100.0	100.0	100.0	100.0

House of Representatives and Senate's unanimous passage of the North Korean Human Rights Act of 2004. In fact, as discussed earlier, North Korea's deplorable human rights record—one of the worst in the world, according to regular reports from Amnesty International—is one of the main pillars underlying the American perception that the North Korean regime is inherently evil or, at the very least, highly problematic. (This issue will be discussed in greater detail later in this chapter.) While Table 6.2 demonstrates that there was clearly more diversity in DPRK coverage than in coverage about U.S.-DPRK relations, it is important to remember that the newspapers accorded far less coverage to the former (510 articles versus 1,443 articles).

The respective prominence of security and human rights issues was similarly reflected in the data on DPRK-related subjects. As previously stated, the DPRK's pursuit of WMD garnered nearly one-third of aggregate U.S. attention to the Korean peninsula over the years of the study. Within DPRK-related news, as shown in Table 6.3, a formidable 64.9 percent of coverage was devoted to this subject. That is, more often than not, when one of the U.S. newspapers published an article on the DPRK, it was about that nation's WMD programs and appeared during one of two nuclear crises—when the North had amassed "a pile of plutonium" and the United States was, once again, faced with the dilemma of how to address the issue of WMD in the DPRK.

According to Table 6.3, at 9.15 percent, the second-foremost subject in DPRK-related news was that country's humanitarian and human rights situation. The U.S.-DPRK military conflict (5.46%) ranked third, other general

TABLE 6.3
U.S. media coverage of subjects within DPRK-related news (percent)

Subject	*New York Times*	*Washington Post*	*Wall Street Journal*	All
ALL DPRK				
DPRK WMD	59.8	69.66	65.99	64.9
Humanitarian/Human rights in the DPRK	10.63	9.66	5.29	9.15
U.S.-DPRK military conflict (unrelated to WMD issues)	7.55	5.1	2.02	5.46
Other general diplomacy	6.02	4.03	2.77	4.58
DPRK politics	3.71	3.76	5.29	4.06

diplomacy (4.58%) fourth, and North Korean politics (4.06%) fifth. No economic topic ranked in the top five most prevalent subjects. Overall, findings show that DPRK coverage was relatively similar among the three newspapers, apparently due to overwhelming concern about North Korea's pursuit of WMD and concern over human rights issues. Thus, the U.S. newspapers portrayed the DPRK in much more consistent terms than the ROK, persistently reinforcing the fixed image of an antagonistic, threatening communist regime with little regard for the well-being of its own people.

As expected, Figure 6.3 shows two clear peaks in DPRK WMD coverage during the nuclear crises. Generally, while the three dailies have varying levels of security coverage, there is remarkably close alignment in coverage trends. That is, for the most part, the three newspapers' coverage increased or decreased in tandem, seemingly in response to events.

It is important to note here that the coding scheme includes missile issues in the DPRK WMD category. North Korea's development of missiles greatly concerned the U.S. government for the length of this study, as Pyongyang's joint drive toward a nuclear capability and medium- and long-range delivery systems exponentially increased the risk of attack on ally Japan, as well as the American homeland. Also, U.S. leaders frequently cited concern about North Korea's providing missiles and missile (and even nu-

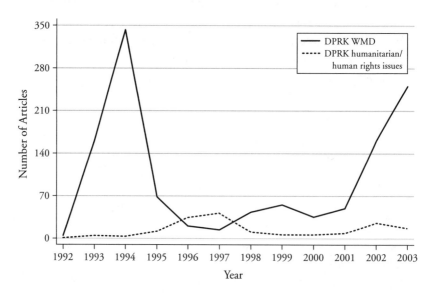

FIGURE 6.3 Number of articles in U.S. newspapers on DPRK-related subjects.

clear) technology to Syria and Iran, actors hostile to Israel. Indeed, in a July 1993 address to South Korea's National Assembly, President Clinton warned, "North Korea appears committed to indiscriminate sales of the Scud missiles that were such a source of terror and destruction in the Persian Gulf. Now it is developing, testing and looking to export a more powerful missile with a range of 600 miles or more; enough for North Korea to threaten Osaka, or for Iran to threaten Tel Aviv."[35] In addition to generating domestic political debate over the best approach to North Korea, this missile threat compounded both the complexity and the newsworthiness of DPRK WMD development from the U.S. perspective.

Compared to WMD coverage, human rights and humanitarian topics in DPRK-related news appear to have received scant attention from the U.S. media. Still, this was the second most prominent issue and subject in U.S. coverage of the North, and even though it garnered a relatively small number of articles, it left a stinging impression on Americans' overall perception of North Korea. Figure 6.3 illustrates that humanitarian and human rights issues received more coverage than WMD topics in two years of this study, 1996 and 1997, which were years of horrific famine in North Korea. This increase in the relevance of human rights issues signals that it was at this time that DPRK humanitarian issues first seemed to infiltrate the popular American consciousness through the media. In contrast, before 1996, including during the first nuclear crisis, there was relatively little, if any, coverage of this subject. In addition to spurring U.S. media attention because of the sheer scale of human suffering, the exodus of hungry North Korean refugees to China during the famine and in the years that followed made it possible for U.S. journalists to procure new information on other forms of human rights abuses in North Korea.[36]

At the onset of President Clinton's first administration, he declared that in the post–cold war era, human rights would stand as a major pillar of U.S. foreign policy; however, most of his attention to this matter was concentrated on China. In general, Asians perceived the Clinton approach as heavy handed, believing that the United States was too impatient and too demanding in urging human rights improvements in the region. In attempting to change China's approach to human rights, Clinton made renewal of most favored nation (MFN) trading status contingent on measurable progress. Beijing perceived this as atrocious interference in its domestic affairs and refused to bend. Pressured by U.S. business interests and recognizing the strategic need to enlist China's assistance in the first North Korean nuclear crisis (as well as in other regional matters), Clinton revamped his approach and excised human rights conditionality. His administration internalized an important lesson: Although in line with American principles, insistence on human rights improvements can at once be ineffective and hinder cooperation on vital strategic imperatives.

Clinton's idealistic approach on human rights concentrated on China and did not extend to the Korean peninsula. In fact, at this time, most U.S. media coverage of human rights in Korea focused on South Korea's healing from its authoritarian years, including President Kim Young Sam's initiative to grant amnesty to more than 41,000 individuals declared criminals and dissidents by his authoritarian predecessors.[37] In dealing with North Korea during the first nuclear crisis, Clinton's negotiators did not raise human rights issues. When pressed on this issue by reporters, the chief U.S. negotiator responded that "the nuclear issue has to come first, and then, if our relations improve, we can move on to other issues."[38] While the Bush administration increased the level of rhetoric on human rights issues, with President Bush himself meeting with the family of Japanese abductee Megumi Yokota and Kang Chol-Hwan, North Korean refugee and author of "The Aquariums of Pyongyang: Ten Years in the North Korean Gulag," the topic remained largely absent from the fundamental U.S. approach to the so-called Six-Party Talks.[39]

As Figure 6.4 demonstrates, the *New York Times* and the *Washington Post* visibly renewed their coverage of human rights in North Korea in conjunction with the most recent nuclear crisis. It appears that the greater focus on the WMD topic led to renewed interest in humanitarian and human right topics.[40] Indeed, as President Bush expressed in his "axis of evil" speech, there is a popular perception that in North Korea, WMD development and human rights are intimately connected. As Senate Foreign Relations Committee Chairman Senator Richard Lugar (R-Ind.) wrote in an editorial in the *Washington Post* in July 2003, "Instead of trying to feed its people, Pyongyang is obsessed with developing nuclear weapons and missiles, and fortifying its one million-man army."[41]

Even during the famine of the late 1990s, U.S. coverage acknowledged natural disasters as contributing factors to the human suffering in the DPRK but focused largely on the government's mismanagement of the economy and defense spending as the primary cause.[42] As noted in Chapter 3, South Korean media coverage of DPRK humanitarian and human rights issues,

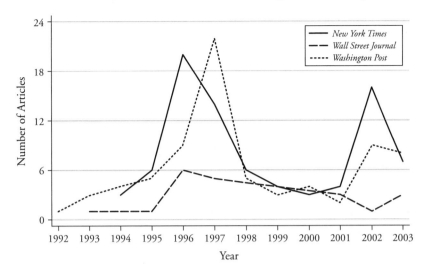

FIGURE 6.4 Number of articles in U.S. newspapers on DPRK humanitarian and human rights issues.

while varied in conservative and progressive publications, generally focused much more on the plight of the North Korean people, as opposed to U.S. coverage, which tended to focus on the culpability of the North Korean regime, including its perceived explicitly evil decision to choose weapons development over rice distribution.

DEEP-ROOTED DISTRUST OF THE "HERMIT KINGDOM"

This section examines how the U.S. media perceive and portray DKRK-related issues and how these dynamics may have changed over time.[43] Interestingly, as shown in Table 6.4, in terms of descriptive tone, DPRK coverage scored more negatively than U.S.-DPRK coverage (–0.75 versus –0.59), whereas in terms of evaluative tone, U.S.-DPRK news rated more negatively than DPRK news (–0.84 versus –0.70). In other words, when it came to descriptions of events, DPRK news was more negative than U.S.-DPRK news. Yet in evaluative terms, the leading U.S. dailies were more critical of the U.S.-DPRK relationship than of the country itself. This likely reflects a very pessimistic assessment of the U.S.-DPRK relations, marked by two nuclear standoffs during the study period.

Within news tone scores for DPRK-related issues and subjects, the issue/subject of humanitarian and human rights was rated very negatively,

TABLE 6.4
U.S. media news tone by focus category, issue, and subject

	Tone	New York Times	Washington Post	Wall Street Journal	Average
Category					
DPRK	Descriptive	−0.72	−0.95	−0.57	−0.75
	Evaluative	−0.52	−0.91	−0.67	−0.70
U.S.-DPRK	Descriptive	−0.54	−0.74	−0.50	−0.59
	Evaluative	−0.72	−0.91	−0.89	−0.84
Issue (all DPRK)					
Security	Descriptive	−0.77	−0.92	−1.00	−0.90
	Evaluative	−0.95	−1.06	−1.12	−1.04
Humanitarian/human rights issues	Descriptive	−0.89	−1.33	−0.67	−0.96
	Evaluative	−1.15	−1.29	−0.94	−1.12
Subject (all DPRK)					
DPRK WMD	Descriptive	−0.74	−0.96	−0.94	−0.88
	Evaluative	−0.97	−1.07	−1.11	−1.05
Humanitarian/human rights issues	Descriptive	−0.57	−1.10	−0.79	−0.82
	Evaluative	−0.80	−1.18	−0.92	−0.97

especially within *Washington Post* coverage (−1.33 for descriptive tone and −1.29 for evaluative tone). The three dailies' evaluative tone scores on human rights showed less variation than their descriptive tone scores and, on average, were more negative. That is, U.S. newspapers evaluated this issue/subject in even more negative terms than they described events related to human rights. Once again, this finding seems to reflect near unanimity among the American pubic and policy makers in their views of the DPRK human rights issue, an issue that energizes both internationalists on the American left and religious conservatives on the right of the American political spectrum.

Security also received very negative descriptive and evaluative scores. Security was by far the most covered issue within DPRK-related news. The *Times* published 491 articles, the *Post* 509, and the *Journal* 199 over the course of this study. Evaluative tone scores on security demonstrated less variation and were also more negative than descriptive tones on the issue. Once again, this demonstrates that the U.S. press viewed North Korean WMD development very critically and emphasizes the relative invariability of American opinion on it.

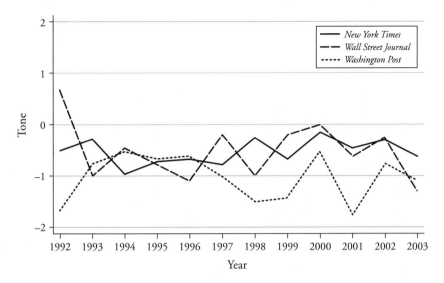

FIGURE 6.5 U.S. newspapers' average evaluative news tone toward DPRK.

Figure 6.5 displays the U.S. media evaluative tone toward the DPRK, and Figure 6.6 illustrates the U.S. media evaluative tone toward the U.S.-DPRK relationship. Compared to the figures on the U.S. newspapers' tones toward the ROK and U.S.-ROK relations (Chapter 5), the most readily apparent difference demonstrated in Figures 6.5 and 6.6 is that tone was never positive, with one noteworthy exception in 2000, which will be discussed later.

It is also interesting to notice that, on the whole, the newspapers generally evaluated the U.S.-DPRK relationship in similar ways, but their coverage of the DPRK itself was characterized by more divergent trends in evaluative tones. Recall that in terms of South Korea, the opposite was true: Coverage of the country itself showed more unified trends among the newspapers' evaluative tones, while coverage of the country's relationship with the United States produced more divergent responses from the U.S. newspapers in this study. Also recall that in terms of news attention, the ROK received much more coverage in the U.S. media than the U.S.-ROK relationship, and the U.S.-DPRK relationship received much more coverage than the DPRK itself. Given these trends, it becomes apparent that the focus categories that receive more coverage also seem to exhibit similar patterns in tone among newspapers during this period of study. The focus categories receiving less coverage—perhaps not driven by clear, easily inter-preted events related to that focus category—tend to produce greater vari-ance among newspapers' evaluative tones.

As noted earlier, the one year in which U.S.-DPRK coverage registered a positive evaluative tone score was 2000. That year, when the *Journal* and *Post* both registered positive evaluative tone scores and *Times* coverage was neutral, marks one of the most dramatic changes in tone seen on any of the graphs (both for 1999 to 2000 and from 2000 to 2001; see Figure 6.6). This boost in the year 2000 likely reflects developing views—spurred by high-level U.S.-DPRK meetings as well as the historic inter-Korean summit—that North Korea might graduate from "rogue regime" status to become a functioning member of the international community, moving toward nor-malization of relations with the United States. The precipitous decline in tone from 2000 to 2001 suggests the quelling of this optimism when the re-cently inaugurated Bush administration departed markedly from the Clin-ton administration's DPRK policy approach, expressing strong skepticism that inter-Korean engagement would yield any real change or positive result and interrupting momentum in bilateral consultations (in effect, nullifying the two U.S.-DPRK communiqués signed in Washington in 2000).

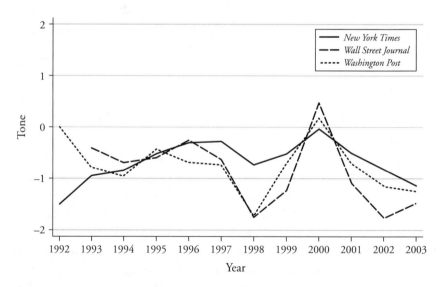

FIGURE 6.6 U.S. newspapers' average evaluative news tone toward the U.S.-DPRK relation-ship.

For tone toward both the DPRK and the U.S.-DPRK relationship, the period 1994–1996 was a time of relative convergence among the U.S. newspapers. While, on average, the tones during this time stayed flat for the DPRK, those toward U.S.-DPRK relations gradually and steadily improved in conjunction with the resolution of the first nuclear crisis. The events of 1997 and 1998—most notably, growing recognition of famine in North Korea and the North's provocative missile launch over Japanese territory—seem to have had a stratifying effect among the newspapers on evaluative tone toward both the DPRK and U.S.-DPRK relations. The negativity of tone toward the U.S.-DPRK relationship in 1998 was nearly matched in the last few years of the study, when evaluative tone showed a steady decline from 2000 to 2003. Within these years, the *Wall Street Journal* has tended to be the most negative news source. The last year of data, 2003, showed relative convergence in the three newspapers' very negative assessments of the U.S.-DPRK relationship.

Of great significance is the extent to which the three U.S. newspapers' tones on U.S.-DPRK relations track closely with one another. Earlier, it was established that U.S.-DPRK coverage seems to be more event driven than coverage of other focus categories, most notably around the two nuclear crises. Thus, it is logical that events surrounding the development of nuclear weapons—certainly an extreme and threatening scenario—would solicit similar coverage across the U.S. newspapers, even among newspapers of varying ideological bents.

Figure 6.7 displays the three U.S. newspapers' average evaluative tones toward the subjects of North Korean WMD development and humanitarian and human rights over time. As shown clearly in the figure, these subjects were rated very negatively throughout the study period. It is interesting to note that neither of these subjects becomes dramatically more negative during the times in which the U.S. media accorded it greatest attention. That is, humanitarian and human rights tone scores are not most negative during the famine, and North Korean WMD development does not yield significantly more negative tones between 1993 and 1994 or 2002 and 2003.

While events and attention to them may vary over time, the U.S. publications maintained fairly consistent negative evaluative tones toward these subjects. Somewhat curiously, during the first nuclear crisis in 1993 and 1994, none of the newspapers' evaluative tones fell below –1 (see Figure 6.6). This slightly less negative coverage of the first nuclear crisis than the second was

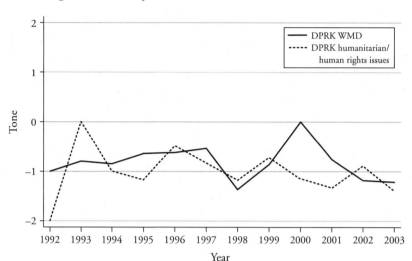

FIGURE 6.7 U.S. newspapers' average evaluative news tone toward North Korean WMD development and humanitarian and human rights.

likely due to a variety of factors, including general U.S.-ROK agreement on the appropriate diplomatic approach to the situation during the first crisis, plus increased U.S. concern over the North's potential connection to global terrorism in a post–September 11 world during the second crisis. This issue will be explored further in the next chapter.

North Korea as a "Dangerous Other"

Chapter 5 and this chapter both examine how the U.S. media portrayed the ROK and the DPRK in terms of news attention and sentiments over time. Overall, there is a good deal of balance in the amount of coverage devoted to Korean peninsula news, with security and trade as top issues. However, there are crucial differences in U.S. media coverage of ROK and DPRK news when examined separately.

For ROK-related news, as presented in the previous chapter, the country itself received more news attention than its relationship with the United States, with American interest in South Korean economic and trade issues driving coverage of this ally. As noted in Chapter 5, the ROK, as a major trading partner, has importance to the United States beyond the security alliance.

On the other hand, for DPRK-related news, the U.S.-DPRK relationship was featured decisively more often than the DPRK itself (a finding certainly influenced by the country's significant information barriers), and nearly three-fourths of North Korea–related coverage focused on security matters. The U.S. media interest in North Korea is tethered to the U.S. government's responses to that nation, and these responses are most often precipitated by security-related provocations. Across newspapers, similar percentages of DPRK-related content devoted to security issues indicate that North Korea is viewed primarily as a security problem and that this view is widely shared. Thus, it is apparent from the study's findings that the U.S. media—and by extension, the U.S. public—see the ROK and DPRK through very different lenses.

News about the U.S.-DPRK relationship recorded highly negative tone ratings, with little variation among the three newspapers' scores. This indicates that the U.S. media are fairly unified in their assessment of U.S.-DPRK relations. Within the three dailies' tone scores for DPRK issues, human rights was the most negative, even more negative than security and domestic politics (which both received very negative scores). This is hardly surprising, given that some humanitarian organizations have named North Korea as one of the world's foremost human rights offenders. While security may be the essential aspect of the North Korea problem from the U.S. perspective, it is the human rights issue that is capable of eliciting strong emotions and contributing to the perspective that the North Korean regime is evil, in nature and in action.

Overall, across news for the Korean peninsula—for the ROK and the DPRK—security is persistently seen as one of the most problematic areas from the perspective of the U.S. media, ostensibly owing to the DPRK's pursuit of nuclear weapons and its missile proliferation. In particular, the U.S. media view of the DPRK is not only very negative but shows little variation, producing a fixed, unfavorable image of the nation. The deep-rooted negative image of the "hermit kingdom" certainly has the potential to be a major obstacle to the normalization of U.S.-DPRK relations.

Although there are serious debates in the United States over the problem of North Korea, they focus on the complexities of security policy and are not related to identity and the politics of identity, as is the case for South Korea. The ostensibly partisan U.S. debate has centered on differences in foreign affairs policy. The ABC ("anything but Clinton") policies put in place by the George W. Bush administration at the outset of its tenure were designed to break the cycle of nuclear blackmail. But in large part, Bush revamped his approach in his second term, essentially seeking denuclearization for normalization (a familiar formulation) through multilateral and bilateral talks and persistent diplomacy. Many believed this course of diplomatic pragmatism was not wholly different from the course followed by the Clinton administration after all. (It should also be remembered that President George H. W. Bush made initial strategic concessions to the North, removing U.S. nuclear weapons from ROK soil, in hopes that the Northern regime would arrest its pursuit of nuclear technologies.)

Thus, the U.S. partisan debate over North Korea is quite different from the partisanship seen in South Korea. Many in South Korea believe their relationship with the North defines the Korean nation in the twenty-first century. The same cannot be said for Americans, however. Among other pressing foreign and security policy challenges, Americans merely seek a policy that is effective in stopping DPRK proliferation and, possibly one day, in bringing the DPRK up to international standards on human rights. Indeed, the findings of this chapter confirm David Sanger's 1993 assertion that North Korea is seemingly only—or at least, mostly—of interest to the United States in any great measure when it is harboring "a pile of plutonium."

Just as North Korea shapes South Koreans' sense of national identity while serving as primarily a policy matter for Americans, the U.S.-ROK relationship—intimately tied to the North Korea problem—is conceptualized through a different framework or lens in each country. While the relationship has been a matter of marked and increasing contention in the ROK for some time, as shown in Chapter 4, only more recently have the U.S. media portrayed the relationship as troubled. The following chapter turns to an examination of these ideas—the identity thesis and the policy rift thesis— to evaluate more precisely how differing perceptions of the DPRK and the U.S.-ROK relationship during this study period can influence the future of the relationship between Seoul and Washington.

SEVEN

Identity and Policy in the Alliance

As discussed in previous chapters, the U.S. and Korean news media view their nations' relationship quite differently. The U.S. media displayed critical views of the relationship only in the later years of the study period, and there was little difference in that regard among the three newspapers. However, the Korean progressive media showed a critical view of the U.S.-ROK relationship much earlier than the U.S. newspapers, and there were sharp differences between the progressive and conservative Korean newspapers in their respective views on the relationship.

These discrepancies in U.S. and Korean media views can be interpreted as reflecting the different framework or lens each nation employs in approaching the alliance. More specifically, the critical views of the U.S. media largely reflect a perceived policy rift between the U.S. and South Korean governments, principally over North Korea, while the South Korean media views are closely related to the larger issue of national identity. In this chapter, these two arguments—the policy rift thesis and the identity thesis—are put to a series of empirical tests using media data from both countries.

First, the news tones of articles about the United States–Republic of Korea (U.S.-ROK) relationship are compared in accordance with combinations of U.S. and Korean administrations. This examination is intended as an empirical test of the *policy rift thesis*, which maintains that the collision between the Kim Dae Jung administration's Sunshine Policy and the George W. Bush administration's hard-line approach toward the Democratic People's Republic of Korea (DPRK) marked a distinct turning point for the U.S.-ROK relationship. If this thesis does, in fact, possess explanatory power, as many experts of Korean affairs have argued, then one should expect a clear downturn in the U.S. media news tone on U.S.-ROK relations during the overlapping period of the Kim and Bush administrations. One should also expect the news tone to remain largely unchanged after the Roh Moo Hyun administration took office, since it continued the engagement policy of Kim Dae Jung.

However, a rather different pattern should be anticipated from the Korean news media. First, critical views of U.S.-ROK relations should appear in the Korean media, especially in the progressive newspaper, much earlier than the Bush-Kim overlap. Second, significant differences in progressive and conservative views of the alliance should also be apparent. And third, these differences should have increased over time. Once again, this is because the progressive critique of the alliance in South Korea gained momentum prior to the Bush-Kim overlap period, reflecting Korean progressives' efforts to reformulate their national identity in the post-authoritarian, post–cold war context. This open and intense contention intensified in the later years of this study period, as demonstrated in Chapter 4. Together, these findings should lend strong support to the *identity thesis* elaborated in the introductory chapter.

Second, this chapter includes a further comparison of news tones regarding U.S.-ROK relations during the two nuclear standoffs. It is suggested that the U.S. media viewed tension between the allies as reflecting policy discord on the North Korean nuclear issue. Consequently, one should expect the news tone about the relationship to have turned significantly more negative during the second nuclear crisis, as compared to the first nuclear standoff in the mid-1990s. That is, during the first crisis, the alliance partners pursued a fairly unified approach toward the North, despite some concerns by the Korean government, whereas during the second standoff, the partners disagreed over the most suitable policy approach, based on fundamental differences over the utility of engaging North Korea. Thus, one should expect the U.S. news media to display more negative tones about the U.S.-ROK relationship during the second crisis.

In contrast, the South Korean media may display different patterns in tone. If the primary impetus for South Koreans' changed views was related to their effort to redefine their nation's relationship with the United States in the post–cold war era, as the identity thesis suggests, then the change in views on U.S.-ROK relations should be expected to occur before the policy disputes over the nuclear issue. This should hold true at least in the case of the progressive newspaper, since progressive forces in South Korea led the challenge to prevailing views of the North and the alliance. In contrast, the conservative newspaper may have become even less critical of U.S.-ROK relations during the second nuclear crisis, primarily because during the later years of this study period, conservative political forces demonstrated significant concern over ostensible alliance deterioration and thus came to stress the importance of the alliance.

Third, as a complementary analysis, the chapter examines U.S. news media tones about the U.S.-Japan relationship during the two nuclear crises. Japan is another important Pacific ally of the United States, and the two nations' relationship has also been subject to change in the post–cold war era. Yet unlike South Korea, Japan shares with the United States a perception that the DPRK is a regional and even a global security threat. Consequently, the Japanese endorsed the Bush administration's policy approach to the current standoff (during the years of this study). That is, Japanese and U.S. threat perceptions were seemingly more congruous than those of the United States and the ROK. If this is the case, then one should expect contrasting patterns in U.S.-ROK and U.S.-Japan relations during the current nuclear crisis—in essence, the weakening of the U.S. alliance with the ROK and the strengthening of the U.S. alliance with Japan. That is, in the terms of the study's empirical tests, the news tones toward the U.S.-Japan relationship should have become more positive during the second nuclear standoff with Pyongyang, in contrast to the news tones toward the U.S.-ROK relationship.

Finally, concerning the South Korean news media, this chapter examines whether changing views of the North have affected views of U.S.-ROK relations in general. As shown in Chapter 3, the Sunshine Policy of the Kim Dae Jung government was crucial to changing South Korean views of the North, which, in turn, is said to have affected views of the U.S.-ROK relationship. If this is the case, then one should expect improved views of the North and more negative views of the alliance after implementation of the Sunshine Policy. These shifts are intimately related, as both reflect South Korean notions of national identity. However, one should expect this correlated change to appear only in the progressive newspaper, as its conservative counterpart held steadfast to more traditional views of the North and the alliance. This is conceived as a complementary test of the identity thesis using South Korean data.[1]

Media Views by Administrations

To begin, this chapter examines the shifts in news tone during the four periods of distinct combinations of U.S. and Korean presidential administrations. Once again, this analysis can offer an empirical assessment of whether the collision between the Kim Dae Jung administration's Sunshine Policy and the George W. Bush administration's hard-line approach marked a distinct turning point in the U.S.-ROK relationship.

South Korea allows a president to serve a single five-year term, while the United States allows a president to serve two four-year terms. During the study period, South Korea saw three different administrations: those of Kim Young Sam (February 1993–February 1998), Kim Dae Jung (February 1998–February 2003), and Roh Moo Hyun (February 2003–end of the study). For the same period, the United States had only one change in president, from Bill Clinton (January 1993–January 2001) to George W. Bush (January 2001–end of study). Thus, the study examines four combinations of South Korean and U.S. administrations: (1) Clinton and Kim Young Sam; (2) Clinton and Kim Dae Jung; (3) Bush and Kim Dae Jung; and (4) Bush and Roh Moo Hyun.

When the policy rift thesis is applied to U.S. data, one should anticipate the U.S.-ROK relationship to have been viewed relatively positively during Clinton–Kim Young Sam (variable name: CLIN1&2*YS) and Clinton–Kim Dae Jung (CLIN2*DJ) and for tone to have turned more negative during Bush–Kim Dae Jung (GWB1*DJ), with tone remaining conflict ridden during Bush–Roh Moo Hyun (GWB1*ROH). In addition to examining U.S. media data in accordance with these administration overlaps, the analysis will also look to the ROK data, which may reveal a different pattern in line with the identity thesis, as described earlier.

U.S. MEDIA

As Figure 7.1 illustrates, prior to the overlap of the Kim Dae Jung and Bush administrations, U.S. media tone (i.e., the average of the tones of the three newspapers: the *New York Times, Washington Post,* and *Wall Street Journal*) on the U.S.-ROK alliance was relatively neutral to positive. During the Kim Young Sam and Clinton administrations, the descriptive tone was close to neutral at 0.09 and the evaluative tone was only slightly negative at −0.26. During the Clinton and Kim Dae Jung years, both descriptive (0.26) and evaluative (0.17) tones were positive. Indeed, these years recorded

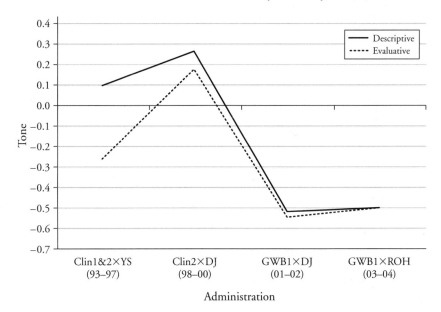

FIGURE 7.1 Average U.S. media tone on the U.S.-ROK relationship by administration overlaps.

the most positive tones of the study period. The Clinton administration largely endorsed the engagement policy of the Kim Dae Jung government. Thus, these years were marked by significant diplomatic accomplishments, from the 2000 summit and Secretary of State's Madeleine Albright's trip to Pyongyang to the establishment of the U.S.-ROK-Japan Trilateral Coordination and Oversight Group (TCOG). The Clinton administration was said to have "great trust and confidence" in Kim Dae Jung.[2]

However, the U.S. media evaluation of U.S.-ROK relations took a striking downward turn when the Bush administration came to power in 2001. During the Bush–Kim Dae Jung period, the descriptive tone was –0.53 and the evaluative tone was –0.56. It had been apparent from the early months of Bush's tenure that he and Kim Dae Jung held different views on the appropriateness of the pace and terms of South Korean engagement of the North, provisions of the Agreed Framework,[3] and later, the outbreak of the second nuclear crisis on the peninsula. This change in news tones supports the policy rift thesis: Kim Dae Jung's policy of engaging North Korea (lacking steadfast demands of reciprocity) was incongruous with the DPRK strategy of the Bush administration. From the U.S. perspective, policy

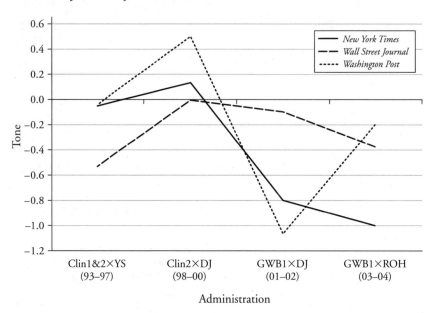

FIGURE 7.2 U.S. media tone on the U.S.-ROK relationship during administration overlaps by newpaper.

differences on North Korea could have a profound impact on perceptions of the alliance.

As Figure 7.2 shows, the Bush-Kim period's deterioration of evaluative tone was most pronounced in the *Washington Post*, while there was little change in the evaluative tone of the *Wall Street Journal*. (The descriptive tone, not reported here, shows a similar pattern.) Both these findings are logical, given that disputes between the two allies were over security and political issues, both major news items for the *Washington Post*. There were no significant economic or trade-related disputes between Presidents Bush and Kim, and thus only a small change in tone for the financial news–oriented *Wall Street Journal* is congruous with this narrative. The inter-newspaper difference lends credence to the assertion that the most salient policy conflict occurred in the realm of security and politics.

Analysis of the Bush–Roh Moo Hyun overlap reveals no significant improvement in tone from the Bush–Kim Dae Jung years. At the same time, it is important to recognize that, on average, tone did not deteriorate further. This finding runs contrary to the assertions of some critics, who blamed the Roh administration for fueling anti-American sentiments and deepening the level of tension within the alliance.

An examination of the newspapers' respective changes in tone from the Bush-Kim period (2001–2002) to the Bush-Roh period (2003–2004) shows mixed results. While the *Washington Post*'s coverage became more positive in both descriptive and evaluative terms during Roh's tenure, the *Wall Street Journal*'s coverage became slightly more negative for both types of tone. This might reflect some concern or apprehension that the financial sector held when the ROK presidency was filled by former human rights lawyer Roh Moo Hyun, who was relatively unknown and ostensibly critical of the United States, as well as market jitters at the inception of the second nuclear crisis on the peninsula. The *New York Times*'s evaluative tone became more negative, although its descriptive tone became less negative. Thus, there is inconclusive evidence that tone clearly improved or deteriorated during Roh's tenure in the Blue House.[4]

KOREAN MEDIA

A very different pattern can be seen from the Korean data. As presented in Figure 7.3, the progressive newspaper consistently displayed negative views of the U.S.-ROK relationship over the study period. In fact, contrary to the U.S. media view, the tone of the progressive *Hankyoreh Shinmoon* on

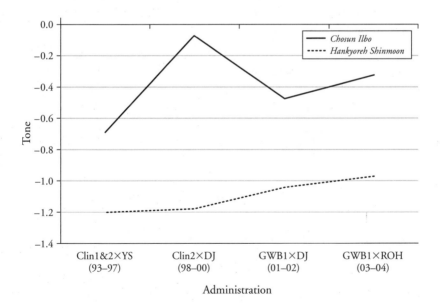

FIGURE 7.3 Korean media tone on the U.S.-ROK relationship during administration overlaps by newspaper.

U.S.-ROK relations was most critical prior to the overlap of the Kim Dae Jung and Bush administrations. During the Clinton and Kim Young Sam administrations, *Hankyoreh*'s average tone was –1.20, and its tone remained similarly negative during the Clinton and Kim Dae Jung years (–1.18). This is in sharp contrast to the U.S. media, which recorded its most positive tones during these years. Indeed, at the time U.S. analysts proclaimed that "Washington and Seoul share a sense that their bilateral relations have never been better."[5] The progressive Korean newspaper's news tone improved slightly during the Bush–Kim Dae Jung years (–1.04) and Bush–Roh Moo Hyun (–0.97) years, but these changes were marginal. Thus, together, these findings from the Korean media do not lend empirical support to the policy rift thesis, which attributes the downward turn in news tone to the discord over North Korea policy during the Bush-Kim era. The progressive tone toward U.S.-ROK relations remained very negative throughout the study period.

The tone of *Chosun Ilbo*, the conservative newspaper, toward U.S.-ROK relations was most negative during the Clinton–Kim Young Sam years (–0.69). Its negative tone may have been related to the Clinton administration's forward-leaning approach to talks with North Korea and Korean conservatives' general concern that the South was being closed out of such diplomacy. The Kim administration had urged the United States to engage in direct negotiations with the North but to limit the scope of the talks to the nuclear issue. Although working-level and behind-the-scenes U.S.-ROK cooperation was quite good, Kim objected to the "package deal" formulation of Clinton, arguing that Seoul had been marginalized.[6] *Chosun*'s critical tone reflects Korean conservatives' concern with U.S. engagement of Pyongyang throughout the Clinton–Kim Young Sam period and sensitivity over the level of Seoul's involvement in this process.[7]

After the Clinton–Kim Young Sam period, *Chosun*'s tone toward the U.S.-ROK relationship seems to have improved and then deteriorated in a pattern similar to that of the U.S. newspapers, although *Chosun*'s tone never became positive. The conservative newspaper's tone improved significantly from the Clinton–Kim Young Sam to the Clinton–Kim Dae Jung years, during which tone was close to neutral (–0.07). This is somewhat surprising, given the conservative critique of the Kim Dae Jung government and its engagement policy, but as noted earlier, those years were marked by significant diplomatic strides. *Chosun*'s tone turned more negative during the Bush–Kim Dae Jung years (–0.47) and then improved slightly during the

Bush–Roh Moo Hyun years. Improvement during the Bush-Roh years—a time characterized by nuclear crisis, anti-American sentiment in Korea, and difficulties in coordination—may seem counterintuitive. But in fact, it seems to reflect conservative efforts to bolster the alliance in accordance with fears that progressive action and expression of sentiment might be undermining the U.S. commitment to South Korean security during an especially dangerous time.

Together, the findings from these analyses demonstrate that the U.S. media's view of the U.S.-ROK relationship deteriorated noticeably after 2001, when the Bush administration began to openly express its skepticism of Kim Dae Jung's engagement policy and the Agreed Framework. This finding offers strong support for the policy rift thesis. On the other hand, findings based on analyses of the South Korean media demonstrate that the progressive newspaper was consistently critical of the relationship, whereas its conservative counterpart reacted to the progressive critique by stressing the importance of the U.S.-ROK relationship in recent years and overall exhibiting a pattern more similar to that of U.S. newspapers. Thus, during these study years, a critical gap existed between the progressive and conservative newspapers in their views of U.S.-ROK relations and the U.S. role on the peninsula. These findings can be interpreted to reflect identity politics, as associated with efforts to reimagine South Korean national identity, including vis-à-vis its traditional ally.

The U.S.-ROK and U.S.-DPRK Relationships During the Nuclear Crises

This section focuses on the state of the U.S.-ROK relationship shown in the newspapers of the two countries during the two nuclear crises on the peninsula, offering additional tests of the policy rift and identity theses. The two nuclear crises are critical periods in which to examine U.S.-ROK relations, as it is during such times of crisis that the essential elements and underlying assumptions of each nation's policy approach are exposed and that policy coordination is, at once, most important and most challenged.

The two nuclear crises unfolded in quite different environments. During the first crisis, the ROK and U.S. administrations worked closely together and shared a similar assessment of the threat presented by North Korea, although the ROK government displayed its concerns over the U.S.

approach, as stated earlier. In contrast, the current nuclear crisis erupted in an environment in which Washington and Seoul no longer viewed the North Korea problem through the same lens and often worked at cross-purposes. While the United States took a global approach to nonproliferation issues, especially in the context of the war on terrorism, and initially saw pressure and isolation as requisites of its diplomatic strategy, South Korea focused most intently on peninsular stability and the continuation of inter-Korean engagement. At the same time that many in the U.S. government worried that North Korea might share nuclear components or technology with other regimes or terrorist groups, many in the South believed that the North Korean threat was exaggerated. In fact, more than Pyongyang's nuclear programs, they feared the potential U.S. military action that these programs might spur.[8]

According to the policy rift thesis, it is these divergent U.S. and ROK threat perceptions and resultant differences in policy approach that have strained relations between the two allies. Thus, more negative views of the U.S.-ROK relationship during the second crisis would lend support to the policy rift thesis. In accordance with previous arguments, this trend should be expected to be evident in the U.S. media data.

However, given the argument (articulated in Chapters 3 and 4) that the identity thesis has greater explanatory power for trends in South Korean coverage of North Korea and U.S.-ROK relations, in this analysis of South Korean media data, increasingly negative tones should not necessarily be expected during the second nuclear crisis. Instead, evidence should be expected of the emergent postauthoritarian, post–cold war progressive perspective, in the form of negative views of U.S.-ROK relations, as early as the first nuclear crisis. The progressive identity has certainly evolved and gained ground since 1994, especially in the context of the North Korean famine and President Kim Dae Jung's engagement policy. However, it was clearly present *before* recent U.S.-ROK policy discord in the second nuclear crisis, especially in an activist, progressive media outlet such as *Hankyoreh*.[9]

In contrast, it should be anticipated that the conservative newspaper, *Chosun*, will display different views of the U.S.-ROK relationship, with its tone being even less critical during the second nuclear standoff, as South Korean conservatives were concerned by the deteriorating alliance and came to stress its importance during the crisis. In accordance with the hardening of these respective conceptions of Korean identities (discussed in Chapter 3), it should be expected that a great gap will be observed in evaluations of U.S.-ROK relations during the second nuclear crisis. In addition to examining media tone, this section also examines media attention to the U.S.-ROK relationship during the two nuclear crises.

However, before examining U.S.-ROK relations in the context of the two nuclear crises, it will be valuable to first evaluate U.S.-DPRK relations during the two nuclear standoffs. Doing so is intended to shed light on how the U.S. and South Korean media perceived the impact of these crises on U.S.-DPRK relations. Together, analyses of the U.S. and Korean media treatment of the U.S. relationship with each Korea should also provide insight into how the U.S.-ROK and U.S.-DPRK relationships pertain to each other during such times of conflict.

DEFINING THE TWO NUCLEAR CRISES

The period between February 1993 and October 1994 can be defined as the first nuclear standoff (NUKE1). In February 1993, the International Atomic Energy Agency (IAEA) demanded that North Korea permit special inspections of two undeclared nuclear-related sites based on its obligations under the Nuclear Non-Proliferation Treaty (NPT). North Korea's refusal spurred suspicions of its nuclear intentions and marked the beginning of its first nuclear standoff with the United States. After a period of high tension and protracted negotiation, the Agreed Framework was finally signed between the United States and North Korea in Geneva on October 21, 1994, finalizing bilateral negotiations that had gone back and forth for more than 18 months.

The current nuclear crisis (NUKE2) began on October 16, 2002, when the United States announced that North Korea admitted, upon being confronted with new U.S. intelligence, that it had been conducting a clandestine uranium enrichment program as an alternative route to nuclear weapons development. The Agreed Framework collapsed, North Korea withdrew from the NPT, and the Six-Party Talks eventually emerged as the prime forum for negotiation on this issue.

In the fall of 2006, the North conducted its first test of a nuclear device. At the time of this writing, the nuclear standoff is still unfolding with no clear sign of resolution in sight, though U.S.-ROK collaboration on the nuclear issue has been improved with the establishment of new governments in both countries. For the purpose of the present study, the data for

NUKE2 cover the period from October 2002 to July 2003 for the ROK data and from October 2002 to January 2004 for the U.S. data.

THE U.S.-DPRK RELATIONSHIP

U.S. Media

Figure 7.4 depicts the number of articles on the U.S.-DPRK relationship published by each of the three U.S. newspapers over the study period. Several observations stand out. First, even though the *New York Times* showed a modest increase in news coverage, overall, there was no substantial increase from the first to the second nuclear crisis. These relatively flat levels of coverage run contrary to expectations, given that the current crisis is generally believed to be more dangerous. Namely, the crisis developed in the post–September 11 context of the U.S. war on terrorism (wherein the possibility of a North Korean transfer of nuclear materials and/or technology to another rouge state or terrorist cell must be taken seriously) and after demonstrated advancements in DPRK long-range missile technology. Both these circumstances mean that a DPRK nuclear device could be delivered—possibly to American soil—in new and more far-reaching ways than was the case during the first nuclear crisis.

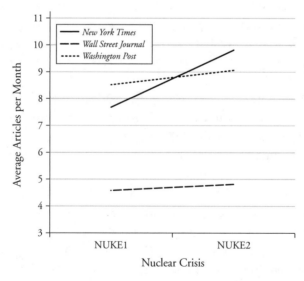

FIGURE 7.4 U.S. media coverage of the U.S.-DPRK relationship during nuclear crises by newspaper.

However, the existence of similar levels of media attention to the first and second nuclear crises does not necessarily signify that the U.S. media viewed these two crises in similar terms. The general media environment during the two crises must also be considered, including other significant stories that competed for space in the "news hole," as it is often called in the news industry. During the present crisis, the U.S. media were occupied with the war in Iraq and with Iran's seeking nuclear capabilities against the will of the international community.

Additionally, while the media have some agenda-setting capacity, many journalists contend that in the realm of U.S. news, the White House carries far greater power in this regard. Throughout the second nuclear standoff, the Bush administration refused to call it a "crisis." Moreover, the amount of time a president and his administration spend talking about an issue generally correlates with how a newspaper covers the issue; that is, there is news if the administration makes a statement on the issue.[10] The Bush administration's channeling of focus toward the case for the war in Iraq clearly stands in contrast to the Clinton administration's high-profile approach to the first North Korean nuclear crisis, one of its first major foreign policy challenges. These differing degrees of presidential attention, or administration focus, provide insight into why there was not an increase in coverage of the second crisis, when it was perceived by many pundits to be more dangerous.

Turning to the U.S. media tone toward the U.S.-DPRK relationship, it is first worthwhile to note that all three newspapers' tones were quite negative during both periods, indicating that the status of U.S.-DPRK relations was generally presented as highly conflict driven. As shown in Figure 7.5, tones during the second nuclear crisis were even more negative than those recorded during the first nuclear crisis in the mid-1990s. Thus, even though the three U.S. newspapers did not increase their volume of coverage from the first to the second nuclear crisis, they registered far more pessimism related to U.S.-DPRK relations in the second standoff.

This finding confirms the U.S. government's greater concern over the nuclear status of North Korea in the post–September 11 world. It may also reflect concern over discord among the five parties attempting to resolve the issue, editors' frustration with and/or criticism of Washington's approach, or a combination thereof.[11] Indeed, tone deterioration was greatest in the *Wall Street Journal*, perhaps indicating that, especially from a more conservative point of view (the perspective most closely associated with most Bush administration

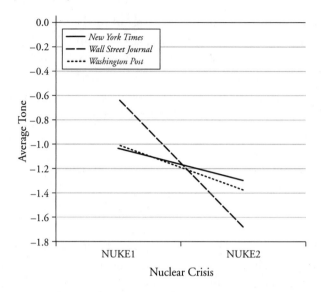

FIGURE 7.5 U.S. media tone for the U.S.-DPRK relationship during nuclear crises by newspaper.

officials during the study period), the threat of a rogue regime with nuclear weapons was more serious than ever in the new strategic landscape.

Korean Media

As illustrated in Figure 7.6, within South Korean press coverage of the U.S.-DPRK relationship, a substantial increase can be observed in the number of articles published in *Hankyoreh Shinmoon* from the first to the second nuclear crisis (a 48% increase, or from 16.2 to 24 articles per month), while a more modest increase can be observed in *Chosun Ilbo*'s coverage (about 15%, or from 15.8 to 18.6 articles per month). The progressive newspaper's pronounced increase in coverage is consistent with the increase over time of the North Korea–related news frame on "U.S. responsibility" (see Chapter 3). Even though *Chosun*'s increase in attention from the first to the second crisis was not as dramatic as that shown by *Hankyoreh*, the Korean conservative newspaper did accord far more attention to the U.S.-DPRK relationship than the U.S. media, and its increase in coverage from the first to the second crisis was larger than that of any of the three U.S. newspapers.

The disparity between Korean and U.S. media attention levels during the standoffs is due, in part, to the pervasiveness of competing stories (i.e., Iraq)

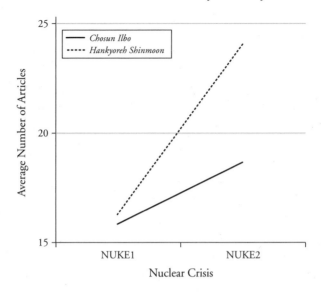

FIGURE 7.6 Korean media coverage of the U.S.-DPRK relationship during nuclear crises by newspaper.

in the U.S. foreign policy news landscape, as well as to a general asymmetry of attention to such issues. At the same time, it is hardly surprising that tensions between two "significant others" receives great attention in the Korean press.

Figure 7.7 demonstrates that the tones of *Chosun* and *Hankyoreh* toward U.S.-DPRK relations deteriorated in relatively equal proportions (from −0.42 to −0.80 and from −0.09 to −0.52, respectively). As discussed in Chapter 4, in the later years of this study period, both *Hankyoreh* and *Chosun* assessed the U.S.-DPRK relationship in more negative terms but owing to different reasons. Progressives had been skeptical of U.S. policy, while conservatives had criticized continuing DPRK provocations. Interestingly, the conservative newspaper, *Chosun*, was consistently more negative on U.S.-DPRK relations than its progressive counterpart, a dynamic that remained valid during the second nuclear crisis, although *Hankyoreh* published more articles during this period. And yet, all three U.S. newspapers were more negative about the U.S.-DPRK relationship than *Chosun* during both crises. This indicates the U.S. media portrayal of greater alarm over DPRK nuclear development, largely confirming the conventional belief (informed by strategic realities as well as identity-related factors) that South Korea does not perceive the nuclear issue to be as serious as the United States does.

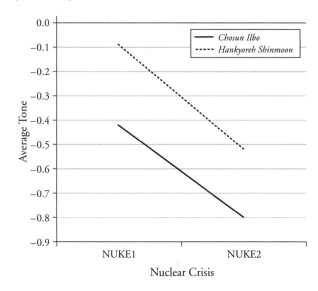

FIGURE 7.7 Korean media tone for the U.S.-DPRK relationship during nuclear crises by newspaper.

THE U.S.-ROK RELATIONSHIP

U.S. Media

As depicted in Figure 7.8, with regard to U.S. media attention to the U.S.-ROK relationship, a modest increase can be observed from the first to the second nuclear crisis. The most significant increase, seen in the *New York Times*, was only slightly more than one article per month.

It is interesting to note that U.S.-ROK relations were featured slightly more prominently in the context of the second nuclear standoff, in which the ROK had a seat at the table in accordance with the Six-Party Talks and the United States and ROK faced policy coordination difficulties. Given the policy conflicts between Seoul and Washington during the time of the second nuclear crisis, one might have expected greater attention to U.S.-ROK relations in the U.S. media, but once again, this lack of significantly increased attention may be due to the pervasiveness of competing stories—namely, Iraq and other facets of the war on terror.

Looking to U.S. media tone on U.S.-ROK relations, the analysis largely confirms the policy rift thesis. First, as expected, news tone on the U.S.-ROK relationship during the first crisis was not very negative. In fact, the *Washington Post* recorded a positive tone. This indicates that the general

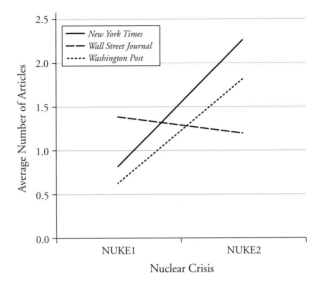

FIGURE 7.8 U.S. media attention to the U.S.-ROK relationship during nuclear crises by newspaper.

status of U.S.-ROK relations was not that unfavorable, at least in the eyes of the U.S. media, as the two allies carried out close coordination throughout the first nuclear crisis, in which Seoul and Washington shared similar threat perceptions. Second, the decline in news tone from the first to the second crisis largely confirms expectations. As shown in Figure 7.9, both the *Washington Post* and the *New York Times* exhibited significant declines in tone toward U.S.-ROK relations.[12] These results are consistent with prior expectations, as well as the shared concern among foreign policy officials in Seoul and Washington. The second nuclear crisis was particularly vexing and dangerous, as it broke out in an environment in which the U.S.-ROK alliance was being contested and in which differences in perception of the common threat—upon which the alliance was founded—were becoming more conspicuous.[13]

Korean Media

In contrast to the U.S. media, the Korean media showed a huge increase in their attention to U.S.-ROK relations, indicating that the alliance became a much more important issue during the second nuclear standoff in South Korea. As shown in Figure 7.10, *Chosun* and *Hankyoreh*'s increases

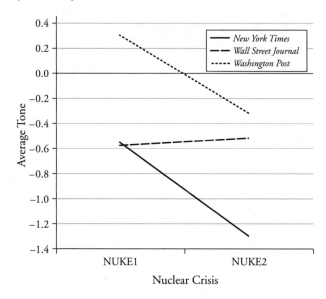

FIGURE 7.9 U.S. media tone for the U.S.-ROK relationship during nuclear crises by newspaper.

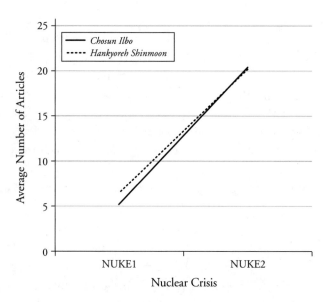

FIGURE 7.10 Korean media attention to the U.S.-ROK relationship during nuclear crises by newspaper.

were indeed dramatic—three- to fourfold. Although South Korea generally pays more attention to the United States than the United States pays to South Korea, the disparity in coverage rates between Korean and U.S. newspapers during the current standoff—approximately 10 times in terms of the monthly number of articles—is truly striking. The U.S.-ROK relationship clearly became a subject of greater discussion and contention in South Korea during the second crisis, when, as observed in past chapters, opposing progressive and conservative forces engaged in intense debate over the role of the United States on the peninsula. The degree of similarity in the two newspapers' attention to U.S.-ROK issues, as depicted in Figure 7.10 (i.e., monthly article count and rate of increase are nearly identical), suggests that, despite their opposing ideological and political views on this subject, *Chosun* and *Hankyoreh* agree that the U.S.-ROK relationship is a critical issue confronting their nation.

While the two Korean newspapers accorded similar levels of attention to U.S.-ROK relations during each nuclear crisis, their respective tones indicate a distinct divergence in opinion on this important allied relationship from the first to the second nuclear crisis. As has been demonstrated through several previous analyses, the two newspapers' respective views of U.S.-ROK relations, already differentiated during the first nuclear crisis, hardened over time. *Hankyoreh*'s tone became even more negative (from −1.0 to −1.18), while *Chosun*'s tone became less negative (from −0.65 to −0.38) from the first nuclear standoff to the second (see Figure 7.11).

Yet perhaps most importantly, this analysis confirms that the progressive newspaper's tone was highly negative during *both* crises. Clearly, the progressive criticism of the U.S.-ROK relationship was already present during the first crisis, whereas this degree of negative coverage was not seen in the U.S. media at the time. Once again, this finding can be interpreted as supporting the identity thesis. This progressive criticism, present during both nuclear crises, was related to efforts to redefine Korea's relationship with the United States in the post–cold war era.

While the conservative newspaper's tone toward U.S.-ROK relations became more positive (i.e., less negative), its tone toward the United States itself (not reported here) declined from the first to the second nuclear standoff. Although these findings may seem inconsistent, the conclusion can be drawn that even as the conservative paper was critical of U.S. foreign policy on a broad level, it valued the U.S.-ROK alliance, especially during times of

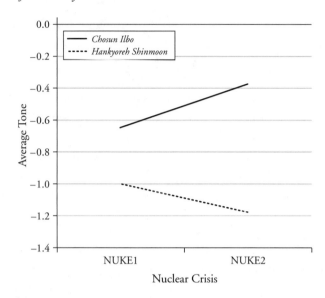

FIGURE 7.11 Korean media tone for the U.S.-ROK relationship during nuclear crises by newspaper.

tension between the United States and the DPRK. As a result of different tone trends in views of the U.S.-ROK relationship, the gap between conservatives and progressives increased, indicating greater division among South Koreans in their views of the nuclear standoff and the alliance. This finding again attests to the need for separating anti-American and anti-alliance sentiment, as discussed in Chapter 4.

Together, these findings from the South Korean news media demonstrate that the U.S.-ROK relationship was both increasingly discussed and increasingly contentious during the second crisis. However, defying the expectation of the policy rift thesis, the South Korean media tone did not deteriorate significantly during the second crisis. While the progressive newspaper displayed a more negative tone during the second nuclear crisis, the tone was only marginally more negative; that is, *Hankyoreh* was consistent in its very negative view of U.S.-ROK relations. Moreover, contrary to expectations associated with the policy rift thesis, the conservative newspaper demonstrated a more positive tone toward U.S.-ROK relations during the second crisis. This increased progressive-conservative gap suggests greater contention within South Korean society in accordance with the arguments that these changes and disagreement reflect the intensification of the politics of national identity.

The U.S.-Japan Relationship During the Nuclear Crises

As a complementary analysis to the policy rift explanation of the strained U.S.-ROK relationship, this chapter now examines coverage of the U.S.-Japan relationship during the two nuclear standoffs. If differences over North Korea policy actually lie at the heart of the strained U.S.-ROK relationship (from the U.S. perspective), then one would expect that changes in the U.S. newspapers' tones about the U.S.-ROK relationship would exhibit a unique pattern—one different from the newspapers' tones on U.S. relations with other nations.

Some experts and pundits, especially those in South Korea, have argued that the United States has seen a marked deterioration in its relations with many other nations (not only South Korea) in recent years, following the Bush administration's launch of the war on terrorism and the war in Iraq.[14] Thus, this comparative examination is important to assess whether changes in the U.S.-ROK relationship reflect a general pattern in U.S. relations with allies or whether unique and specific circumstances are, in fact, at work in the U.S.-ROK case.

Thus, U.S.-ROK relations will be compared to U.S.-Japan relations as a test of this general thesis of the deterioration of relations under the Bush administration. Like South Korea, Japan is an important Pacific ally of the United States, and U.S. troops have been stationed in that country since the end of World War II. The United States, Japan, and South Korea have cooperated closely on regional security issues for much of the post-1965 period, especially since the initiation of the Perry Process in 1998. Japan's security is affected by North Korea's missile and nuclear development, and Tokyo is a participant in the Six-Party Talks.

During the study period, there was a strong sense that, unlike South Korea, Japan shared the U.S. perception that the North is a regional and even a global security threat. Through the end of this study period (2004), Japan endorsed the Bush administration's policy, including multilateral dialogue and pressure, during the second nuclear standoff. Indeed, Japan not only agreed with the U.S. approach to the current standoff, but as Ambassador Michael Armacost has pointed out, "Anxieties about North Korea's nuclear ambitions and missile tests have prompted Japan to expand collaboration with the U.S."[15]

This is true regarding missile defense, especially since the DPRK's 1998 missile test, which prompted a societywide reevaluation of Japan's security.

That is, while the U.S.-Japan alliance experienced strategic confusion and coordination difficulties in the wake of the post–cold war, a series of developments in the mid to late 1990s prompted path-breaking cooperation and coordination.[16] This led to development of an environment in which the Japanese and U.S. threat perceptions were seemingly more closely aligned than those of the United States and the ROK during the later years of this study period. If the congruity of threat perceptions actually differed in this way, then one would expect to observe contrasting patterns in U.S.-ROK and U.S.-Japan relations during the second nuclear crisis. That is, from the first to the second nuclear crisis, news tones about U.S.-Japan relations would be expected to become more positive, while those regarding U.S.-ROK relations would be expected to become more negative.

Indeed, the finding empirically demonstrates a contrasting pattern in the U.S. media's view of the U.S.-Japan relationship compared with that of the U.S.-ROK relationship during the two nuclear crises. As Figure 7.12 shows (also see Figure 7.9), U.S. media tones on the U.S.-ROK and U.S.-Japan relationships during the first nuclear standoff fell within a similar range.[17] They were slightly negative, perhaps reflecting surface-level tension between the Kim Young Sam and Clinton administrations, as well as U.S. frustration

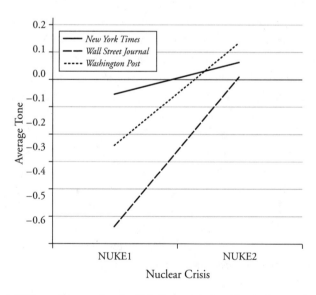

FIGURE 7.12 U.S. media tone for the U.S.-Japan relationship during nuclear crises by newspaper.

over Japan's reluctance to even discuss the first nuclear crisis and its possible implications with its alliance partner.[18]

However, the progression of media tone from the first crisis to the second crisis showed opposing patterns. In contrast to the tone toward U.S.-ROK relations, the U.S. media tone toward U.S.-Japan relations revealed a healthy improvement from the first to the second nuclear crisis, actually turning positive in the case of all three newspapers. This improvement was likely due, at least in part, to U.S.-Japanese congruence in policy toward the North and, more broadly, to a shared imperative for a closer alliance, spurred primarily by North Korea's provocative 1998 missile launch over Japan and operationalized under two leaders with similar visions for the alliance.[19]

Thus, these findings may be considered further evidence of the efficacy of the policy rift thesis, as associated with the U.S. media perspective. The U.S. media evaluation of the U.S.-Japan relationship demonstrates that deteriorating U.S. views of the U.S.-ROK relationship cannot be attributed to the general loosening of alliances in the post–cold war era or to disapproving reactions to Bush administration policies among friendly and allied governments.

The DPRK and the U.S.-ROK Relationship

Finally, the South Korean media data can be used in a test of the identity thesis that examines the correlation between perceptions of the DPRK and the U.S.-ROK relationship. In accordance with the identity thesis, it can be argued that the U.S.-ROK alliance entered a new phase when former South Korean President Kim Dae Jung began to pursue an aggressive engagement policy toward the North—an event that occurred years before President Kim and President Bush clashed over policy toward North Korea.

The Sunshine Policy was not intended to challenge U.S.-ROK relations. In fact, quite to the contrary, President Kim emphasized strong deterrence and the importance of the alliance as a base from which South Korea could capably pursue engagement with the North.[20] Yet once implemented, this policy had the unintended consequence of significantly altering South Koreans' perception of the North and the alliance. Findings presented in Chapters 3 and 4 clearly showed such a change in attitudes, especially in the progressive media, which forcefully advocated a forward-leaning form of engagement not premised on reciprocity along with an "independent

TABLE 7.1
South Korean media views of the DPRK and the U.S.-ROK relationship

	Tone			
	Before Kim Dae Jung		Kim Dae Jung and after	
	Chosun Ilbo	*Hankyoreh Shinmoon*	*Chosun Ilbo*	*Hankyoreh Shinmoon*
DPRK	−0.34	−0.19	−0.30	−0.08
Inter-Korean relations	−0.28	0.07	−0.30	0.20
United States	−0.03	−0.15	−0.16	−0.40
U.S.-ROK relationship	−0.03	−0.22	−0.06	−0.33

way" from the United States. Using headline data from the South Korean media, this section further probes the question of whether altered views of the North were responsible for changing attitudes toward the alliance in the Sunshine era.[21]

As shown in Table 7.1, the conservative newspaper *Chosun* showed little change in tone toward North Korea and inter-Korean relations after the launch of the Sunshine Policy, as both tones remained very negative (from −0.34 to −0.30 on North Korea and from −0.28 to −0.30 on inter-Korean relations). Additionally, *Chosun's* tone toward the U.S.-ROK relationship showed little change (from −0.03 to −0.06), even though its tone toward the United States became more critical in the Sunshine era (from −0.03 to −0.16).

These findings suggest that during the study period, South Korean conservatives continued to view the North as a threat and remained critical of inter-Korean relations. As a result, the conservatives continued to stress the importance of the alliance in accordance with their perception of South Korea's security interests, not because of any idealized view of the United States. As articulated by *Chosun Ilbo*, this was an environment characterized by a South Korean "administration and much of its support base [that had], without end, acted in a way to weaken the Korea-U.S. alliance."[22] In this environment, "a hasty reduction of [U.S. Forces Korea] or discussions of rearrangement [could] bring about disastrous results to security and peace on the Korean peninsula."[23]

On October 5, 2004, four months after the U.S. decision to reduce its presence on the peninsula, *Chosun's* lead headline was "Seoul Could Fall to North Korean Army in 16 Days without U.S. Troops." According to Daniel Sneider, in more recent years, this fear of abandonment or concern over the durability of the U.S. strategic commitment, harbored principally by Korean conservatives, has intensified with the withdrawal of U.S. forces, the pending dissolution of the Combined Forces Command, and following the North's July 2006 missile tests.[24]

In contrast to its conservative counterpart, the progressive newspaper showed substantial change in its views of North Korea as well as the United States, and the two are related. First, *Hankyoreh*'s tones toward the North and inter-Korean relations, both of which were approximately neutral prior to President Kim Dae Jung's tenure, improved in the Sunshine era (from −0.19 to −0.08 on North Korea and from 0.07 to 0.20 on inter-Korean relations). In sharp contrast, *Hankyoreh*'s views of the United States and the U.S.-ROK relationship became more negative, deteriorating from −0.15 to −0.40 and from −0.22 to −0.33, respectively. These findings demonstrate empirically that as South Korean progressives perceived North Korea and inter-Korean relations in a more positive light, they became more critical of U.S.-ROK relations and the United States, adding further support to the argument regarding progressives' reassessment of national identity in relation to these two significant others.

It is interesting to compare these findings with the U.S. media's view of the DPRK. As shown in the previous chapter, all three U.S. newspapers' tones were highly negative during the entire length of this study, from 1992 to 2003. Most of the changes in tone scores reflected particular events. For example, tone was relatively less negative during the inter-Korean summit in 2000, while tone was significantly more negative around the time that President Bush characterized the DPRK as part of an axis of evil. Unlike the Korean media, the U.S. media exhibited no direct correlation between views of the North and views of U.S-ROK relations. Rather, in the later years of this study period, U.S. media tones toward the U.S.-DPRK and the U.S.-ROK relationships both declined, in accordance with the second nuclear crisis and correspondent policy discord between Seoul and Washington.

Once again, these differences in ROK and U.S. media views can be interpreted as reflecting the differing prisms through which the two nations perceive the alliance, its relevance, and North Korea. The U.S. media regard the U.S.-ROK relationship as a policy issue, and a downturn in tone reflects policy differences on specific issues between the two allies. On other hand, the Korean media approach the relationship in accordance with Korean national identity, and consequently, changes in tone tend to be protracted evolutions (and less event specific) related to trends that reflect Koreans' efforts to redefine their national identity.

Divergences in Perception and Paradigm

The analyses presented in this chapter offer an excellent opportunity to examine contending arguments regarding the ostensibly deteriorated U.S.-ROK alliance. Before this study, experts on Korean affairs had identified a number of factors responsible for recent changes in the U.S.-ROK relationship, but such assertions were essentially general statements, based on personal observations and anecdotal evidence and thus lacking specificity as well as rigorous empirical testing. As a way of concluding this chapter, this section will compare a number of these arguments against the evidence gathered from the U.S. and South Korean news media.

First, the loosening of alliances is put forward as a general trend in the post–cold war era, with some positing that changes within the U.S.-ROK alliance should be seen as part of this larger trend.[25] In particular, adherents to this notion contend that U.S. arrogance and unilateralism in world affairs—especially in the context of the war on terrorism and the military action in Iraq—have alienated many nations, and Seoul's increasing distance from Washington during the final years of this study period is part of this larger trend. Yet the ROK, albeit reluctantly, has deployed troops to Afghanistan and Iraq to demonstrate support for the U.S.-led war against terrorism and to secure the alliance in a troubled time. Also, U.S. media views of the U.S.-Japan relationship, as described earlier, have turned more positive in recent years, casting doubt on the U.S. unilateralism thesis (although Japan, the United Kingdom, and Australia may be exceptions to a broader trend). While general dissatisfaction with U.S. policies in the September 11 era may have been an exacerbating factor in the Korean case, findings from the Korean and U.S. media data indicate the need to be more specific in explaining evident strains in the U.S.-ROK relationship.

Second, some scholars and experts have focused on South Korean domestic political factors to explain changes in bilateral relations. Katherine Moon, for instance, argues that the changing U.S.-ROK relationship is an inevitable outcome of Korean democratization, under which Koreans have demanded more equality in their nation's relations with the United States.[26] This argument is valid to the extent that democratization created an environment within Korea that was conducive to questioning and debate about U.S.-ROK relations. However, the argument fails to explain how democratization has specifically affected U.S.-ROK relations. In a similar vein, the progressive Roh government, which came to power supported by the ascension of the 386 generation into politics, has been blamed. Yet the findings presented earlier show that news tones about the U.S.-ROK relationship largely remained unchanged from the Kim Dae Jung to the Roh government. That is, the difficulty of coordination persisted under the Roh government. President Roh was not able to bridge this gap, but at the same time, he should not be blamed as its impetus. In addition, during the last years of his presidency, Roh sought to strengthen and broaden U.S.-ROK relations through an ambitious bilateral free trade agreement.

Third, anti-Americanism in South Korea has received significant attention in studies of the changing U.S.-ROK relationship during the critical period toward the end of the study years.[27] Once again, the importance of this factor is not being disputed, especially when conceived of as an exacerbating factor. Still, the view that anti-Americanism is principally responsible for tension in the alliance lacks the specificity required for empirical inquiry. First, it fails to identify why recent anti-Americanism strained the U.S.-ROK alliance, while the arguably more widespread and even violent anti-American movements of the 1980s did not have a similar effect. Second, while both conservative and progressive newspapers in Korea became critical of the United States in the later years of the study period, their respective views of the U.S.-ROK relationship were increasingly divergent. The progressive media were the primary critics of the relationship, while conservative forces in journalism sought to stress the importance of the alliance, presumably because of their concern with growing anti-Americanism within Korean society. This suggests that there are not necessarily any links between anti-American sentiment and anti-alliance view. Finally, the anti-Americanism thesis fails to view the change in the U.S.-ROK relationship as an interactive process involving both nations, not simply a reflection of events or sentiments in one country. A more fundamental factor must be identified that led to both anti-American sentiments/movements and erosion in the U.S.-ROK alliance during these critical years.

In this chapter, two arguments have been advanced: the policy rift thesis and the identity thesis. In sum, the policy rift thesis best explains the American view of the changing U.S.-ROK relationship, while the identity thesis is most persuasive with respect to the Korean view. That is, from the American perspective, the strain in the U.S.-ROK alliance had much to do with the clashes of the two nations' differing approaches to DPRK policy. However, from the Korean viewpoint, the strain had more to do with the intensification of identity politics in their society.

The findings presented in this chapter confirm the policy rift thesis with the U.S. media data. They clearly show that policy disputes between the proengagement Kim Dae Jung government and the hard-line Bush administration were a significant factor in producing critical views of the bilateral relationship in the U.S. news media. The policy rift thesis is also supported by the fact that the second North Korean nuclear standoff had a decidedly more negative impact on U.S.-ROK relations. This was not the case during the first nuclear crisis, when both nations shared a common approach to the North Korea issue, in contrast to the early years of the second crisis, when the two nations saw the issue through fundamentally different lenses. This divergent perception of the North Korean threat is most responsible for the recent deterioration in U.S.-ROK relations and has crucial policy implications.

The policy rift thesis is further supported by analysis of the U.S.-Japan relationship during the two nuclear standoffs. In contrast to the U.S. media view of the U.S.-ROK relationship, their view of the U.S.-Japan relationship turned more positive during the second nuclear crisis, reflecting a common interest and approach in dealing with the North in addition to other alliance initiatives.

However, the policy rift thesis does not sufficiently explain the Korean view of changing relations between the United States and the ROK. First, critical views of the relationship appeared in the progressive newspaper much earlier than the Bush–Kim Dae Jung overlap, well before critical policy discord became salient. Second, the Korean media displayed no significant difference in news tones about U.S.-ROK relations between two nuclear standoffs, especially in the progressive newspaper. In fact, the progressive newspaper's view of U.S.-ROK relations was negative during both crises. In contrast, the conservative newspaper became even less critical during the second nuclear crisis, primarily because it was concerned over the perceptibly deteriorating alliance and thus came to stress its importance, especially during the crisis. As a result, a widened gap was discovered between the two newspapers during the second crisis compared with the first standoff.

All these findings indicate that what was most crucial to the changing view of the alliance among Koreans involved changing views of the North, and this was clearly revealed in the progressive newspaper. Further analysis indeed shows that the Sunshine Policy of the Kim Dae Jung government was instrumental in changing South Korean views of the North and, though perhaps unintentionally, affecting views of the U.S.-ROK relationship. These findings can be interpreted to reflect identity politics vis-à-vis North Korea and the United States within South Korea.

In conclusion, the findings presented in this chapter clearly demonstrate that the United States and the ROK approach their bilateral relationship from different paradigms. The difference is not simply accidental or situational but rather deeply rooted in the two allies' differences in power, perception, historical experience, and policy approach. With the establishment of the Lee and Obama administrations, alliance collaboration has improved, but as both nations seek to chart a course for their strategic alliance, they must take into account these differing perceptions and frameworks. The next chapter will address a number of important policy implications as a way of concluding this study.

EIGHT

A New Era in the U.S.-ROK Relationship

In the months before North Korea's test of a nuclear device on October 9, 2006, there was a groundswell of policy and scholarly discussion of this prospect, especially in the wake of the North's provocative test of seven ballistic missiles in July of that year and amid strident North Korean rhetoric and diplomatic deadlock. While some analysts believed a nuclear test to be Pyongyang's "last card," which it would threaten to use but ultimately not play, others viewed a test as likely for both technical and political reasons. Analysts worried that the effects of such a test could be catastrophic. A demonstrated North Korean nuclear capability might prompt a new Asian arms race, with Japan, Taiwan, and perhaps South Korea eschewing U.S. extended deterrence in favor of their own nuclear status.[1]

Conventional wisdom, especially in U.S. policy circles, held that a North Korean nuclear test was a "red line" that, if crossed, would yield a uniform, punitive response from Washington's partners in the Six-Party Talks—a diplomatic construct that, like the United States–Republic of Korea (U.S.-ROK) alliance, had been plagued by differences in fundamental assumptions about the appropriate combination of pressure and dialogue. Just before President Roh's September 14 visit to Washington, DC, the *Economist* took stock of the strained alliance and asserted, as if an article of faith, that "America and South Korea would no doubt be brought closer together" in the event of a nuclear test by North Korea.[2] While in Washington, Roh seemed to reinforce this perception. He told a group of Korea experts that a nuclear test would be "far more devastating" than the missile tests and "would certainly cause a major re-evaluation of [inter-Korean] relations,"[3] suggesting that perhaps this would finally lead Seoul to utilize its purported leverage over the North.

On the day that President Roh met President Bush at the White House, I happened to be in Washington, DC, for a seminar co-hosted by my center, the Walter H. Shorenstein Asia-Pacific Research Center at Stanford University, and the Brookings Institution entitled "North Korea: 2007 and Beyond," based on my co-edited book.[4] During a question-and-answer session, I was asked about the likelihood of a nuclear test and its effects, particularly the impact a test might have on South Korean views of the North. Could it snap U.S. and South Korean threat perceptions back into alignment? I responded that I would not be surprised if North Korea did conduct a test. Yet even in the face of such a dramatic event, I would not expect any fundamental change in inter-Korean relations, since South Korean perceptions of the North are intimately tied to national identity, and national identity does not change quickly or easily.[5]

These thoughts were in line with the larger argument that I made that day, an argument also put forward in this book. That is, while the North is a relatively narrowly conceived policy matter for Americans, it is central to issues of national identity for South Koreans. Moreover, the nationalist identity that underpinned the Roh government's world view would not—indeed, could not—change overnight.

Within a month of that seminar, the North did, in fact, surprise the world by testing a nuclear weapon. Despite feeling great skepticism, I still harbored some hope that the conventional wisdom was right—that this event would be catastrophic enough to bring the United States and the ROK closer together.[6] In the first few days after the test, events in Seoul seemed to indicate this might occur. Analysts observed that the ROK government's reaction was "firmer and quicker" than its response to the missile tests in July.[7] As discussed in Chapter 3, there was a growing sense within South Korea that its engagement policy—designed, in large part, to improve North Korean behavior and coax it into the international system—had fallen far short of achieving its aims. Roh himself stated that it had become "difficult . . . to stick to [a] policy of engagement" and "difficult to argue that such a policy is effective."[8] The *Financial Times* bluntly argued that with the nuclear test, it had become "patently clear that South Korea has gained next to nothing for its [engagement] efforts."[9]

However, these early signs that the ROK government might reassess its engagement policy and pursue an approach similar to that of the United States proved misleading. A string of resignations, policy disputes, and confusions within the Roh administration demonstrated a lack of accord over how to respond to the nuclear test.[10] By the time U.S. Secretary of State Condoleezza Rice arrived in Seoul in mid-October, the "South Korean power elite [had] yet to build a consensus among them, not to mention reach any common ground with the opposition." While President Roh had initially implied that inter-Korean economic projects might be suspended in the wake of the test, his administration appeared to be quickly "backpedaling."[11] Rice's request for South Korea to join the Proliferation Security Initiative (PSI) was flatly denied. Although the conservative party held Roh's government and the engagement policy partly responsible for the North's test, progressives, including former President Kim Dae Jung, heaped blame on the Bush administration and its unwillingness to hold bilateral talks with the North.[12] Ultimately, the Roh administration decided it had no choice but to continue pursuing engagement and shun Washington's punitive approach.

For many, U.S.-ROK disagreement in the wake of the nuclear test seemed ominous. If these two seasoned alliance partners could not coordinate effectively in the face of such a dramatic and dangerous event, under what circumstances could robust cooperation be restored? In short, what had happened to this alliance?

Identity Versus Policy

This book has argued that an incongruence in identities and thus interests arose between the United States and the ROK in the post–cold war, postauthoritarian era and that this incongruence was exacerbated with the Sunshine Policy and in the wake of September 11. Although the period examined in this study may well represent the height of identity politics in South Korea, the incongruence in identities and interests pervading U.S.-ROK relations is more than a temporary or passing phenomenon. Rather, it presents a major, persistent challenge for the bilateral relationship over the long term, through administrations of any political stripe on either side.

During the cold war, the anticommunist (even anti–North Korean) years, the South shared the United States' world view and interests on the peninsula. However, the end of the cold war and South Korea's subsequent engagement with communist countries—first, China and Russia, and later, the Democratic People's Republic of Korea (DPRK)—transformed South Korean views about their nation's place in emerging global and regional orders. Such revitalized thinking about national identity necessarily included reevaluation of South Korea's two most important relationships: those with "significant others" North Korea and the United States. Consequently, identity plays an increasingly important role in shaping Korea's relations with them.

In South Korea, democratization provided the domestic context that facilitated the rethinking of national identity. During the authoritarian years, the state implicitly advocated the anticommunist conception of identity and suppressed any alternative on security grounds.[13] In the process of democratization, civil society challenged the authoritarian state's sanctioned notion of identity, opening debate over the proper form of Korean identity for a self-governed nation entering a new era. In this new environment, South Korean progressives began to conceptualize the DPRK not as a staunch enemy but rather as a suffering sibling to be helped and a partner to engage. These constituencies focused on dangers associated with the weakness of North Korea, and the rationale for the security alliance with the United States—including the burdensome U.S. troop presence in the ROK—was increasingly questioned. The intense debate between conservatives and progressives over the North and the U.S.-ROK relationship, as documented in this study, offers empirical evidence of substantial and prolonged contention over national identity.

During this critical time, the elections of the Kim Dae Jung and the Roh Moo Hyun governments institutionalized progressive ideas about South Korean identity vis-à-vis the DPRK and the United States. These presidents were able to convert their ideas into state policies—most notably, the Sunshine Policy. The progressive conceptions of national identity and policies of the two administrations were incongruent with a conservative Bush administration, which was focused on the war on terror and believed that South Korean and Clinton administration engagement of the North had been naïve and ineffective. At the same time that South Korean views of the North and the alliance were significantly evolving, the U.S. view of North Korea as a threat continued unmitigated. In the latter half of the 1990s, the United States became increasingly concerned over the DPRK's production and proliferation of ballistic missiles, and in the post–September 11 era, the North's fresh pursuit of nuclear capabilities significantly heightened American threat perceptions, especially in light of the Bush administration's concerns over regional nuclear proliferation and potential linkages to global terrorism. Thus, in understanding the changing nature of the U.S.-ROK relationship and the disparity in views during the study years, one must consider the weight of historical timing and how events in both nations—the end of the cold war, Korean democratization, September 11, and the second nuclear crisis—have been internalized and thus altered identities and interests.

Beyond calculating the impact of significant events, this study shows that the United States and South Korea use different frameworks or lenses in viewing their relationship. For South Koreans, the U.S.-ROK relationship is an issue central to their national identity, whereas for Americans, the relationship is conceived as one of many important alliances the United States maintains in line with its security interests and obligations. In South Korean society, relations with the nation's two significant others are not only divisive and prone to politicization but tangled and complicated.

For instance, as shown in Chapters 3 and 4, during the study period, the Korean media devoted a great deal of news attention to the United States and North Korea. They engaged in intense point and counterpoint debates in editorials and columns and were clearly polarized along well-defined political and ideological lines. The results of the study also illustrate that over the course of that period, especially after implementation of the Sunshine Policy, opposing points of view on the North Korea problem and the U.S.-ROK alliance have intensified. This is certainly consistent with the larger trend of a contemporary Korean society that is sharply divided in its views of critical foreign policy issues in accordance with generational lines and political ideology.[14]

Not surprisingly, this ingroup debate over the identity of the nation often became bitter and emotional, hindering rational discussion. As experts on Korean affairs have shown, during this period, South Korea became caught between two conflicting identities. Political scientist J. J. Suh has termed them the *conservative identity*, which holds the traditional view of the United States as a key ally and partner in national security, and the progressive *nationalist identity*, which pits Korean identity against the United States.[15]

As presented in Chapters 3 and 4, the gap between these conflicting identities grew in the later years of the study period. Even if the intensity of contention over South Korean national identity does not return to the levels witnessed during the pivotal period examined here, continued disputes over identity are likely. In fact, the recent return to power by conservatives has not alleviated the intensity of identity politics. On the contrary, progressive forces continue to contend with the conservative Lee government on almost every key issue related to the U.S.-ROK alliance and inter-Korean relations.

As has been argued elsewhere, Korean politics of identity can be traced back to a century ago and have shown themselves to be durable.[16] Neither democratization nor globalization has uprooted the politics of identity in more recent times. Instead, democratization makes the processes of contention over identity more messy and complicated, especially when combined with the rhetoric of ethnic nationalism.[17] While a particular administration in Seoul can dampen or amplify the expression of the politics of identity, societal contention over national identity is fundamentally connected to sociological forces larger than any particular occupant of the Blue House.

It is apparent, however, that American views of the DPRK and the U.S.-ROK alliance do not play a major role in defining American identity but rather are matters conceived of within the context of U.S. policy and security interests. The U.S. newspapers are not locked in a bitter emotional debate over the ROK, the bilateral relationship, or the alliance; rather, the newspapers' divergent coverage stems from their varied interests in particular issues, such as finance and diplomacy, not ideology. For the United States, South Korea is not a significant other that informs American notions of its identity in the world. South Korea is not even a top policy issue for the U.S. government. Indeed, a recent report from a group of American and Korean experts stated, "One of the key characteristics defining ROK-US bilateral relations is an asymmetry of attention" in favor of the ROK.[18] Findings in this study have empirically confirmed this assumption.

While the security alliance and the U.S.-ROK relationship have produced fervent debate in South Korea, in the United States, the alliance draws relatively little coverage. As shown in Chapter 6, even the current nuclear standoff with the DPRK did not receive significant coverage due to competing stories, particularly those on the Middle East. North Korea is narrowly conceived of as a security matter, and policy toward the Koreas is only part of a larger framework of U.S. policy toward East Asia.

Generally, scholars of international relations have debated the salience and importance of power sources and structures that shape international relations in the modern world. *Realists* have stressed the importance of power and its distribution among states, while *institutionalists* have emphasized international institutions or regimes (i.e., explicit and implicit norms, rules, principles, and procedures[19]) as key influences on state behavior. *Constructivists* accord attention to processes associated with identities and values. Yet in large part, these three paradigms tend to treat power and identity as conceptually separate, neglecting how they may be related and interact.[20]

In arguments that bridge realist and constructivist notions of state behavior, Henry Nau asserts that both power and national identity shape relations between states and that states' conceptions of their own national identities are often unacknowledged but vital factors in the making of foreign policy.[21] Although Nau argues for greater consideration of national identity in international relations, he conceives of national identity in largely static, narrow terms—maintaining that states' identities either converge or diverge—rather than as an evolving construct influenced over time by state-to-state relations and the changing structure of the international system.

It is not hard to imagine that two nations in a relationship or alliance characterized by an asymmetry in power or status may have different perceptions of one another and thus approach and influence one another differently. James Morrow, for instance, contends that in an asymmetric alliance, both the patron and the client view each other through different lenses, driven by different motivations and interests based on power and role in the international system.[22]

This book argues that, depending on the disparity in power, the stronger nation can very well become a significant other for the weaker nation, while the converse would seem unlikely. As a result, the more powerful nation, as a significant other, can shape the weaker nation's collective identity, while the stronger nation is able to conceive of its relationship with the weaker nation in narrower terms. It is no coincidence that the United States and the ROK conceive of their relationship and the North through the different lenses (i.e., *policy* for the United States and *identity* for South Korea) given power imbalance or asymmetry that exists between the two. As South Koreans in the post-authoritarian era began to rethink their place in a newly emerging regional and global order, identity has gained more significance in defining their relationship with the United States.

In sum, the United States is seen as a significant other by Koreans, and for them, the U.S.-ROK relationship is tied to issues of national identity.

On the Korean side, the evident strain in bilateral relations during the later years of the study period stemmed from a new Korean identity challenging the alliance (the *identity thesis*). However, Korea is neither large enough nor important enough to shape U.S. national identity as a significant other. (Indeed, no nation currently seems to occupy this role.) Therefore, Washington's frustrations with Seoul were subsequently over divergent policy preferences (the *policy rift thesis*), underpinned by differing perceptions of essential circumstances and effective methods of inducing change. Thus, the asymmetry in power explains why the Korean debate focuses on the larger terms and purpose of the alliance, while the scope and depth of examination by Americans remains limited.

Anti-American and Anti-alliance Sentiment

This study also demonstrates through empirical evidence that there has been an increase in anti-American coverage in both conservative and progressive Korean newspapers since the year 2000. Although the ROK had experienced waves of anti-American sentiment in the past, previous instances were closely connected with specific issues, such as the Carter administration's plan to withdraw U.S. troops from the peninsula and alleged U.S. support for authoritarian South Korean regimes. More a function of fear of U.S. abandonment than entrapment, these waves of anti-American sentiment did not question the rationale of the U.S.-ROK alliance.

In this respect, the anti-American and anti-alliance sentiment from 2000 to 2003 examined here may be unique. During this time, an increasing number of Koreans explicitly questioned the rationale of the alliance and expressed deep resentment toward the United States, charging that the nation and the alliance stood as stumbling blocks to inter-Korean relations and eventual unification. Believing that the United States, not the DPRK, was the greater threat to peace on the peninsula,[23] these critics asserted that the alliance actually ran counter to Korean interests. As the South Korean electorate installed the two successive progressive administrations, anti-American themes entered institutional politics and "criticism of United States policy moved into the mainstream," according to a report by the Congressional Research Service.[24] Yet this report's assessment of anti-American sentiment as "less ideological and more issue-specific" is misleading, because it fails to appreciate the depth of identity politics.

According to the view espoused by this book, Korean anti-Americanism at the time reflected identity politics and was indeed ideologically driven. This ideological underpinning and connection to national identity explains why a variety of policy issues from seemingly different realms—from the Lone Star scandal[25] and the KORUS free trade agreement (FTA) to U.S. Forces Korea (USFK) troop realignment and the PSI—are connected to larger progressive and conservative narratives about the United States and North Korea. It also explains why even complex issues and seemingly straightforward accidents have the potential to be immediately polarizing along predictable lines—a category of phenomena dubbed earlier as *identity-invoking events.*

Some experts believe that this most recent tide of anti-Americanism was an expression of South Koreans' increased national pride.[26] This argument focuses on the decreased disparity in the material power gap between the ROK and the United States in accordance with the ROK's impressive economic development following the inception of the alliance. In 1953, ROK per capita income was less than $100, but today, that figure has risen to around $20,000, and the ROK boasts the thirteenth-largest economy in the world. Having experienced a dramatic change in national status, many Koreans have sought recognition and respect from their longtime patron, the United States. Put another way, Korea's enhanced economic position, together with its status as a democracy, has led to new expectations for how the United States should relate to this ally.

This line of argument holds that the United States has lagged in appropriately recognizing South Korea's new status and that this has spurred antipathy toward what is presumed to be an unequal alliance. Does the United States acknowledge the increased economic importance of the ROK to American interests? In this study, economic and trade issues were by far the most represented category in U.S. media coverage of South Korea and the bilateral relationship. But how did coverage of South Korea compare to coverage of other nations? As shown in Chapter 5, while nations such as France, Israel, and India all had lower trade volumes with the United States than did the ROK, they received more coverage in the U.S. media.

News coverage is based on a variety of factors, and trade level constitutes only one of them. Given the nature of news, it is difficult to assert that any one nation should receive a certain amount of coverage relative to other nations. Yet beyond empirical data on news, it is important to recognize that in the eyes of many Koreans, their nation, especially during this study period, did not receive proper recognition and due respect from the United States, thus engendering a sense of injustice and resentment. Whether this perception is valid is difficult to judge and also another matter. Regardless, the existence of this strongly felt perception helps to explain the growth of anti-American nationalism in South Korea since the late 1990s. As suggested by scholars of identity politics, perception can foment "a reality of [its] own, for it is seldom *what is* that is of political importance, but what people *think is*."[27]

In assessing anti-Americanism in Korea, it is important not to conflate anti-U.S. sentiment with anti-alliance sentiment. Chapter 4 clearly demonstrated that the two are not synonymous and do not always change together. While both the progressive and conservative Korean newspapers became more critical of the United States following the Kim Dae Jung era, *Chosun Ilbo*, for instance, assessed the U.S.-ROK relationship more positively from year to year over the same period. This was likely due to conservatives' concern that a progressive government and increasingly loud progressive voice in Korean society might undermine the alliance. Motivated to respond in the face of the increasing progressive rhetorical volume on the alliance, *Chosun* increased its number of editorials and columns stressing the importance of the alliance, which were significantly more positive than those published by *Hankyoreh*. This reflects, as Daniel Sneider argues, the conservative fear of "strategic abandonment" by the United States, ostensibly a result of displeasure at progressive criticism of the United States and the alliance.[28]

It is regrettable that most discourse on this topic, including the *anti-American thesis* presented in the introductory chapter, conflates anti-U.S. and anti-alliance sentiment. Such discourse obscures valuable insight into the full composition of Korean sentiment and how, over time, such sentiment has influenced Korean identity. It also implies that Korean conservatives' return to power does not preclude continued questioning of the United States' approach to the world and to Asia. The U.S. policy makers and analysts of Korean affairs should not overlook the complexities of Korean sentiment in formulating policy toward the peninsula.

As proven earlier in this book, there is no comparable anti-Koreanism or anti-alliance sentiment in the United States. To be sure, various U.S. policy makers and media outlets have expressed their displeasure with South Korean policy toward the North and Korean attitudes toward the alliance.

However, Chapters 5 and 6 demonstrated that this displeasure is related to specific policy issues and is hardly ideological. Ordinary Americans, in particular, may not be well informed about Korean issues; South Korea may not be consequential enough to be on their so-called mental map (and it is far from the only country or even ally that fits this description). According to Ambassador Michael Armacost, "The domestic politics of our Asian alliances is like the story of the dog that didn't bark. . . . The value of these alliances is rarely contested in our national politics."[29] Korea is certainly one such case.

The Media, Public Diplomacy, and International Relations

This study examined U.S.-ROK relations through the prism of the news media. According to U.S. media scholar Stephen Hess, "Until the Vietnam War caused the beginning of a reassessment, scholars generally agreed that the making of the country's foreign policy was rarely affected by public opinion." At this time, the notion that foreign policy was exclusively the domain of elites was amended to allow for the idea of popular influence, particularly that "an energized public had the power to narrow policymakers' range of options."[30]

This study confirms the media's role in that process by way of shaping public discourse and opinion on foreign policy issues. Moreover, the study of the Korean press demonstrates that the media can be an important medium in the process of forging national identity, a finding in line with a growing consensus taking hold across the social sciences that identity is "something actively and publicly created through discourse."[31] Embedded in the concept of state power, national identity affects the course of a nation's strategy and policy on international issues. As constructivists have pointed out, identity can provide a cognitive framework for shaping interests, preferences, world views, and, consequently, foreign policy actions.[32]

However, less investigative attention has been paid to how identity develops in a way that affects international relations. Research in other fields has shown the importance of the media in identity formation, and these findings should be readily applicable to the field of international relations. For instance, scholars of nationalism have argued that "print capitalism" was instrumental to the rise of nation as an "imagined community" in the modern era.[33] Likewise, Korean scholarship has pointed to the importance of the mass media in the rise and development of Korean identity in the 1920s under Japanese rule.[34]

The analysis presented in this book suggests that the deep divide and heated debate in the Korean media reflect more than just domestic politics. The division appears to be related to different identities vis-à-vis the North and the United States, which can be forged and reinforced through intense debate in the national media. This also explains why debate in the Korean media has been so emotionally charged and consensus so rarely achieved, reminiscent of ethnic conflict in multiethnic societies.[35] In short, it is necessary to pay closer attention to the media's role in identity formation, as national identity is a powerful construct, capable of influencing state behavior, strategy, and policy.

The findings of this study also have implications for U.S. and South Korean public diplomacy efforts. In the post–September 11 era, the U.S. government increased its public diplomacy activities to get the nation's true message out to the world. Within a month of the terrorist attacks, a former advertising executive with more than 40 years of experience, Charlotte Beers, became undersecretary of state for public affairs and public diplomacy, and Congress injected $497 million annually into the public diplomacy budget with passage of the Freedom Promotion Act of 2002.[36] At the working level, the U.S. State Department continued to regularly conduct surveys in foreign countries to assess popular sentiment and gauge perception of the United States. These were all important elements of U.S. public diplomacy efforts designed to win the approval and favor of people in other nations.

Yet in addition to the more general limits of public diplomacy,[37] the United States has found such efforts to be particularly challenging in recent years in South Korea. According to former diplomat David Straub, by 1999 and into the early 2000s, the Korean media had come to portray "the U.S. government, especially USFK, [as having] disrespected the Korean people to the extent of not caring about their safety or even their very lives. . . . Items that fit into the ugly American storyline were reported; those that did not weren't; and as popular anger grew, so did the appetite for even more negative stories about the U.S."[38] While some urged better public diplomacy in response to the situation, American diplomats felt as if they were fighting a losing battle. Again, according to Straub, the South Korean media had become "so tendentious that U.S. statements and explanations were almost uniformly greeted with disbelief and anger, making the situation even worse. The South Korean media reported, and the public agreed, that the U.S. had no sense of shame. The U.S., they felt, was trying to defend the indefensible."[39]

These years correspond with the rise of identity politics in South Korea and the creation of powerful narratives about the United States and the U.S.-ROK relationship that lumped together many seemingly disparate events. Under such circumstances, it is difficult for official U.S. explication—for example, of USFK crime statistics (as Straub cites, crime rates actually went down during this period)—to have much of an impact in the face of heightened emotion and the strong momentum of narratives propelled by civic groups and the media.

In fact, the analysis of the Korean media presented in this book shows that during the initial years of the second (i.e., current) nuclear standoff, as the conflict between the United States and North Korea intensified, the progressive press raised its anti-American editorial tone, blaming the United States for the escalation of tension on the peninsula. These patterns in news coverage coincided with similar temporal fluctuations in South Korean public perceptions of the North Korea problem and attitudes toward the United States. In the short term, the differing approaches of these alliance partners on the nuclear issue represented a problem of policy coordination, one that has improved with the establishment of the Lee and Obama administrations.

From a more long-term perspective, however, the problem is not primarily one of policy coordination. South Koreans are reevaluating their national identity, and the progressive media, which gained substantial influence in policy making over the study years, is a venue for and has even led such efforts.[40] When anti-American protests filled the streets of Seoul in 2002 during the presidential campaign, the United States (both government officials and journalists, as shown in Chapter 5) failed to fully appreciate the impetus of these larger forces. South Korean voters' decision in 2007 to send a conservative candidate to the Blue House reflected their fatigue with 10 years of progressive rule, not necessarily their desire for fundamental change.

While Lee's presidency may well result in improved U.S.-ROK policy coordination, the United States must recognize the changing South Korean views of the United States and North Korea and the fact that Korean progressives will continue to press their message, encouraging active opposition. The candlelight protests over the importation of American beef in the summer of 2008 has proven that. As Ambassador Michael Armacost points out, "One key to America's public diplomacy problem depends on whether it can persuade elements of the progressive camp in South Korea that Washington is on the right track, without in the process alienating the conservatives. That'll be a trick."[41]

The South Korean government has likewise sought to improve its national image in the world, especially in the United States. The government has been using the slogan "Dynamic Korea" to enhance the country's image overseas, and the Korean Embassy in Washington, DC, has been hosting the KORUS House Forum, inviting Korean experts to speak on various issues related to Korea and the alliance. Yet despite such improved efforts at promotion, there is still the sense that "a certain degree of continued international obscurity . . . keeps Korea in the realm of the not remembered."[42] Moreover, in terms of popular culture, the so-called Korean wave has not reached American audiences in the same way it has those in Asia.

According to a group of U.S. and Korea experts, to address the asymmetry of attention in U.S.-ROK relations, "South Korea needs to actively promote its national image to U.S. officials and opinion-makers and to a wider American public."[43] This group goes on to recommend legislative exchanges, diversifying channels of communication to be bipartisan, and hiring a savvy K Street public relations firm. According to the experts of this group, "South Korea has a great story to tell, . . . but sadly, it has been punching well below its weight in terms of conveying its accomplishments and its importance." These experts cite the ROK's troop deployment to Iraq as one of the most glaring examples of the under-publicizing of Korea.[44]

Yet at the same time, the progressive media's challenging of the alliance has offered it one advantage, although it is perhaps counterintuitive. As Straub notes, the asymmetry of attention combined with the Korean (particularly, progressive) perspective yield the loudest voice within U.S.-ROK alliance politics. According to Straub, "The result is that South Korea frames issues and sets the agenda for the bilateral relationship to a significant degree, in spite of the asymmetry in raw power in favor of the U.S."[45] Recognizing the different patterns of asymmetry in power and attention is crucial to understanding the dynamics within the U.S.-ROK relationship.

The variation in news tone by issue discussed in the previous chapters makes it possible to discern the relative degree to which each issue poses challenges to the public image of two Koreas in the United States and the image of the United States in Korea. This exhaustive statistical approach provides an index that might be useful to public diplomacy professionals in both nations. For instance, press coverage in South Korea and the United States clearly shows that security is persistently one of the most problematic issues for both nations, largely owing to the DPRK's pursuit of nuclear weapons and ballistic missile proliferation. On the other hand, more positive (and less negative) tones on other issues, such as economics, may imply that the United States and the ROK have bases on which to build a more robust, strengthened relationship, even apart from their partnership in countering the threat presented by the DPRK. It is in this regard that the KORUS FTA has been advocated by the Bush, Roh, and Lee governments.

Certainly, public diplomacy is a complex exercise that cannot be considered apart from the substance of policy. Fundamentally, "public diplomacy cannot be effective unless the foreign policy it supports is farsighted and reasonable."[46] Given this, the findings of the study should be taken into account as Seoul and Washington each seek to improve its image in the other country.

Pyongyang, however, faces a truly monumental challenge in attempting to counter Americans' deep-rooted negativity toward the North, as detailed in Chapter 6. In the U.S. press, nations often come to have "preassigned roles."[47] This is particularly so in the case of North Korea, a state that some media critics contend has suffered from a notable lack of nuanced, well-researched coverage.[48] To change such monolithic coverage, the DPRK may need to grant better access to foreign correspondents. As noted by Caroline Gluck, a former BBC correspondent based in Seoul who has made seven reporting trips to North Korea, Pyongyang "should use the opportunity of foreign media visits to tell the world their viewpoint, to show us a side of the country that rarely gets told, as they often complained about negative reporting by visiting reporters."[49]

The Future of the U.S.-ROK Relationship

As discussed in this book, the U.S.-ROK alliance has faced many challenges over the years and must evolve in a new environment created by changing domestic and international situations. International relations theorist Stephen Walt specifies certain conditions under which alliances become less likely to endure. They include cases in which the state posing the original threat becomes weaker, an alliance member becomes "convinced that their adversaries are not as bellicose as they once feared," the passage of time makes "shared historical experiences" less relevant, and elites seek to improve their domestic political position through attacks on an alliance, especially when sovereignty issues are at stake.[50]

Although reasonable arguments can be made that *all* these conditions applied to the study period, the U.S.-ROK alliance has endured. In fact, despite identity politics and policy disputes, the Bush and Roh administrations worked together to address concerns of the alliance (such as relocation of the USFK headquarters from Yongsan to Pyongtaek and transfer of wartime operational control [OPCON]) and to offer a new base of the alliance (such as the KORUS FTA). In addition, polls show South Korean public support of the alliance. According to a June 2006 World Gallup Poll, although less than half (43%) of Koreans feel seriously threatened by North Korean nuclear weapons, two-thirds (66%) believe that U.S. withdrawal from their country would greatly impact the stability of Northeast Asia. Indeed, over 70% of Koreans state a preference for retaining the U.S. presence.[51]

Both Washington and Seoul acknowledge the imperative to work closely together to develop a broader rationale for the alliance that reflects new realities. Beyond the defense of South Korea and Japan, U.S. alliances with these nations have contributed significantly to regional stability in East Asia. Indeed, the Mutual Defense Treaty commits the two nations to work together to "strengthen the fabric of peace in the Pacific area."[52] Putting greater focus on this long-enshrined imperative would necessarily involve political will from Seoul, given that the United States would likely emphasize increased ROK-Japan cooperation and multilateral initiatives, such as the PSI, in pursuit of this goal. Stressing regional—or even global—peace and stability as an organizing principle would also serve as meaningful U.S. recognition of Korea's economic and diplomatic stature and identity.

Victor Cha has suggested that the broadening of the alliance's rationale could be fortified by efforts to bolster a shared identity within the alliance— that is, to emphasize "commonly held norms, values, beliefs, and conceptions of how security is best achieved." Cha argues that "a key determinant of alliance resiliency is the degree to which shared identities underpin interaction," as this type of commitment allows alliances to outlive and extend beyond their original rationales.[53]

In the first meeting of Presidents Bush and Lee Myung Bak, at Camp David in April 2008, the leaders stressed the allies' common values and shared challenges in the twenty-first century, calling for a broad-based "strategic alliance" that on the basis of "freedom, democracy, human rights and the principle of market economy . . . will contribute to global peace and security."[54] Many noted analysts, including those belonging to the Korea Society–Shorenstein APARC "New Beginnings" group, believe that this is a very positive development,[55] commensurate with South Korea's enhanced standing in the world, although they stress the importance of early bilateral agreement on the substance and details of such a proposal.[56]

There are cautiously optimistic expectations on both sides of the Pacific that the four-year period of the Lee and Obama administrations represents an opportunity to strengthen the U.S.-ROK relationship. This seems especially true, considering that the last five years featured the overlap of President Roh and the 386ers with President Bush and the neoconservatives, which was, at least in the early years, possibly the least workable combination of leadership for the alliance. New hope is justified, and both sides have reason to be optimistic.

President Lee has stressed the importance of the U.S.-ROK alliance and said that he will attempt to promote trilateral collaboration among South Korea, the United States, and Japan. Lee has also promised that, unlike his predecessor, he will take a pragmatic, interest-based approach to foreign affairs and national security issues, a message that was well-received in both Washington and Tokyo during Lee's first presidential trip abroad.[57]

President Obama has similarly stressed the importance of consulting with key U.S. allies in pursuing a foreign policy agenda, and early indications of his policy suggest that he will take a more realist approach to international relations. As to the U.S.-ROK alliance, Obama said:

> Forged in blood during the Korean War more than a half-century ago, the alliance has sustained itself through the crucible of the Cold War and remains central to U.S. security policy in East Asia. . . . We need to work with South Korea on a common vision for the alliance to meet the challenges of the 21st century, not only those on the Korean Peninsula but in the region and beyond.[58]

At their summit in Washington on June 16, 2009, Presidents Lee and Obama announced a "Joint Vision for the Alliance," highlighted by the U.S. commitment to provide nuclear protection to South Korea to counter a growing nuclear threat from the North. The two leaders, referring to the planned transition of wartime military control, agreed to advance a plan to restructure their half-century-old military alliance to allow the ROK to "take the lead role in the combined defense" of the peninsula, supported by an enduring and capable U.S. military force presence."[59] The two administrations seem to have repaired some of the past strains on the alliance and currently enjoy a higher level of policy collaboration.

Nonetheless, the United States should be wary of raising expectations for a dramatic change in South Korea as a result of this power shift to a conservative government. As shown in this book, the Korean political landscape has evolved significantly since democratization, with the development of a vibrant and institutionalized left and civil society. These groups and their ideas (particularly about the North and the United States) persist, and identity politics could reemerge quite quickly in line with events, as what happened with China's claim on Koguryo[60] and the 2002 USFK accident. Indeed, the controversy over the agreement to begin reimportation of U.S. beef to Korea represents the first such case under the new Lee administration. The president has viewed the spread of public anxiety over U.S. beef as politically motivated,[61] and *Chosun Ilbo* has compared the outpouring of emotion and the holding of candlelight vigils to the sweeping anti-American reaction to the 2002 schoolgirl incident.[62]

The divided political landscape is not likely to change in the near term, and this dynamic may hinder the ability of ROK governments to think and act strategically. In fact, as clearly displayed during Lee's first visit to Washington, DC, in April 2008, his ostensibly pragmatic policy is firmly grounded in the alliance identity, provoking strong reaction from progressive forces that have promoted the nationalist identity. Although the voice of Korean progressives was weakened by defeat in recent elections, this constituency still remains important in Korean society, and the United States should not underestimate it or its ideas.

This is particularly true given the possibility that establishment of a conservative administration in South Korea may galvanize the opposition in challenging the government's policy agenda, including—and perhaps foremost—its approach to the North (especially if the Lee administration's attempt to enforce greater conditionality only produces worse North Korean behavior and/or inter-Korean cooperation bogs down). In a sense, progressives were co-opted by the governments of Kim Dae Jung and Roh Moo Hyun, as they reluctantly agreed on policies such as sending troops to Iraq. In the face of a conservative administration, however, the progressives could become more aggressive in advancing their agenda. This may mean intensification of identity politics, and the United States could easily be caught between a conservative presidential administration and progressive activists.

It is also important to acknowledge that there is not necessarily a direct relationship between policy preferences associated with the alliance identity and those preferable to the United States, although progressive notions of identity and policy preferences clearly pose a more fundamental challenge to the alliance. For example, throughout the 2007 Korean presidential campaign, the conservative Grand National Party (GNP) indicated its desire to renegotiate the agreed date for the transfer of wartime operational control from U.S. to Korean military commanders. Yet the U.S. Department of Defense repeatedly signaled that this (and other alliance military reform issues) had already been resolved to mutual satisfaction through extensive bilateral negotiations and was not open for renegotiation. In the eyes of U.S. defense professionals, the alliance is moving forward, and increased South Korean responsibility is a reflection of the nation's excellent, capable forces.

Likewise, policy makers associated with the nationalist identity may pursue initiatives in line with U.S. interests. For example, former President Roh Moo Hyun may have expressed anti-American sentiment to get elected, but as president, he took many steps to shore up the alliance. He visited USFK units and stressed his support for the alliance; he cooperated with the U.S.-led plan for USFK reduction and realignment, including relocation of Yongsan; he initiated negotiations for the U.S.–ROK free trade agreement; and he dispatched ROK troops to Iraq and Afghanistan (even if motivated primarily not by shared regional interests but by anxiety over potential U.S. military action against North Korea). Indeed, Roh administration officials regard themselves as having worked hard and in good faith to strengthen the alliance for the long term by resolving many outstanding issues and making it a more equal partnership.

The social and political dynamics that built up during the years of the study period signal that even though a conservative administration has assumed power, this is new political terrain. Despite having proalliance intentions, the Lee government must operate within a transformed context, molded by the recent contesting of Korean identity. In particular, as this book has demonstrated, South Koreans, particularly progressives, have come to use a different lens from that of the Americans in viewing the alliance. Perhaps the development is inevitable in a new era marked by Korean democratization, the end of the cold war, inter-Korean rapprochement, and U.S. preoccupation with the struggle against global terrorism. It must also be noted that having different lenses is not unusual for the states in an alliance, especially one of asymmetry, and it will not necessarily undermine the bilateral relationship if there is mutual appreciation and if, as is possible, the differing lenses produce compatible visions.

The main challenge stems from the fact that the South Korean lens is divided and that the U.S. lens is clouded. As shown throughout the book, Koreans are sharply divided in their view of the alliance, while Americans view Korean policy with confusion at times, as well illustrated by the Bush administration's policy toward the DPRK. Korea's divided polity is unlikely to change in the near future, and the new Obama administration will be preoccupied with the Middle East and South Asia, leaving Korean affairs as major but nevertheless secondary policy issues.

Thus, the main task for the ROK is to build a national consensus on its policy toward the North and the alliance, while the main task for the United States is to present a coherent policy toward the peninsula in close collaboration with its ally. Ultimately, if the U.S.-ROK relationship is to evolve to meet these new challenges, leaders and policy makers in both countries must recognize that this is a new era, in which they may employ different lenses in approaching the alliance driven by their own national interests and identities. In particular, the United States needs to respect the ROK as a legitimate partner, not just a dependent client in the alliance, as it has in the past, and to acknowledge the political constraints imposed on the ROK government by identity politics. Just as Americans need to take this into account, Koreans must understand that American thinking about security issues, including the Korean peninsula and the U.S.-ROK alliance, has significantly changed since the September 11 terrorist attacks. To construct a viable alliance that meets the challenges of a new era, both nations must march together, treating their partner as it is, not as it was or as they might wish it to be.

Reference Matter

Appendix: Code Book

Variable Number	Variable Name	Coding Categories
ARTICLE ATTRIBUTE BLOCK		
AR1	ARTICLE NUMBER	{Ranges from 1 to xxxxx}
AR2	CODER ID	
AR3	NEWS OUTLET CODE	1 = *New York Times* 2 = *Washington Post* 3 = *Wall Street Journal*
AR4	DATE	mm/dd/yyyy
AR5	NEWSWIRE	1 = Original 2 = AP 3 = Reuter 4 = Other (Specify:_____)
AR6-1a	REPORTER 1: (LAST NAME)	{Name} -99 = Not Given
AR6-1b	REPORTER 1 (FIRST NAME)	{Name Middle Initial} -99 = Not Given
AR6-2a	REPORTER 2 (LAST NAME)	{Name} -99 = Not Applicable
AR6-2b	REPORTER 2 (FIRST NAME)	{Name Middle Initial} -99 = Not Applicable
AR7	PICTURE	1 = Picture 0 = No Picture
AR8	LOCATION OF REPORTER	0 = Unspecified 1 = Seoul/S. Korea 2 = Pyongyang/N. Korea 3 = Panmoonjum 4 = Washington, DC 5 = Other U.S. Cities 6 = Other (Specify:_____)

Variable Number	Variable Name	Coding Categories
AR9	LOCATION OF ARTICLE: SECTION	{Ex: "Section A", "First Section} -99 = Not Given
AR10	LOCATION OF ARTICLE: PAGE	{Ex: "A13", "13"} -99 = Not Given
AR11	LOCATION OF ARTICLE: COLUMN	{Ranges from x to xx} -99 = Not Given
AR12	DESK	1 = "Editorial Desk" 2 = "Foreign Desk" 3 = "National Desk" 4 = "Money and Business/Financial Desk" 5 = "Society Desk" 6 = "Metropolitan Desk" 7 = "Sports Desk" 8 = "Arts and Leisure Desk" 9 = "Travel Desk" 10 = Other (Specify:_____) -99 = Not Given
AR13	LENGTH OF ARTICLE(WORDS)	{Ranges from x to xxxx} -99 = Not Given
AR14	TYPE OF ARTICLE	1 = News Story 2 = News Analysis 3 = Special Feature Story (Specify_____) 4 = Regular Column (Identify Author Position_____) 5 = Guest Column (Identify Author Position_____) 6 = Unsigned Newspaper Editorial 7 = Letters: 8 = Other (Specify:_____)
AR15	AUTHOR ETHNICITY	0 = Non-Korean/Korean American 1 = Korean/Korean American -99 = Cannot be determined
CONTENT BLOCK		
C1	MAJOR FOCUS OF COUNTRY	1 = S. Korea 2 = N. Korea 3 = U.S.-ROK Relationship 4 = U.S.-DPRK Relationship 5 = Inter-Korea Relations 6 = Other (Specify:_____)
C2	ORIGIN OF STORY (WHO INITIATED IT?)	1 = S. Korean government officials 2 = S. Korean nongovernment sources 3 = N. Korean government officials 4 = N. Korean nongovernment sources 5 = U.S. government officials 6 = U.S. non-government sources 7 = Journalist 8 = Other (e.g., other news reports, etc.) (Specify:_____)

Variable Number	Variable Name	Coding Categories
C3	DESCRIPTIVE OR ANALYTICAL STORY	1 = Mostly descriptive 2 = Both (equally descriptive and evaluative) 3 = Mostly evaluative
C4-1	TOPIC AREA 1 (THE MOST IMPORTANT)	1 = Security/Military Issues in E. Asia 2 = Domestic Politics 3 = Economy/Trade 4 = General Diplomacy 5 = Human Rights/Humanitarian Issues 6 = Social Issues (e.g., social security, crime, poverty, etc.) 7 = Science and Technology 8 = Arts/Culture/Religion 9 = Sports 10 = Korean American Community Issues 11 = Other (Specify:_____)
C4-2	TOPIC AREA (THE 2nd MOST IMPORTANT)	1 = Security/Military Issues in E. Asia 2 = Domestic Politics 3 = Economy/Trade 4 = General Diplomacy 5 = Humanitarian/Human Rights Issues 6 = Social Issues (e.g., social security, crime, poverty, etc.) 7 = Science and Technology 8 = Arts/Culture/Religion 9 = Sports 10 = Korean American Community Issues 11 = Other (Specify:_____)
C5-1	SPECIFIC ISSUE 1	1 = N. Korea's WMD (including nuclear and missile programs, chemical/biological weapons) 2 = Inter-Korea Military Conflict (unrelated to WMD issues) 3 = U.S.-N. Korea Military Conflict (unrelated to WMD issues) 4 = U.S. Troops in S. Korea (protests are not the focus) 5 = N. Korea's Arms Trafficking/Drug Sales/Smuggling 6 = S. Korea Domestic Defense Issues (military spending, etc.) 9 = U.S. Arms Sales to S. Korea 10 = Other Security/Military Issues (Specify:_____) 11 = S. Korea Civic Movement (including non–labor related protest and demonstration) 12 = Anti-U.S. Protests 13 = S. Korea Elections (presidential and congressional) 14 = S. Korea Domestic Politics (other than election related)

Variable Number	Variable Name	Coding Categories
C5-1	SPECIFIC ISSUE 1	15 = N. Korean Politics 16 = S. Korea-U.S. Trade 17 = Korean Economic (financial) Crisis 18 = S. Korean Economy/Industry (general) 19 = S. Korea's Labor Relations 20 = N. Korean Economy 21 = Inter-Korea Economic Relations 22 = Other Economy (Specify:_____) 23 = S. Korean President's Visit to United States 24 = Other General Diplomacy 25 = Humanitarian/Human Rights Issues in N. Korea 26 = S. Korea Social Issues (e.g., crime, poverty, social problems) 27 = Other S. Korea Society Issues (Specify:_____) 28 = Science and Technology 29 = Arts/Culture/Religion 30 = Sports 31 = Korean American Community Issues (e.g., immigration) 32 = Other Issues (Specify:_____)
C5-2	SPECIFIC ISSUE 2	1 = N. Korea's WMD (including nuclear and missile programs, chemical/ biological weapons) 2 = Inter-Korea Military Conflict (unrelated to WMD issues) 3 = U.S.-N. Korea Military Conflict (unrelated to WMD issues) 4 = U.S. Troops in S. Korea (protests are not the focus) 5 = N. Korea's Arms Trafficking/Drug Sales/Smuggling 6 = S. Korea Domestic Defense Issues (military spending, etc.) 9 = U.S. Arms Sales to S. Korea 10 = Other Security/Military Issues (Specify:_____) 11 = S. Korea Civic Movement (including non–labor related protest and demonstration) 12 = Anti-U.S. Protests 13 = S. Korea Elections (presidential and congressional) 14 = S. Korea Domestic Politics (other than election related) 15 = N. Korean politics 16 = S. Korea-US Trade 17 = Korean economic (financial) crisis

Variable Number	Variable Name	Coding Categories
C5-2	SPECIFIC ISSUE 2	18 = S. Korean Economy/Industry (general) 19 = S. Korea's Labor Relations 20 = N. Korean Economy 21 = Inter-Korea Economic Relations 22 = Other Economy (Specify:_____) 23 = S. Korean President's Visit to United States 24 = Other General Diplomacy 25 = Human Rights/Humanitarian Issues in N. Korea 26 = S. Korea Social Issues (e.g., crime, poverty, social problems) 27 = Other S. Korea Society Issues (Specify:_____) 28 = Science and Technology 29 = Arts/Culture/Religion 30 = Sports 31 = Korean American Community Issues (e.g., immigration) 32 = Other Issues (Specify:_____)
C6-1	REFERENCE: SOURCE 1 (>3)	0 – No Source 1 {→ GO TO C7} 1 = U.S. President 2 = Former U.S. President (Specify:_____) 3 = White House Secretary of Press 4 = U.S. Elected Officials/Politicians (Specify:_____) 5 = Other U.S. Public Officials (Specify:_____) 6 = U.S. Experts/Pundits (Specify:_____) 7 = S. Korean President 8 = Former S. Korean Presidents (Specify:_____) 9 = S. Korean Press Secretary 10 = S. Korean Elected Officials/Politicians (Specify:_____) 11 = Other S. Korea Public Officials (Specify_____) 12 = S. Korean experts/pundits (e.g., professors and analysts, etc.) 13 = Kim Il Sung 14 = Kim Jong-Il 15 = N. Koran public officials (Specify:_____) 16 = N. Korean Experts (Specify:_____) 17 = S. Korean Journalist (Specify:_____)

Variable Number	Variable Name	Coding Categories
C6-1	REFERENCE: SOURCE 1 (>3)	18 = American Journalist (Specify:_____) 19 = Other Foreign Journalist (Specify:_____) 20 = International Organization/Agency/ Banks (Specify:_____) 21 = Other (Specify:_____)
C6-1T	SOURCE 1 TONE ON C1	−1 = Mainly Negative 0 = Mixture 1 = Mainly Positive 4 = Indifferent/Neutral
C6-2	REFERENCE: SOURCE 2 (>3)	0 = No Source 1 {→ GO TO C7} 1 = U.S. President 2 = Former U.S. President (Specify:_____) 3 = White House Secretary of Press 4 = U.S. Elected Officials/Politicians (Specify:_____) 5 = Other U.S. Public Officials (Specify:_____) 6 = U.S. Experts/Pundits (Specify_____) 7 = S. Korean President 8 = Former S. Korean Presidents (Specify_____) 9 = S. Korean Press Secretary 10 = S. Korean Elected Officials/Politicians (Specify:_____) 11 = Other S. Korea Public Officials (Specify:_____) 12 = S. Korean Experts/Pundits (e.g., professors and analysts, etc.) 13 = Kim Il Sung 14 = Kim Jong-Il 15 = N. Korean Public Official (Specify:_____) 16 = N. Korean Experts (Specify:_____) 17 = S. Korean Journalist (Specify:_____) 18 = American Journalist (Specify_____) 19 = Other Foreign Journalist (Specify:_____) 20 = International Organization/Agency/ Banks (Specify:_____) 21 = Other (Specify:_____)
C6-2T	SOURCE 2 TONE ON C1	−1 = Mainly Negative 0 = Mixture 1 = Mainly Positive 4 = Indifferent/Neutral

Variable Number	Variable Name	Coding Categories
C6-3	REFERENCE: SOURCE 3	0 = No Source 1 {→ GO TO C7}
		1 = U.S. President
		2 = Former U.S. President (Specify:_____)
		3 = White House Secretary of Press
		4 = U.S. Elected Officials/Politicians (Specify:_____)
		5 = Other U.S. Public Officials (Specify:_____)
		6 = U.S. Experts/Pundits (Specify:_____)
		7 = S. Korean President
		8 = Former S. Korean Presidents (Specify:_____)
		9 = S. Korean Press Secretary
		10 = S. Korean Elected Officials/Politicians (Specify:_____)
		11 = Other S. Korea Public Officials (Specify:_____)
		12 = S. Korean Experts/Pundits (e.g., professors and analysts, etc.)
		13 = Kim Il Sung
		14 = Kim Jong-Il
		15 = N. Korean Public Officials (Specify_____)
		16 = N. Korean experts (Specify:_____)
		17 = S. Korean Journalist (Specify:_____)
		18 = American Journalist (Specify:_____)
		19 = Other Foreign Journalist (Specify:_____)
		20 = International Organization/Agency/Banks (Specify:_____)
		21 = Other (Specify:_____)
C6-3T	SOURCE 3 TONE ON C1	−1 = Mainly Negative
		0 = Mixture
		1 = Mainly Positive
		4 = Indifferent/Neutral
C7	DESCRIPTIVE ARTICLE TONE (ON C1)	−2 = Primarily Negative
		−1 = Somewhat Negative
		0 = Mixture/Indifferent (Neutral)
		1 = Somewhat Positive
		2 = Primarily Positive
		6 = No DESCRIPTIVE statements on C1
C8	EVALUATIVE ARTICLE TONE (ON C1)	−2 = Primarily Negative
		−1 = Somewhat Negative
		0 = Mixture/Indifferent (Neutral)
		1 = Somewhat Positive
		2 = Primarily Positive
		6 = No EVALUATIVE statements on C1

Notes

Chapter 1

1. Norimitsu Onishi, "South Korean President Pledges Pragmatism," *New York Times*, February 26, 2008.

2. Burt Herman, "Chillier Winds Blow across Korean Border," Associated Press, March 6, 2008. It is important to note that at the time of this writing, no expert on North Korea occupies a senior security policy position in the Lee government. This stands in sharp contrast to the Roh government, in which North Korea expert Lee Jong-Seok was in charge of national security policy.

3. George Wehrfritz, "Angry at the Yanks: Strange Times for U.S. Troops Helping to Defend South Korea," *Newsweek*, January 13, 2003, www.newsweek.com/id/62765 (accessed June 17, 2009).

4. Steven R. Weisman, "Threats and Responses: East Asia: South Korea, Once a Solid Ally, Now Poses Problems for the U.S.," *New York Times*, January 2, 2003.

5. This also occurred after U.S. Secretary of Defense Donald Rumsfeld announced that he would likely reduce and reorganize the U.S. troop presence on the peninsula, which many Koreans perceived as a direct response to anti-American protests. See Doug Struck, "Anti-U.S. Sentiment Abates in South Korea: Change Follows Rumsfeld Suggestion of Troop Cut," *Washington Post*, March 14, 2003.

6. Pew Research Center, Pew Global Attitudes Project Survey, "Views of a Changing World, June 2003," http://people-press.org/reports/pdf/185.pdf (accessed January 7, 2009). See also David Steinberg, "Korean Attitudes towards the United States: The Complexities of an Enduring and Endured Relationship" (paper presented at the Georgetown Asian Studies Program Conference, Washington, DC, January 30, 2003).

7. Eric V. Larson, Norman D. Levin, Seonhae Baik, and Savych Bogdan, *Ambivalent Allies? A Study of South Korean Attitudes toward the U.S.* (San Diego: RAND Corporation, 2004).

8. Daniel Sneider, "The U.S.-Korea Tie: Myth and Reality," *Washington Post*, September 12, 2006.

9. For example, after meeting with South Korean President Roh Moo Hyun in May 2003, President Bush said, "I have found the president to be an easy man to talk to. He expresses his opinions very clearly and it's easy to understand." President Roh was even more effusive: "Now, after having talked to President Bush, I have gotten rid of all my concerns, and now I return to Korea only with hopes in my mind."

10. Victor D. Cha, "Shaping Change and Cultivating Ideas in the US-ROK Alliance," in *The Future of America's Alliances in Northeast Asia*, ed. Michael H. Armacost and Daniel I. Okimoto (Stanford, CA: The Walter H. Shorenstein Asia-Pacific Research Center, 2004); Victor D. Cha and David C. Kang, *Nuclear North Korea: A Debate on Engagement Strategies* (New York: Columbia University Press, 2003); Victor D. Cha, "Korea's Place in the Axis," *Foreign Affairs* 81, no. 3 (2002): 79–92; and Ted Galen Carpenter and Doug Bandow, *The Korean Conundrum: America's Troubled Relations with North and South Korea* (London: Palgrave Macmillan, 2004).

11. It should be noted that President Bush's skepticism about the North was not the sole point of disagreement. Before traveling to Washington, DC, President Kim Dae Jung had met with President Vladimir Putin and joined the Russian leader in opposing the Bush administration's missile defense plan, a major priority for the new U.S. president. This unnecessary swipe at a major administration policy initiative, coming from a treaty ally on the eve of the leaders' first meeting, soured the atmosphere even before talking points were exchanged.

12. Michael H. Armacost, "The Future of America's Alliances in Northeast Asia," *The Future of America's Alliances in Northeast Asia*, ed. Michael H. Armacost and Daniel I. Okimoto, 19 (Stanford, CA: The Walter H. Shorenstein Asia-Pacific Research Center).

13. Gi-Wook Shin and Kristin Burke, "A Mandate with Caveats: Lee Myung Bak's Election, Politics, and Policy," http://aparc.stanford.edu/publications/a_mandate_with_caveats_lee_myung_baks_election_politics_and_policy (accessed December 28, 2007).

14. This term refers to a generation of Koreans that includes those when the term was coined in their 30s, those born in the 1960s, and those who attended university during the 1980s, when student movements for democratization reached their zenith. Members of this generation have assumed the mantle of leadership during the Roh administration.

15. See Derek Mitchell, ed., *Strategy and Sentiment: South Korean Views of the United States and the U.S.-ROK Alliance* (Washington, DC: Center for Strategic and International Studies, 2004); David Steinberg, ed., *Korean Attitudes toward the United States: Changing Dynamics* (New York: M. E. Sharpe, 2005); Larson et al. (2004); Katharine Moon, "Korean Nationalism, Anti-Americanism, and Democratic Consolidation," in *Korea's Democratization*, ed. Samuel S. Kim (New York: Cambridge University Press, 2003); Young-Shik Bong, "Anti-Americanism and the U.S.-Korea Military Alliance," *Confrontation and Innovation on the Korean Peninsula* (Washington, DC: Korea Economic Institute, 2003), 18–29; Sook Jong Lee, "Allying with the United States: Changing South Korean Attitudes," *Korean Journal of Defense Analysis* 17, no. 1 (Spring 2005), 81–104; Robert Marquand, "How S. Korea's View of the North Flipped," *Christian Science Monitor*, January 22, 2003. www.csmonitor.com/2003/0122/p01s02-woap.html (accessed June 17, 2009); and Nae Young Lee and Jung Han-oorl, "Panmi yŏron kwa hanmi tongmaeng" [South Korean Public Opinion on Anti-Americanism and the U.S.-ROK alliance]," *Kukka chŏllyak* [National Strategy] 9, no. 3 (2003): 58–32. www.sejong.org/Pub_ns/PUB_NS_DATA/kns0903-03. pdf (accessed June 17, 2009).

16. "U.S.-Korea Relations: Opinion Leaders Seminar" (Korea Economic Institute, Washington, DC, July 2003), 7.

17. See Bruce Cumings, *The Origins of the Korean War*, vol. 1 (Princeton, NJ: Princeton University Press, 1981); Gi-Wook Shin, "South Korean Anti-Americanism," *Asian Survey* 36, no. 8 (1996): 787–803.

18. As summarized in a Pew report, "The war [in Iraq] has widened the rift between Americans and Western Europeans, further inflamed the Muslim world, softened support for the war on terrorism, and significantly weakened global public support for the pillars of the post-World War II era, the U.N. and the North Atlantic alliance" (Pew Research Center for the People and the Press, 2003).

19. Joseph S. Nye Jr., *Soft Power: The Means to Success in World Politics* (New York: Public Affairs, 2004).

20. See Philip Yun and Gi-Wook Shin, eds., *North Korea: 2005 and Beyond* (Stanford, CA: Shorenstein Asia-Pacific Research Center, 2006).

21. For instance, almost half of the ruling Uri party assemblymen had activist pasts.

22. Mitchell (2004), 107.

23. "U.S.-Korea Relations: Opinion Leaders Seminar," 3.

24. Taek-Young Hamm, "North Korea: Economic Foundations of Military Capability and the Inter-Korean Balance," in *North Korea: 2005 and Beyond*, ed. Philip Yun and Gi-Wook Shin (Stanford, CA: Shorenstein Asia-Pacific Research Center, 2006); Mitchell (2004).

25. Stephen Walt, "Why Alliances Endure or Collapse," *Survival* 39, no. 1 (Spring 1997), 156–79.

26. See Kenneth Neal Waltz, *Theory of International Politics* (Reading, MA: Addison-Wesley, 1979); John J. Mearsheimer, *The Tragedy of Great Power Politics* (New York: Norton, 2001); Stephen M. Walt, *Origins of Alliances* (Ithaca, NY: Cornell University Press, 1987).

27. Walt (1987).

28. James D. Morrow, "Alliance and Asymmetry: An Alternative to the Capacity Aggregation Model of Alliances," *American Journal of Political Science* 35, no.4 (1991): 904–33.

29. See Glenn H. Snyder, *Alliance Politics* (Ithaca, NY: Cornell University Press, 1997), particularly page 166. Note that while Snyder focuses on short-term policy bargaining, I seek to examine broader, longer-term trends associated with an uneven distribution of power between allies.

30. For an excellent example of how "othering" shapes identity, see Iver B. Neumann, *Uses of the Other: "The East" in European Identity Formation* (Minneapolis: University of Minnesota Press, 1999).

31. According to Peter Hays Gries, national identities are "not autonomous, but instead evolve through international encounters" and also "the stories that we tell about our national pasts." Peter Hays Gries, "The Koguryo Controversy, National Identity, and Sino-Korean Relations Today," *East Asia* 22, no. 4 (Winter 2005): 3–17.

32. China and Japan also influence Korean identity. For more on the role of China in South Korea's recent politics of identity, see Gi-Wook Shin, "Asianism and Korea's Politics of Identity," *Inter-Asia Cultural Studies* 6, no. 4 (2005): 610–24.

33. See Chae-Jin Lee, *The Troubled Peace: U.S. Policy and the Two Koreas* (Baltimore, MD: Johns Hopkins University Press, 2006), 376. Lee chronicles how domestic developments in both the United States and South Korea have influenced policy. While I believe his reasoning holds true for the United States, in the case of South Korea, we must consider identity, a construct that is deeper and more durable than domestic political disputes and outcomes.

34. Key-Hiuk Kim, *The Last Phase of the East Asian World Order* (Berkeley: University of California Press, 1980).

35. See Hyung Il Pai, *Constructing Korean Origins* (Cambridge, MA: Asia Center, Harvard University); Gi-Wook Shin, *Ethnic Nationalism in Korea* (Stanford, CA: Stanford University Press, 2006).

36. Although the Northern regime promotes anti-Americanism, we also need to note that this regime has been seeking to normalize its relationship with the United States, which would give it access to resources, lessen the security threat, and provide more diplomatic space to maneuver, especially vis-à-vis China.

37. More subtly, the United States' close alliance with the ROK also helped develop a more cooperative relationship with another important ally in East Asia, Japan. As former U.S. Ambassador to Japan Michael Armacost noted, Japan would have found it difficult politically to sustain support for U.S. bases if it were the United States' only ally in the region. This situation may have changed in recent years, as Japan has become increasingly concerned by the rising power and influence of China. See Armacost (2004).

38. Between the mid-1950s and the early 1960s, for example, roughly 50 percent of the ROK's annual budget came from U.S. aid. South Korea received a total of $6 billion in economic aid from the United States between 1946 and 1978. For comparison, during the same period, the United States provided only $6.9 billion to all the African countries combined and $14.9 billion to all the Latin American countries combined. Furthermore, the United States provided $9 billion in military aid to the ROK between 1955 and 1978; during this period, all the countries in Africa and Latin America combined received only $3.2 billion in military aid.

39. Alice H. Amsden, *Asia's Next Giant: South Korea and Late Industrialization* (Oxford: Oxford University Press, 1989).

40. Even to an American public opposed to expanding U.S. bases overseas after World War II, U.S. defense officials could argue that South Korea was one case where the presence of U.S. troops was truly welcomed and effective.

41. Tim Shorrock, "The Struggle for Democracy in South Korea in the 1980s and the Rise of Anti-Americanism," *Third World Quarterly* 8, no. 4 (1986): 1198–99.

42. See Gi-Wook Shin and Kyung Moon Hwang, *Contentious Kwangju: The May 18 Uprising in Korea's Past and Present* (Boulder, CO: Rowman and Littlefield, 2003). For accounts of the uprising from a U.S. perspective, see William H. Gleysteen Jr., *Massive Entanglement, Marginal Influence: Carter and Korea in Crisis* (Washington, DC: Brookings Institution Press, 1999).

43. Gi-Wook Shin (1996), 787–803.

44. Sun Hyuk Kim, *The Politics of Democratization in Korea* (Pittsburgh, PA: University of Pittsburgh Press, 2000).

45. For a thorough explanation of the principles and assumptions of the Sunshine Policy, see chapter 3, "The Sunshine Policies: Principles and Main Activities," in *Sunshine in Korea: The South Korean Debate over Policies toward North Korea*, ed. Norman D. Levin and Yong-Sup Han (Santa Monica, CA: RAND, 2003).

46. Hong Soon-Young, "Thawing Korea's Cold War: The Path to Peace on the Korean Peninsula," *Foreign Affairs*, May/June 1999, 8–12.

47. For example, see Do-Yeong Kim, "After the South and North Korea Summit: Malleability of Explicit and Implicit National Attitudes of South Koreans," *Peace and Conflict: Journal of Peace Psychology* 9, no. 2 (2003): 159–70, www.informaworld.com/smpp/title~content=g785828770~db=all.

48. Calvin Sims, "New (Friendly) Craze in South Korea: The North," *New York Times*, June 20, 2000.

49. *JoongAng Ilbo*, January 3, 2001, as cited in Levin and Yong-Sup Han (2003), 106.

50. See, for example, Marquand (2003); Kurt Achin, "South Korea-US Alliance in Difficult Transition," *Voice of America*, May 2, 2005; and Balbina Y. Hwang, "Minding the Gap: Improving U.S.-ROK Relations," *Backgrounder*, no. 1814, December 21, 2004, Heritage Foundation, http://author.heritage.org/Research/AsiaandthePacific/bg1814.cfm.

51. Chung-In Moon, "ROK-DPRK Engagement and US-ROK Alliance: Trade-off or Complementary?" (paper presented at the U.S.-DPRK Next Steps Workshop, Nautilus Institute and the Carnegie Endowment for International Peace, Washington, DC, January 27, 2003), www.nautilus.org/fora/security/0237A_Moon.htm (accessed January 7, 2009).

52. Concern among U.S. experts and the Bush administration registered even before Roh's election, including reaction to candidate Roh's comments that if war broke out between the United States and North Korea, South Korea would not automatically side with the United States and might consider neutrality. See Anthony Spaeth, "Roh Moo Hyun Takes Center Stage," *Time*, February 24, 2003, 2.

53. See David C. Kang, "Rising Powers, Offshore Balancers, and Why the US-Korea Alliance Is Undergoing Strain," *International Journal of Korean Unification Studies* 14, no. 2 (2005): 115–40; Scott Snyder, "The China-Japan Rivalry: Korea's Pivotal Position?" in *Cross-Currents: Regionalism and Nationalism in Northeast Asia*, ed. Gi-Wook Shin and Daniel Sneider, 241–58 (Stanford, CA: Walter H. Shorenstein Asia-Pacific Research Center, 2007).

54. This change also reflects growing business opportunities in China, which replaced the United States as the ROK's largest trading partner in 2004.

55. Gilbert Rozman, *Northeast Asia's Stunted Regionalism: Bilateral Distrust in the Shadow of Globalization* (Cambridge: Cambridge University Press, 2004), 364.

56. Shin (2005).

57. Polls consistently show that a high percentage of Koreans back engagement. For example, a poll published by *Joongang Ilbo* on October 13, 2006, found that even after the North's nuclear test, substantial support for the engagement policy continued, with over 70 percent of Koreans agreeing that "Dialogue between North and South Korea was the best way to resolve the current crisis." This poll was conducted by "Joins P'unghyang-gae" (research.joins.com) polling company, and its publication in *Joongang Ilbo* was cited in Sheila Miyoshi Jager, "Time to End the Korean War: The Korean Nuclear Crisis in the Era of Unification," *Japan Focus*, October 24, 2006.

58. Conservatives were enraged when they found that the Kim Dae Jung government had paid cash to Pyongyang to facilitate the breakthrough with the North (i.e., the summit), and the under-the-table payoffs became a big issue in debates over engagement.

59. Hahm Chaibong, "The Two South Koreas: A House Divided," *Washington Quarterly* 28, no. 3 (Summer 2005): 57–72; Byung-Hoon Suh, "Kim Dae Jung's Engagement Policy and the South-South Conflict in South Korea: Implications for U.S. Policy," *Asian Update*, Summer 2001, www.asiasociety.org/publications/update_southkorea.html (accessed January 7, 2009).

60. J. J. Suh, Peter J. Katzenstein, and Allen Carlson, *Rethinking Security in East Asia* (Stanford, CA: Stanford University Press, 2004), 169. In using Suh's terms, *alliance identity* and *nationalist identity*, I am not rendering any judgment on the relative patriotism of these two groups, which are both devoted to the Korean nation and the protection of its interests.

61. Victor D. Cha, "Shaping Change and Cultivating Ideas in the US-ROK Alliance," in *The Future of America's Alliances in Northeast Asia*, ed. Michael H. Armacost and Daniel I. Okimoto (Stanford, CA: The Walter H. Shorenstein Asia-Pacific Research Center), 121.

62. Victor D. Cha, *Alignment Despite Antagonism: The US-Korea-Japan Security Triangle* (Stanford, CA: Stanford University Press, 1999), 2–3.

63. Ibid., 67. Cha also cites in this quote a personal interview with Park Sang Yong, Yonsei University Professor of Business Administration.

64. Joel S. Wit, *Going Critical: The First North Korean Nuclear Crisis* (Washington, DC: Brookings Institution Press, 2004), xv.

65. Don Oberdorfer, *The Two Koreas: A Contemporary History* (New York: Basic Books, 1997), 193.

66. Report to the Speaker U.S. House of Representatives, North Korea Advisory Group, November 1999, www.fas.org/nuke/guide/dprk/nkag-report.htm (accessed January 7, 2009).

67. Richard L. Armitage, "A Comprehensive Approach to North Korea," *Strategic Forum* 159 (March 1999), Institute for National Strategic Studies, National Defense University, www.globalsecurity.org/wmd/library/news/dprk/1999/forum159.html (accessed January 7, 2009).

68. Andrew Moens, The Foreign Policy of George W. Bush: Values, Strategy and Loyalty (Burlington, VT: Ashgate, 2004), 109–11; Sebastian Harnisch, "U.S.-North Korean Relations under the Bush Administration: From 'Slow Go' to 'No Go,'" Asian Survey 42, no. 6 (November/December 2002): 856–82.

69. See Larry Niksch, "North Korea's Nuclear Weapons Program," Congressional Research Service Report no. IB 91141 (Washington, DC: CRS for Congress, 2001); James A. Kelly, "United States Policy in East Asia and the Pacific:

Challenges and Priorities" (testimony before the Subcommittee on East Asia and the Pacific, House Committee on International Relations, June 12, 2001).

70. As is now well known, there were ongoing policy disputes between State Department pragmatists and White House/Pentagon ideologues. In March 2001, for instance, under pressure from hard-liners, Secretary of State Colin Powell was obliged to retract his comment that the Bush administration would "pick up where Clinton left off" on talks with North Korea over missiles. As Barbara Slavin, senior diplomatic reporter of *USA Today*, notes, "In the first Bush term, the ideologues kept winning and US-Korean relations continued to deteriorate." See Barbara Slavin, "Reporting the North Korea Nuclear Crisis and More: Adventures in the 'Axis of Evil,'" in *First Drafts of Korea: The U.S. Media and Perceptions of the Last Cold War Frontier* (KSP Conference, Stanford, CA, July 13, 2007).

71. Victor D. Cha, "Korea: A Peninsula in Crisis and Flux," in *Strategic Asia 2004–2005: Confronting Terrorism in the Pursuit of Power*, ed. Ashley J. Tellis and Michael Willis, 150–52 (Washington, DC: National Bureau of Asian Research, September 2004).

72. According to former U.S. diplomat David Straub, President Roh agonized over the decision to send ROK troops to Iraq, believing that the U.S. invasion was unwarranted. President Roh's appeal to the National Assembly on this issue made "perfectly clear to all South Koreans that . . . he feared that the U.S. might take unilateral military action against North Korea's nuclear program if the ROK did not support the U.S. in Iraq." See David Straub, "Public Diplomacy and the Korean Peninsula," in *First Drafts of Korea: The U.S. Media and Perceptions of the Last Cold War Frontier* (KSP Conference, Stanford, CA, July 13, 2007).

73. The Bush administration shifted from a confrontational to a more diplomatic approach after the midterm elections and hawks such as Donald Rumsfeld and John Bolton left office.

Chapter 2

1. Key examples include Derek Mitchell, ed., *South Korean Views of the United States and the U.S.-ROK Alliance* (Washington, DC: Center for Strategic and International Studies, 2004); and Eric V. Larson et al., *Ambivalent Allies? A Study of South Korean Attitudes toward the U.S.* (Santa Monica, CA: RAND Corporation, 2004).

2. For example, even though the Larson et al. (2004) study provides an excellent analysis of South Korean opinion of the United States and U.S.-ROK relations, it does not empirically demonstrate the kind or degree of impact that this sentiment has had on the alliance.

3. Although the media have an agenda-setting capacity, many journalists con-

tend that the government also affects the media's selection and coverage of key issues in crucial ways. See David Sanger, "Covering North Korea's Nuclear Program: A Very Different WMD Problem," *First Drafts of Korea: The U.S. Media and Perceptions of the Last Cold War Frontier Conference*, Shorenstein Asia-Pacific Research Center, Stanford, CA, 13 July 2007.

4. See Shanto Iyengar, *Is Anyone Responsible? How Television Frames Political Issues.* (Chicago: University of Chicago Press, 1991); David K. Perry, "The Mass Media and Inference about Other Nations," *Communication Research* 12 (1985); David K. Perry, "The Image Gap: How International News Affects Perceptions of Nations," *Journalism Quarterly* 64 (1987): 416–21; Robert B. Albritton and Jarol B.Manheim, "News of Rhodesia: The Impact of a Public Relations Campaign," *Journalism Quarterly* 60 (1983): 622–28; Robert B. Albritton and Jarol B. Manheim, "Changing National Images: International Public Relations and Media Agenda Setting," *American Political Science Review* 78, no. 3 (September 1984): 641–57.

5. See Bruce Russett, "Doves, Hawks, and U.S. Public Opinion," *Political Science Quarterly* 105, no. 4 (1990): 515–38; Philip Powlick, "The Attitudinal Bases for Responsiveness to Public Opinion among American Foreign Policy Officials," *Journal of Conflict Resolution* 35, no. 4 (1991): 611–41.

6. Leonard A. Kusnitz, *Public Opinion and Foreign Policy: America's China Policy* 1949–1979 (Westport, CT: Greenwood Press, 1984).

7. Alan D. Monroe, "Consistency between Public Preferences and National Policy Decisions," *American Politics Quarterly* 7, no. 1 (1979): 3–19; Benjamin I. Page and Robert Y. Shapiro, "Effects of Public Opinion on Policy," *American Political Science Review* 77, no.1 (1983): 175–90.

8. Bernard C. Cohen, *The Public's Impact on Foreign Policy* (Boston: Little, Brown, 1973); Philip J. Powlick, "The Sources of Public Opinion for American Foreign Policy Officials," *International Studies Quarterly* 39 (1995): 427–51.

9. Norman D. Levin and Yong-Sup Han, *Sunshine in Korea: The South Korean Debate over Policies toward North Korea* (Santa Monica, CA: RAND, 2002); Larson et al. (2004); Scott Snyder, "The Role of the Media and the U.S.-ROK Relationship," in *Strategy and Sentiment: South Korean Views of the United States and the U.S.-ROK Alliance*, ed. Derek Mitchell, 73–81 (Washington, DC: Center for Strategic and International Studies, 2004).

10. Larson et al. (2004), 13.

11. There are some studies of media coverage and framing of anti-American sentiments and themes in South Korea; see, for example, Jae-Kyoung Lee, Anti-Americanism in South Korea: The Media and the Politics of Signification (Ph.D. dissertation, University of Iowa, 1993). Yet no study has examined news media coverage of U.S.-ROK relations in both nations and their interactions, as I attempt to do here.

12. In a study of partisan bias in the *Chicago Tribune* from 1900 to 1992, Burgos found that headlines attacking Democratic candidates at the turn of the century were 10 times more prevalent than headlines attacking Republicans. See Russell Burgos, "The Second Hands of History: Partisanship and the Corporate Transformation of American Journalism" (unpublished paper, University of California Los Angeles, 1996); and John Zaller, *A Theory of Media Politics: How the Interests of Politicians, Journalists, and Citizens Shape the News.* Forthcoming. www.sscnet. ucla.edu/polisci/faculty/zaller/media%20politics%20book%20.pdf (accessed June 17 2009). (Zaller quotes Burgos's figure of "10 times more frequent.") www.polisci. ucla.edu/people/faculty-pages/faculty-cvs/zaller_cv_08.pdf

13. In the current journalistic environment, even high-profile, well-respected journalists may lose their jobs if a lack of solid research (or another factor) contributes to a perception of bias. That was the case with CBS news anchor Dan Rather, who, during the 2004 presidential election, used memos of questionable credibility to suggest that President Bush had received preferential treatment in the National Guard during the Vietnam War.

14. See Snyder (2004).

15. Levin and Han (2002).

16. Note that 'the United States' journalistic agenda is still influenced by the government. See Sanger (2007).

17. Until the late 1980s, when Korea made a transition to democracy, the media were under the tight control of authoritarian-military regimes and largely conservative, supporting the government on major policy issues. When the media resisted, as in the case of *Dong-A Ilbo* in the 1970s, they were severely repressed by the government. Of particular importance to the study was the rise of progressive newspapers that occurred as South Korea became democratized in the late 1980s. They criticized the existing newspapers as "complicit with authoritarian regimes" and also focused on representing more progressive views. As has happened elsewhere, in South Korea, the media have become key players in the public discussion of foreign policy issues.

18. Of course, this was not always the case. For instance, the progressive newspapers fiercely criticized the Roh government's decision to send ROK troops to Iraq in support of the U.S. war against terrorism.

19. *USA Today* is distributed nationwide, but its limited circulation makes it a secondary newspaper, at most, in all areas of the country. It is also worth noting that circulation figures do not capture the Internet readership of newspapers.

20. The main U.S. news organizations that have bureaus in South Korea are wires and the *Wall Street Journal*. Most others, including the *New York Times*, use stringers there.

21. Herbert J. Gans, *Deciding What's News* (New York: Pantheon, 1979); see

also Todd Gitlin, *The Whole World Is Watching* (Berkeley: University of California Press, 1980).

22. Arguably, in both the United States and Korea, the public learns more about foreign affairs from newspapers than from broadcast news, although they may rely heavily on television news to stay informed about national politics. See Craig Leonard Brians and Martin P. Wattenberg, "Campaign Issue Knowledge and Salience: Comparing Reception from TV Commercials, TV News and News-papers," *American Journal of Political Science* 40, no. 1 (February 1996): 172–93.

23. One of my main research objectives is to assess the extent to which news influences investor confidence in South Korea. Although I do not address this issue in this book, the data collected here can be used for that purpose, and I intend to pursue it elsewhere.

24. For a brief history of the *Hankyoreh*, see Chaebong T'ŭl ŭiKugŏbang: *Hankyoreh Shinmoon* (The Sewing Machine Korean Language Class: The Han-kyoreh Newspaper) http://blog.naver.com/kwank99?Redirect=Log&logNo=300311 58107 (accessed May 17, 2008).

25. Robert M. Entman, "Blacks in the News: Television, Modern Racism and Cultural Change," *Journalism Quarterly* 69 (1992): 341–61; Thomas Patterson, *Out of Order* (New York: Knopf, 1993).

26. Scott L. Althaus, Jill A. Edy, and Patricia F. Phalen, "Using Substitutes for Full-Text News Stories in Content Analysis: Which Text Is Best? Workshops," *American Journal of Political Science* 45, no. 3 (2001): 707–23.

27. See later in this chapter for definitions of descriptive and evaluative articles.

28. A full description of all the other major variables for the U.S. data is provided in the Appendix. A similar coding book was used for the Korean data, although some categories had to be different.

29. More refined coding schemes were initially tried but after some testing, we adopted the current, simpler coding scheme to maximize intercoder reliability.

30. This descriptive/evaluative distinction has been adopted by many researchers studying the press and politics in the United States. The rise of so-called interpretative journalism is a well-known phenomenon in the United States.

31. See William D. Perreault Jr. and Laurence E. Leigh, "Reliability of Nominal Data Based on Qualitative Judgments," *Journal of Marketing Research* 26 (1989): 135–48.

32. All coders were native Korean speakers and graduate or mature undergraduate students at a major university in Korea and went through extensive training. Additionally, all articles were randomly assigned to coders according to the articles' publication dates to prevent coder-specific attributes from confounding temporal trends in the data. For assessing reliability, all coders examined 100 common editorials and columns. Based on these data, the kappa statistic reached

roughly 0.65 (*Chosun Ilbo*) and 0.69 (*Hankyoreh*) in the two newspapers, showing a satisfactory level of reliability.

Chapter 3

Parts of this chapter appeared elsewhere and are published here in modified form with permission: "North Korea and Politics of Identity in South Korea," in *Brown Journal of World Affairs* 15, no. 1 (2008): 27–303; "North Korea and Contending South Korean Identities," in *Academic Paper Series on Korea* (Korea Economic Institute) 1 (2007): 150–69. Both publications were coauthored with Kristin Burke.

1. Sang-Hun Choe "Seoul Torn over Response to Test: Critics Take Aim at 'Sunshine Policy,'" *International Herald Tribune*, October 13, 2006.

2. Jin Ryu, "US-North Korea Enmity Imperils South Korea," *Korea Times*, October 13, 2006.

3. Kurt Achin, "Senior South Korean Official Apologizes for North's Nuclear Test," *Voice of America News,* Federal Information and News Dispatch, October 10, 2006.

4. Quoted in Anna Fifield, "Clouds over South Korea's 'Sunshine Policy,'" *Financial Times*, October 10, 2006.

5. Quoted in "Let the Sunshine Policy Set," Yonhap News Agency, October 12, 2006.

6. Sang-Hun Choe, "South Korea Grapples with Competing Pressures as It Weighs Its Response to North Korea," *New York Times*, October 12, 2006.

7. Jae-Soon Chang, "South Korean President Pledges to Keep Relations with North Korea 'Friendly,'" Associated Press Worldstream, November 2, 2006; "North Korean Leader Kim Tours Fertilizer Factory Amid Halt in South Korean Aid," Associated Press Worldstream, November 13, 2006.

8. Thom Shanker and Martin Fackler, "South Korea Says It Will Continue Projects in North," *New York Times*, October 19, 2006; "South Korea Slides into Political Dispute for Rejecting U.S. Nonproliferation Drive," Yonhap News Agency, November 15, 2006; Sheila Miyoshi Jager, "Time to End the Korean War: The Korean Nuclear Crisis in the Era of Unification," Policy Forum Online, 06-93A (San Francisco: Nautilus Institute for Security and Sustainable Development, November 2, 2006), www.nautilus.org/fora/security/0693MiyoshiJager.html (accessed January 7, 2009).

9. A number of thoughtful works address these issues. For example, see Balbina Hwang, "Defusing Anti-American Rhetoric in South Korea," *Backgrounder,* no. 1619, January 23, 2003, Heritage Foundation, www.heritage.org/research/asiaandthepacific/bg1619.cfm; Derek Mitchell, ed., *Strategy and Sentiment: South Korean Views of the United States and the U.S.-ROK Alliance* (Washington, DC:

Center for Strategic and International Studies, 2004); Mark E. Manyin, "South Korean Politics and Rising 'Anti-Americanism': Implications for U.S. Policy toward North Korea," *Report for Congress*, Congressional Research Service, May 6, 2003; Testimony of L. Gordon Flake, Hearing on "U.S.-Republic of Korea Relations: An Alliance at Risk?" House Committee on International Relations, September 27, 2006; and Seung-Hwan Kim, "Anti-Americanism in Korea," *Washington Quarterly* 26, no. 1 (Winter): 109–22.

10. Much of this historical context is discussed in my earlier work, Gi-Wook Shin, *Ethnic Nationalism in Korea: Genealogy, Politics, and Legacy* (Stanford, CA: Stanford University Press, 2006), chapters 8 and 9.

11. Shin (2006), 2.

12. See Ernest Gellner, *Nations and Nationalism* (Ithaca, NY: Cornell University Press, 1983).

13. Chaibong Hahm, "The Two South Koreas: A House Divided," *Washington Quarterly* 28, no. 3 (Summer 2005): 57–72; Byung-Hoon Suh, "Kim Dae Jung's Engagement Policy and the South-South Conflict in South Korea: Implications for U.S. Policy," *Asian Update*, Summer 2001, www.asiasociety.org/publications/update_southkorea.html (accessed January 7, 2009).

14. Although I will discuss the conservative and progressive newspapers' different attitudes toward North Korea–related issues later in this chapter, I first note that, over the length of this study, the two dailies covered most North Korea–related focus and topic categories with similar frequency. Thus, in Figures 3.1 and 3.2, I present the total article count for each focus and topic category as a percentage of the total article count from the two newspapers.

15. There has been relatively little news since Kim Jong Il assumed the mantle of leadership after his father's death in 1994. Nonetheless, it is clear from data on tone that the two newspapers' sentiments toward the DPRK are quite distinct.

16. See Taek-Young Hamm, "North Korea: Economic Foundations of Military Capability and the Inter-Korean Balance," in *North Korea: 2005 and Beyond*, ed. Philip Yun and Gi-Wook Shin, eds., 167–96 (Stanford, CA: Shorenstein Asia-Pacific Research Center, 2006).

17. See Shin (2006), chapter 10.

18. Reflecting this thinking, the Korean government has a Ministry of Unification that is separate from the Ministry of Foreign Affairs and Trade.

19. Note here that *peace* and *unification* are not synonymous; indeed, they represent two different strategies that have spurred serious political debate in the ROK. Unification is most often regarded as a long-term goal, while many argue that establishing a peace regime on the peninsula is the more immediate objective. In fact, after the historic inter-Korean summit in 2000, much of the discussion focused on prospects for transitioning from a continuing state of war to a peace

regime, and many felt that talk of unification was premature. The coding scheme does not distinguish between discussion of a peace regime and unification but rather pairs these concepts in this category, which speaks to visions for the future of the peninsula.

20. As quoted in "Editorials Split on Results of Inter-Korean Ministerial Talks," Yonhap News Agency, September 4, 2000.

21. Signed into law by President Bush, the act seeks to focus international attention on the plight of North Koreans, make the human rights issue an integral part of the U.S. approach to North Korea, increase transparency of humanitarian assistance, and assert that defectors from North Korea should receive the protection accorded refugees. Although a broadly popular measure in the United States, this bill was severely criticized by South Korean progressive forces. See Karin J. Lee, "The North Korean Human Rights Act and Other Congressional Agendas," October 7, 2004, www.nautilus.org/fora/security/0439A_Lee.html (accessed January 7, 2009); Balbina Y. Hwang, "Spotlight on the North Korean Human Rights Act: Correcting Misperceptions," *Backgrounder*, no. 1823, February 10, 2005, Heritage Foundation, www.heritage.org/research/asiaandthepacific/bg1823.cfm

22. The year 2001 generally represents an aberration in security-related coverage, owing to the diverse and poignant issues related to the September 11 terrorist attacks on the United States. This seems to be especially true in the case of *Hankyoreh*, which is a smaller newspaper and does not have the capacity of the more comprehensive *Chosun* to cover multiple big stories simultaneously.

23. The year 1994 shows some modest increase in media coverage. It was the year of the first nuclear crisis, the conclusion of the Agreed Framework, and Kim Il Sung's death and the resultant transition of leadership.

24. The tone scale ranges from −2 to +2.

25. "Yonhap Reviews ROK Dailies' View of Prospective N-S Summit," World News Connection, NTIS, U.S. Department of Commerce, April 11, 2000.

26. In my survey taken in the fall of 2000, 80 percent of the respondents agreed that "North and South must form a unitary nation-state," and 71 percent agreed that "Unification means the recovery of ethnic homogeneity." See Shin (2006), chapter 10; Roy Grinkler, *Korea and Its Futures: Unification and the Unfinished War* (New York: St. Martin's Press, 1998).

27. See Don Oberdorfer, *The Two Koreas: A Contemporary History* (New York: Basic Books, 1997), 387–91.

28. Shanto Iyengar, *Is Anyone Responsible? How Television Frames Political Issues* (Chicago: University of Chicago Press, 1991); William G. Jacoby, "Issue Framing and Public Opinion on Government Spending," *American Journal of Political Science* 44, no. 4 (2000), 750–67.

29. William A. Gamson, *Talking Politics* (New York: Cambridge University Press, 1992).

30. For a complete list of the North Korea–related media frames coded in this study, please contact the author.

31. The same six news frames described in Figures 3.6 and 3.7 were also the most prevalent in the time period before Kim Dae Jung's presidency and in the time period after his inauguration. This was true in both newspapers.

32. Although grounded in identity, Kim Dae Jung's Sunshine Policy necessarily included interest-based calculations, including its bid to prolong peaceful coexistence (or even delay unification) to prevent the South from bearing the enormous financial burden suggested by the case of Germany. In the 1990s, there was extensive discussion and fear of the possibility of the collapse of the DPRK, laying the groundwork for this precept of the Sunshine Policy, but in more recent years, a collapse has seemed less likely. Ambassador Michael Armacost astutely points out that with a declining perception of the possibility of collapse, "conservatives [have] more reasons to question the appropriateness or necessity of a policy of unreciprocated engagement" (personal correspondence, May 12, 2008).

33. Kim Dae Jung's election was not the product of such an environment. Rather, according to Hahm (2005, p. 63), "The financial crisis created widespread panic and disgust among the population with the ruling conservative coalition's corruption and mismanagement of the economy"; this provided the opportunity for Kim Dae-Jung to overcome significant obstacles that would normally have kept him from winning a presidential election. Thus, Kim Dae Jung's election helped shape an environment in which progressive ideas were gaining credence.

34. A view held only by those on the extreme far left asserts pride in North Korea's nuclear development, believing that the Korean bomb will ensure the security of a united Korea. Satisfaction at North Korea's 1998 missile test over Japan, which set off a wave of security anxiety in that country, is related to this far-left perspective, which is held by very few South Koreans yet can still raise U.S. alarm when expressed.

35. See Shin (2006), 175–81, as well as select chapters from Mitchell (2004), including the following: chapter 3, Kim Seung-Hwan, "Yankee Go Home? A Historical View of South Korean Sentiment toward the United States, 2001–2004"; chapter 4, Bak Sang-Mee, "South Korean Self-identity and Evolving Views of the United States"; and chapter 5, Lee Sook-Jong, "Generational Change in South Korea: Implications for the U.S.-ROK Alliance."

36. Shin (2006), 159, 180.

37. "Religious and Civic Leaders Call for Aid to N. Korea," *Hankyoreh*, June 3, 2008.

Chapter 4

1. See K. Connie Kang, "Roh Cautions U.S. on North Korea," *Los Angeles Times*, November 13, 2004; Anthony Faiola, "South Korea Weighs Allowing Once-Taboo Support for the North; Debate Reflects Division over Détente," *Washington Post*, November 22, 2004; and Selig S. Harrison, "South Korea-U.S. Alliance under the Roh Government," Nautilus Institute Policy Forum Online 06-28A, April 11, 2006.

2. Jim Lobe, "Now Neo-Con Hawks Push Regime Change in North Korea," Inter Press Service, November 22, 2004.

3. Nicholas Eberstadt, "Tear Down This Tyranny: A Korea Strategy for Bush's Second Term," *Weekly Standard* 10, no. 11 (November 29, 2004).

4. As quoted in William Walker, "Bush's 'Axis of Evil' Warning Sparks Fire," *Toronto Star*, January 31, 2002.

5. *Chosun Ilbo*, November 14, 2004.

6. *Hankyoreh*, November 16, 2004.

7. Daniel Sneider, "The U.S.-Korea Tie: Myth and Reality," *Washington Post*, September 12, 2006.

8. Policy Research Group, chaired by Kongdan Oh Hassig and James Przystup, "Moving the U.S.-ROK Alliance into the 21st Century," Special Report, Institute for National Strategic Studies and Institute for Defense Analyses, September 2007, www.spark946.org/bugsboard/index.php?BBS=pds_2&action=viewForm&uid=130 &page=1 (accessed January 7, 2009).

9. The U.S. media accorded less than one-quarter of ROK-related coverage to U.S.-ROK relations, as presented in Chapter 5.

10. One might instinctively attribute this disparity in prevalence, or perceived importance, to the nature of the data (i.e., editorials/columns, or opinion pieces, from the Korean press data versus all types of articles from the U.S. press). However, when all types of U.S.-related articles in the Korean papers (using the headline data) are examined, this disparity holds.

11. Statement by Doo-Shik Park, editorial writer of *Chosun Ilbo*, as quoted in "Media Reps Focus on Anti-US Feelings," *Korea Times*, January 9, 2003.

12. David R. Sands, "Anti-American Stance Troubles South Koreans: Troops Blame Faulty Intelligence," *Washington Times Seoul*, December 18, 2002.

13. "Rumsfeld's Curse," *Korea Herald*, September 1, 2004.

14. "No Reason to Stay in Iraq," *Hankyoreh*, October 22, 2007.

15. Some may argue that the data, which include editorials and columns, are naturally less event specific and thus biased. However, the headline data that include regular news articles, as well as editorials and columns, show the same pattern (not reported here). Namely, U.S.-ROK relations have become increasingly newsworthy in recent years.

16. "Hankyoreh Sides with Ruling Camp, Other Dailies Support Opposition," *Yonhap News Agency*, July 14, 2000.

17. "ROK Summit Coverage Rekindles Debate between Liberals, Conservatives," *Yonhap News Agency*, June 15, 2000.

18. David Straub, "Public Diplomacy and the Korean Peninsula," in *First Drafts of Korea: The U.S. Media and Perceptions of the Last Cold War Frontier* (KSP Conference, Stanford, CA, July 13, 2007).

19. Sung Joo Han, "Perceived Korean Thaw Draws Diplomatic Challenges," *Korea Herald*, August 8, 2000.

20. Doug Struck, "As Alliances Shift, Japan's Military Role Is Widening," *Washington Post*, September 28, 2001.

21. As described in Chapter 2, the five-point scale of media sentiments ranges from −2 (very negative) to +2 (very positive).

22. See Gi-Wook Shin and Paul Chang, "The Politics of Nationalism in US-Korean Relations," *Asian Perspectives* 28, no. 4 (2004): 119–45.

23. "International Public Concern about North Korea, but Growing Anti-Americanism in South Korea," Commentary, Pew Research Center for the People and the Press, August 22, 2003.

24. It is interesting to make note of events in the year 1994. At the time, the first nuclear crisis was unfolding; there was serious tension between the United States and the DPRK, which had threatened to turn Seoul into "sea of fire." After a period of high tension and protracted negotiation, including a visit by former President Jimmy Carter to Pyongyang in the summer, the Agreed Framework was signed between the United States and North Korea in Geneva on October 21, 1994. The findings indicate that the two newspapers reacted very differently to the crisis and its resolution in that year. As presented in Figure 4.4, *Hankyoreh* published editorials and columns that were very critical of the United States, whereas *Chosun* published materials in which the tone was practically neutral. Accordingly, it was the year of the greatest tone disparity between the two newspapers. This disparity seems to reflect contrasting views of the U.S. approach to the first nuclear crisis.

25. Exceptions include 1998, when the Kim Dae Jung government came to power and progressives may have been more positive on prospects for a more equitable relationship, and 2001, which does not necessarily indicate a positive tone but rather a lack of a very negative tone.

26. "ROK Summit" (2000).

27. Specifically, as shown in Tables 4.3 and 4.4, the presence of U.S. troops in South Korea was the most discussed subject within U.S.-ROK coverage (50.34%), and it received the most negative tone rating (−1.34) in *Hankyoreh*. Yet as shown in Figure 4.3, there was a big drop in coverage of the troop issue from 2000 to 2001

in the progressive newspaper (from 40 to 13 articles). As a consequence, far fewer cases received the very negative rating (–2) in 2001. In fact, in 2000, 57.78 percent of *Hankyoreh*'s editorials and columns on U.S.-ROK relations received a tone rating of –2. In comparison, in 2001, only 12.5 percent scored –2, and most of these were related to the troop issue. Once again, the drop in coverage of U.S. troops in the ROK in 2001 was most likely due to the effects of the September 11 terrorist attacks. Even progressives felt that this was not an appropriate time to criticize this alliance partner, especially when its troops were stationed in their country. Thus, the less negative average tones on the U.S.-ROK relationship in *Hankyoreh* in 2001 seemed to reflect the drop in troop coverage. However, this abatement in troop coverage was only temporary; it was specific to the unique situation of 2001. In 2002, as the progressive newspaper's coverage of the U.S. troop issue returned to its 2000 level, so did its tone toward the U.S.-ROK relationship become more negative.

28. Daniel Sneider, "Strategic Abandonment: Alliance Relations in Northeast Asia in the Post-Iraq Era" (paper presented at the annual symposium of the Korea Institute for International Economic Policy and the Korea Economic Institute, September 2007).

29. The United States largely failed to understand the broader context. In the words of Doug Struck, who covered Korean affairs for the *Washington Post* at the time, "In hindsight, perhaps we missed the mark." Doug Struck, Conference Paper, Session I, "Democracy, Anti-Americanism, and Korean Nationalism," in *First Drafts of Korea: The U.S. Media and Perceptions of the Last Cold War Frontier* (KSP Conference, Stanford, CA, July 13, 2007).

Chapter 5

Some of the descriptive data used in this chapter appeared as "Two Koreas in American News," a chapter in Gi-Wook Shin, Daniel Sneider, and Donald Macintyre, eds., *First Drafts of Korea: The U.S. Media and Perceptions of the Last Cold War Frontier* (Stanford, CA: Shorenstein Asia-Pacific Research Center, 2009). This chapter was coauthored with Kristin Burke.

1. To make the graph readable, available data points for Spain, the Czech Republic, Singapore, Portugal, Switzerland, and the Philippines have been excluded. (All fell in the lower-left portion of the graph.)

2. Martin Fackler, "First Drafts of Korea—Experience of a Business Journalist," in *First Drafts of Korea: The U.S. Media and Perceptions of the Last Cold War Frontier* (KSP Conference, Stanford, CA, July 13, 2007).

3. It is also noteworthy that two of the three countries that so capture U.S. news interest—Japan and China—are in Asia. Often, U.S. newspapers assign one

foreign correspondent to cover Japan and the ROK or sometimes all three countries. This practice sets up a zero-sum dynamic (i.e., a single journalist can only
cover so many stories) that may further entrench preference for news on Japan and
China over the ROK. As *New York Times* correspondent Martin Fackler has written, "South Korea must live in the shadows of two far larger news stories, Japan
and China." See Fackler (2007).

4. William F. May, "Containing Fear in Foreign Policy" (lecture sponsored
by the Kluge Center, U.S. Library of Congress, November 29 2007), http://www.
loc.gov/today/pr/2007/07-228.html (accessed January 8, 2009). See also Walter A.
McDougall, *Promised Land Crusader State: The American Encounter with the World
Since 1776* (Boston: Houghton Mifflin, 1997).

5. Whereas Chapters 3 and 4 evaluated data composed of Korean editorials and
columns, Chapters 5 and 6 look at U.S. data that include many types of newspaper articles, because examining only editorials and columns would have yielded a
sample too small from which to draw conclusions. See Chapter 2.

6. The coverage of inter-Korean relations was done largely from the perspective of South Korea, given lack of access to the North. In fact, 209 articles on inter-Korean relations were reported from Seoul, while only 2 were from Pyongyang.

7. Note that the *Post* has relatively few articles in either focus category, compared to its counterparts: 149 articles on the ROK, compared to 742 in the *Times*
and 999 in the *Journal*; 97 articles on U.S.-ROK relations, compared to 166 in the
Times and 191 in the *Journal*.

8. At least in part, these disparate trends in news volume may be attributed
to the samples utilized in this study. The U.S. data may show more event-driven
coverage of the Korean peninsula, since they are predominantly composed of news
stories, in addition to some editorials and columns. The ROK data may more
closely reflect particular newspapers' political agendas and may be less prone to
events, as they are comprised of editorials and columns. That is, since the U.S.
data predominantly contain news stories—on the whole, more a barometer of
events than opinion, in contrast to editorials and columns—they are likely to exhibit greater sensitivity to events.

9. It may also not be a coincidence that two main Western financial papers,
the *Wall Street Journal* and the *Financial Times*, have full-time correspondents in
Seoul. See Fackler (2007).

10. It is interesting to note that the *Wall Street Journal* recorded even higher
volumes of coverage in 1993 and 1994 than in 1997. For this economic and financial
newspaper, Korea's booming economy was a major story throughout the early
1990s. The *Journal* was unique in this respect, as before 1997, the *Times* and the
Post published very few articles on South Korean economic issues. Indeed, 1997
was the only year in which the *Post* gave any attention at all to ROK economic

issues. In contrast, in the wake of the Asian financial crisis, the *Times*'s appetite for ROK economic news persisted, as it covered this issue at more than twice the average rate it did in the early to mid-1990s. It seems the dramatic financial crisis had made the issue significant for the *Times*. In fact, in the late 1990s and early 2000s, the *Times*'s rate of coverage of economic issues was on par with that of the *Journal*, whose coverage had gradually receded over time, even though the ROK economy remained a significant story.

11. The *Journal* and the *Post* each published 5 articles on security, while the *Times* published 20. (The three newspapers returned to near parity the following year, publishing between 8 and 10 articles each.)

12. It should also be noted that this study's coding scheme examined the number of articles "mainly about" a given topic. While there were few articles mainly about anti-American sentiment and protests, anti-Americanism was mentioned in journalistic shorthand in many articles in connection with the events they principally described. For example, see James Brooke, "Threats and Responses: Nuclear Politics; South Korea Criticizes U.S. Plan for Exerting Pressure on North," *New York Times*, December 31, 2002.

13. Doug Struck, Conference Paper, Session I, "Democracy, Anti-Americanism, and Korean Nationalism," in *First Drafts of Korea: The U.S. Media and Perceptions of the Last Cold War Frontier* (KSP Conference, Stanford, CA, July 13, 2007).

14. David Straub, Conference Paper, Session IV, "Public Diplomacy and the Korean Peninsula," in *First Drafts of Korea: The U.S. Media and Perceptions of the Last Cold War Frontier* (KSP Conference, Stanford, CA, July 13, 2007).

15. Struck (2007).

16. This is according to a search using Lexis-Nexis Academic.

17. Straub (2007).

18. Gi-Wook Shin, "Korea Faces Challenges of Multiethnic Society," *Korea Herald*, July 16, 2007.

19. In examining the *Post*'s negative tone scores on economic matters, recall that this newspaper published dramatically fewer articles on economic topics than its counterparts did, and most of those articles were about the 1997 financial crisis.

20. Struck (2007).

21. Recall that the majority of security coverage occurred within news about the U.S.-ROK relationship, rather than news about the ROK. This was true to a lesser extent in the Korean press, where newspapers, especially the progressive *Hankyoreh*, devoted a fair amount of security coverage not only to bilateral security issues but also to U.S. security, including Iraq, security of the homeland, and other U.S. security interests around the world.

22. Mary McGrory, "Shadow on 'Sunshine Policy,'" *Washington Post*, March 15, 2001.

23. Daniel Sneider, Conference Paper, Session I, "Covering Korea in the 1980s: The Democracy Story," in *First Drafts of Korea: The U.S. Media and Perceptions of the Last Cold War Frontier* (KSP Conference, Stanford, CA, July 13, 2007).

24. Struck (2007).

Chapter 6

Some of the descriptive data used in this chapter appeared as "Two Koreas in American News," a chapter in Gi-Wook Shin, Daniel Sneider, and Donald Macintyre, eds., *First Drafts of Korea: The U.S. Media and Perceptions of the Last Cold War Frontier* (Stanford, CA: Shorenstein Asia-Pacific Research Center, 2009). The chapter was coauthored with Kristin Burke.

1. Italics added. "President Delivers State of the Union Address," Text of speech, News Release, Office of the Press Secretary, January 29, 2002, www.whitehouse. gov/news/releases/2002/01/20020129-11.html (accessed January 13, 2009).

2. This remark was intended to be tough rhetoric in the model of Ronald Reagan. According to the *Economist*, like Reagan's "evil empire" slogan, Bush's strong words were "meant to galvanize support by turning a long and tricky foreign-policy challenge into a simple, moral issue." See "George Bush and the Axis of Evil," *The Economist*, February 2, 2002.

3. David Sanger, "North Korea's Game Looks a Lot Like Nuclear Blackmail," *New York Times*, December 12, 1993.

4. Mohamed ElBaradei, "No Nuclear Blackmail," *Wall Street Journal*, May 22, 2003.

5. Glenn Kessler and John Pomfret, "North Korea's Threats a Dilemma for China; Ally's Nuclear Gamesmanship Rankles Beijing," *Washington Post*, April 26, 2003.

6. Victor Cha, "Mr. Kim Has Our Attention. But He Won't Be Able to Keep It," *Washington Post*, May 4, 2003.

7. As quoted in Sanger (1993).

8. Vilho Harle, *The Enemy with a Thousand Faces* (Westport, CT: Greenwood Press, 2000), 197.

9. For a specific account of the powerful effects of the pictures of the famine, see Barbara Slavin, "Reporting the North Korea Nuclear Crisis and More: Adventures in the Axis of Evil," in *First Drafts of Korea: The U.S. Media and Perceptions of the Last Cold War Frontier* (KSP Conference, Stanford, CA, July 13, 2007).

10. Caroline Gluck, "Reporting North Korea" in *First Drafts of Korea: The U.S. Media and Perceptions of the Last Cold War Frontier* (KSP Conference, Stanford, CA, July 13, 2007). See also Donald Macintyre and Anna Fifield's papers on, "Tales of the Hermit Kingdom: The Challenges of Covering North Korea," in *First*

Drafts of Korea: The U.S. Media and Perceptions of the Last Cold War Frontier (KSP Conference, Stanford, CA, July 13, 2007).

11. Don Oberdorfer, *The Two Koreas: A Contemporary History* (New York: Basic Books 2001), 6.

12. Ibid., 154.

13. Joel S. Wit, "North Korea: Leader of the Pack," *Washington Quarterly* 24, no. 1 (2001): 77–92.

14. Oberdorfer (2001), 143–44.

15. Emphasis added. As quoted in Mark Whitaker with Zofia Smardz, Thomas M. DeFrank, and Gloria Borger, "Loud Talk—And a Little Stick," *Newsweek*, July 22, 1985. According to this article, "Congressional experts also expressed skepticism about the notion of a terrorist 'confederation,'" interestingly, just as experts and commentators expressed skepticism about links among the axis of North Korea, Iran, and Iraq in the wake of President Bush's 2002 State of the Union address.

16. Daryl M. Plunk, "For the Bush Administration, a Policy Challenge on the Korean Peninsula," *Backgrounder*, no. 83, Heritage Foundation, December 9, 1988.

17. Oberdorfer (2001), 250–59.

18. Wit (2001), 78.

19. State Department memorandum, Kartman to Anderson, Subject: Next steps for North Korea, July 17, 1992, State Department FOIA release, National Security Archive Electronic Briefing Book no. 164, ed. Robert A. Wampler, www.gwu.edu/~nsarchiv/NSAEBB/NSAEBB164/EBB%20Doc%201.pdf (accessed January 13, 2009).

20. State Department memorandum, Tarnoff and Davis to Secretary of State Christopher, Subject: North Korea: Options for next steps, November 6, 1993, State Department FOIA release, National Security Archive Electronic Briefing Book no. 164, ed. Robert A. Wampler, www.gwu.edu/~nsarchiv/NSAEBB/NSAEBB164/EBB%20Doc%203.pdf (accessed January 13, 2009).

21. For the complete text of the Agreed Framework, go to www.kedo.org/pdfs/AgreedFramework.pdf.

22. Oberdorfer (2001), 249–50.

23. Before 1993, the DPRK received even less media attention.

24. Jamie McIntyre, "Washington Was on the Brink of War with North Korea Five Years Ago," CNN.com, October 4, 1999, www.cnn.com/US/9910/04/korea.brink (accessed January 13, 2009).

25. Wit (2001), 78.

26. James P. Rubin, "No Time to Delay on North Korea," *Washington Post*, May 18, 2001, and "Engaging North Korea," editorial, *Washington Post*, June 16, 2001.

27. In response, the DPRK mocked Condoleezza Rice by characterizing her

as "a hen strutting around in the White House, crowing arrogantly" and later as "a bitch running riot on the beach." This obscene discourse is not unusual in the context of U.S.-DPRK relations.

28. Bob Woodward, *Bush at War* (New York: Simon & Schuster, 2002), 340.

29. See Macintyre (2007) and Fifield (2007).

30. B. R. Myers, "The Obsessions of Kim Jong Il," *New York Times*, May 19, 2003.

31. See the 2007 KSP conference papers of Barbara Slavin, Donald Macintyre, Caroline Gluck, and Anna Fifield for more information on the restrictions faced by journalists once inside North Korea.

32. See Macintyre (2007), 13–14.

33. David E. Sanger, "Covering North Korea's Nuclear Program: A Very Different WMD Problem," in *First Drafts of Korea: The U.S. Media and Perceptions of the Last Cold War Frontier* (KSP Conference, Stanford, CA, July 13, 2007). In this paper, Sanger also discusses a relevant moral dilemma faced by journalists: "Is it possible to conduct sustained coverage of a problem like the North Korea nuclear crisis without appearing to be pushing [the United States] toward a specific response, including military action?"

34. Karl Schoenberger, "Hot-spot Journalism and the Problem with Coverage of South Korea," in *First Drafts of Korea: The U.S. Media and Perceptions of the Last Cold War Frontier* (KSP Conference, Stanford, CA, July 13, 2007).

35. Remarks by President Clinton in an address to the National Assembly of the Republic of Korea, press release, Office of the Press Secretary, White House, July 10, 1993.

36. See Macintyre (2007) and Fifield (2007).

37. "Thousands in Korea Are Given Amnesty by New President," *New York Times*, March 7, 1993.

38. T. R. Reid, "Dispute Could Hurt U.S.-N. Korea Talks," *Washington Post*, September 15, 1994.

39. This approach is not without controversy, even within the Bush administration. Internal differences of opinion over including the human rights issue was laid bare for public view in January 2008, when Jay Lefkowitz, Bush's special envoy for human rights in the DPRK, publicly criticized the Six-Party Talks for not linking security and human rights issues. Secretary Rice responded in harsh terms, insisting that Lefkowitz did not speak for the administration.

40. As alluded to earlier, the first nuclear crisis did not spur human rights coverage because the famine that awakened the American public to human rights conditions in North Korea had not yet occurred.

41. Richard G. Lugar, "A Korean Catastrophe," *Washington Post*, July 17, 2003.

42. See Stephen Haggard, Marcus Noland, and Amartya Sen, *Famine in North Korea: Markets, Aid, and Reform* (New York: Columbia University Press, 2007).

43. As in the previous chapter, evaluative tone is the focus here, but where relevant, discrepancies between evaluative and descriptive tones are also discussed.

Chapter 7

1. The full-text data are used from the Korean and U.S. media for comparing news tones about the U.S.-ROK relationship in accordance with combinations of the U.S. and ROK administrations and during the two nuclear crises. The headline data are used for analysis of media attention to the U.S.-DPRK relationship and the U.S.-ROK relationship in the Korean media during the two nuclear standoffs. The headline data are also used in the analysis of news tone regarding the U.S.-Japan relationship and the correlation of views of the North with views of the alliance. See Chapter 2 for a detailed discussion of the data sets.

2. Don Oberdorfer, *The Two Koreas: A Contemporary History* (New York: Basic Books, 2001), 420.

3. David E. Sanger, "Korean to Visit Bush, But They Could Be at Odds," *New York Times*, March 7, 2001.

4. This inconclusive result might also be related to the fact that the data cover only one year of overlap between Bush and Roh.

5. David Brown, "Never Better! . . . But Can It Last?" U.S.-ROK Relations, *Comparative Connections* 1, no. 3 (CSIS Pacific Forum, January 2000).

6. The U.S. approach was also difficult for President Kim politically, as it looked remarkably similar to a recent proposal made by Kim Dae Jung, his long-time opponent on the domestic political front. See Oberdorfer (2001), 283–96.

7. It should also be noted that because this analysis examines tone for all U.S.-ROK news, including economic news, news of the financial crisis during this period is a factor in these tone scores.

8. For example, see Barbara Demick, "South Koreans Shrug Off Nuclear Threat," *Los Angeles Times*, December 26, 2002.

9. Recall that *Hankyoreh* emerged out of the democratic movement in 1987. The newspaper endorsed Kim Dae Jung in the 1992 election.

10. *First Drafts of Korea: The U.S. Media and Perceptions of the Last Cold War Frontier* (KSP Conference, Stanford, CA, July 13, 2007). Conference participants also discussed a specific instance in which they believe the Bush administration willfully repressed major news on North Korea to keep Congress and the public focused on Iraq. In October 2002, when Assistant Secretary of State James Kelly traveled to Pyongyang and confronted his North Korean interlocutors about a highly enriched uranium program, the U.S. side believed it received confirmation

of such a program. Yet it was more than a week before the administration confirmed journalists' suspicion of these events. These journalists believe, having been told by administration sources, that the White House kept a close hold on this information to ensure that all attention was focused on its case for a war in Iraq and the upcoming Senate vote authorizing President Bush to declare war.

11. At this juncture in the analysis, it is important to recognize that the data may be affected by the fact that the second nuclear standoff is still ongoing, whereas the crisis during the mid-1990s has ended. This means that NUKE1 includes the final stage of the crisis, in which the United States and the DPRK worked out a solution in the form of the now-defunct Agreed Framework. During this final stage of the crisis, the news tone about the U.S.-DPRK relationship would likely have been coded more positively when compared to the peak of the crisis. Accordingly, the difference in news tone between NUKE1 and NUKE2 may reflect that the current standoff appeared intractable at the end of the study period.

12. The *Wall Street Journal* showed little change in tone from the first to the second crisis (the same as to media attention, shown in Figure 7.8). This might be related to the fact that the strains in the U.S.-ROK relations were over security issues (i.e., DPRK policy), not over trade or economic matters, which the financial paper is most interested in covering.

13. Although not reported here, the news tone toward the ROK was more negative during the second crisis than it was during the first. This suggests that the United States became more critical of the ROK policy toward the North during the current nuclear standoff.

14. See Derek Mitchell, ed., *Strategy and Sentiment: South Korean Views of the United States and the U.S.-ROK Alliance* (Washington, DC: Center for Strategic and International Studies, 2004).

15. Michael H. Armacost, "The Future of America's Alliances in Northeast Asia," in *The Future of America's Alliances in Northeast Asia*, ed. Michael H. Armacost and Daniel I. Okimoto, 14 (Stanford, CA: Walter H. Shorenstein Asia-Pacific Research Center, 2004).

16. See Ralph A. Cossa, "US-Japan Defense Cooperation: Can Japan Become the Great Britain of Asia? Should It?" in *The Future of America's Alliances in Northeast Asia*, ed. Michael H. Armacost and Daniel I. Okimoto, 91–104 (Stanford, CA: Walter H. Shorenstein Asia-Pacific Research Center, 2004).

17. The scale of tone ranges from −1 to +1.

18. Cossa (2004).

19. In this case, U.S. media coverage of U.S.-Japan relations includes all articles related to bilateral matters, not only security-related news items. Thus, this finding should be interpreted with some degree of caution, as a significant portion of the articles in this sample focus on economics.

20. See the University of Pennsylvania speech by Ambassador Yang Sung Chul, Republic of Korea's Position on North Korea's Nuclear Issue, October 17 2002, www.icasinc.org/lectures/yang1.html (accessed January 6, 2002).

21. Kim's Sunshine Policy embodied decades-old progressive views, which had become increasingly mainstream in the 1990s, and challenged conventional wisdom about the North and the alliance. This evolving attitude toward the North led, for instance, the ROK Ministry of National Defense (MND) to cease describing the DPRK as the "main enemy" in its 2004 defense white paper. The ministry's decision to drop the label from its publication (once the publication itself was reinstated) frustrated many policy makers in the United States, as it signaled a widening Seoul-Washington gap in threat perception of the North. Much more than a simple rhetorical adjustment, this significant change to an important defense policy document represented an evolution of attitude set in motion by Kim Dae Jung's Sunshine Policy. The impact of this policy on South Koreans' view of the North has had crucial implications for the U.S.-ROK alliance.

22. *Chosun Ilbo*, as quoted in Khang Hyun-Sung, "South Koreans Fear American Troop Shift Is Start of Downsizing," *South China Morning Post*, May 20, 2004.

23. *Chosun Ilbo* editorial, "Restoring the Alliance," as quoted in "ROKG Urged to Put 'National Interest' before 'Pride' Where USFK Alliance Is Concerned," World News Connection, February 17, 2003.

24. Daniel Sneider, "Strategic Abandonment: Alliance Relations in Northeast Asia in the Post-Iraq Era," in *Toward Sustainable Economic and Security Relations in East Asia: U.S. and ROK Policy Options* (Joint U.S.-Korea Academic Studies Korean Economic Institute, 18 (February 28, 2008), 14.

25. Joseph S. Nye Jr., *Soft Power: The Means to Success in World Politics* (New York: Public Affairs, 2004).

26. Katharine Moon, "Korean Nationalism, Anti-Americanism, and Democratic Consolidation," in *Korea's Democratization*, ed. Samuel S. Kim (New York: Cambridge University Press, 2003).

27. See Chapter 1, note 14.

Chapter 8

1. For a brief description of such commentary from Korean analysts and Secretary of State Donald Rumsfeld, see Hans Griemel, "North Korea Nuke Test Fans Fears of East Asian Nuclear Arms Race," Associated Press, October 9, 2006.

2. "Awkward Bedfellows; South Korea and America," *Economist*, September 9, 2006.

3. "North Korean Nuclear Test 'Far More Devastating' Than Missile Test—Roh," Yonhap News Agency, September 15, 2006 (as supplied by BBC Monitoring Asia Pacific—Political, September 16, 2006).

4. This seminar was based on my co-edited book, Philip Yun and Gi-Wook Shin, eds., *North Korea: 2005 and Beyond* (Stanford, CA: Walter H. Shorenstein Asia-Pacific Research Center, 2005).

5. *North Korea: 2007 and Beyond* (Conference, Shorenstein Asia Pacific Research Center at Stanford University and the Brookings Institution, September 14, 2006), http://iis-db.stanford.edu/evnts/4585/CNAPSTrans.pdf (accessed November 22, 2007).

6. Gi-Wook Shin and Daniel Sneider, "U.S. and Allies Must Stand Up to North Korea's Threat," Opinion-Editorial, *San Jose Mercury News*, October 8, 2006.

7. Norimitsu Onishi, "Tough Talk from Seoul, If Little Will for a Fight," *New York Times*, October 10, 2006.

8. Choe Sang-Hun, "Seoul Joins Tokyo in Bid to Get Tough with North," *International Herald Tribune*, October 10, 2006.

9. Anna Fifield, "Clouds over Seoul's 'Sunshine Policy'," *Financial Times*, October 11, 2006.

10. Khang Hyun-Sung, "Political Fallout Still Hangs over Seoul; Confusion over Engagement Policy Follows Nuclear Test," *South China Morning Post*, October 26, 2006.

11. "Rice's Seoul Visit," Editorial, *Korea Herald*, October 19, 2006.

12. Kim Rahn, "Conservatives Blame Roh, Progressives Blame Bush," *Korea Times*, October 11, 2006.

13. See Gi-Wook Shin, *Ethnic Nationalism in Korea: Genealogy, Politics, and Legacy* (Stanford, CA: Stanford University Press, 2006).

14. Sook-Jong Lee, "Generational Change in South Korea: Implications for the US-ROK Alliance," in *Strategy and Sentiment: South Korean Views of the United States and the U.S.-ROK Alliance* (Washington, DC: Center for Strategic and International Studies, 2004), 43–49.

15. See J. J. Suh, "Bound to Last? The U.S.-Korea Alliance and Analytical Eclecticism," in *Rethinking Security in East Asia: Identity, Power, and Efficiency*, ed. J. J. Suh, Peter J. Katzenstein, and Allen Carlson (Stanford, CA: Stanford University Press, 2004), 169.

16. Gi Wook Shin, "The Paradox of Korean Globalization" (APARC Working Paper, January 2003), http://iis-db.stanford.edu/pubs/20125/Shin.pdf (accessed January 8, 2009).

17. See Shin (2006).

18. "The Search for a Common Strategic Vision: Charting the Future of the U.S.-ROK Security Partnership" (U.S.-ROK Strategic Forum, co-directed by G. John Ikenberry, Chung-In Moon, and Mitchell Reiss, February 18, 2008), www.wm.edu/news/?id=8681 (accessed January 8, 2009).

19. See Stephen D. Krasner, ed., *International Regimes* (Ithaca, NY: Cornell University Press, 1983), 2.

20. See Michael Barnett and Raymond Duvall, "Power in International Politics," *International Organization* 59 (Winter 2005): 39–75; John Gerald Ruggie, "What Makes the World Hang Together: Neo-utilitarianism and the Social Constructivist Challenge," *International Organization* 52 (Autumn 1998): 855–85.

21. Henry Nau, *At Home Abroad: Identity and Power in American Foreign Policy* (Ithaca, NY: Cornell University Press, 2002), 336.

22. James D. Morrow, "Alliance and Asymmetry: An Alternative to the Capacity Aggregation Model of Alliances," *American Journal of Political Science* 35, no. 4 (1991): 904–33.

23. Young-Lim Hong "U.S. More Dangerous Than North Korea," *Chosun Ilbo*, January 12, 2004.

24. Mark E. Manyin, "South Korean Politics and Rising 'Anti-Americanism': Implications for U.S. Policy toward North Korea" (Congressional Research Service, May 6, 2003).

25. *New York Times* journalist Martin Fackler has written, "For example, in covering the opponents of Lone Star and other American funds, I visited offices of activists and social groups festooned with posters showing torn American flags and large fists on the head President Bush. In their writings and speeches, they describe Lone Star as a symbol of American economic domination, and a form of cultural imperialism as the United States tries to impose its brand of capitalism upon smaller South Korea. Resistance to Lone Star is cast in terms of heroic defense of South Korean identity and autonomy." From Martin Fackler, "Experiences of a Business Journalist," Conference Paper, in *First Drafts of Korea: The U.S. Media and Perceptions of the Last Cold War Frontier* (KSP Conference, Stanford, CA, July 13, 2007).

26. See, for example, Sook Jong Lee, "Allying with the United States: Changing South Korean Attitudes," *Korean Journal of Defense Analysis* 17, no. 1 (Spring 2005), 81–104; Sang-Mee Bak, "South Korean Self-Identity and Evolving Views of the United States," in *Strategy and Sentiment: South Korean Views of the United States and the U.S.-ROK Alliance* (Washington, DC: Center for Strategic and International Studies, 2004), 36–42; and Robert Marquand, "How S. Korea's View of the North Flipped," *Christian Science Monitor*, January 22, 2003.

27. Walker Connor, *Ethnonationalism: The Quest for Understanding* (Princeton, NJ: Princeton University Press, 1994), 140; emphasis in original.

28. Daniel Sneider, "Strategic Abandonment: Alliance Relations in Northeast Asia in the Post-Iraq Era," *Toward Sustainable Economic and Security Relations in East Asia: U.S. and ROK Policy Options*, vol. 18 (Korea Economic Institute, February 28, 2008), www.keia.org/joint_studies.php.

29. Michael Armacost, "Asian Alliances and American Politics" (APARC Working Paper, February 1999), 5, 12.

30. Stephen Hess, *International News and Foreign Correspondents* (Washington, DC: Brookings Institution Press, 1996), 1.

31. See Bethan Benwell and Elizabeth Stokoe, *Discourse and Identity* (Edinburgh: Edinburgh University Press, 2006).

32. See William Bloom, *Personal Identity, National Identity and International Relations* (Cambridge: Cambridge University Press, 1990); Jill Krause and Neil Renwick, eds., *Identities in International Relations* (New York: St. Martin's Press, 1996); Yosef Lapid and Friedrich Kratochwil, eds., *The Return of Culture and Identity in IR Theory* (Boulder, CO: Lynne Rienner, 1996); Gilbert Rozman, *Northeast Asia's Stunted Regionalism: Bilateral Distrust in the Shadow of Globalization* (New York: Cambridge University Press, 2004); Jae Jung Suh et al., eds., *Rethinking Security in East Asia* (Stanford, CA: Stanford University Press, 2004).

33. Benedict Anderson, *Imagined Communities: Reflections on the Origins and Spread of Nationalism* (London: Verso, 1983).

34. Michael Robinson, *Cultural Nationalism in Colonial Korea, 1920–25* (Seattle: University of Washington Press, 1988).

35. See Shin (2006).

36. See the House International Relations Committee for a summary of the bill (http://foreignaffairs.house.gov/archives/107/fpa0617.htm).

37. David Straub articulates three impediments to effective U.S. public diplomacy. First, "embassy officials usually have a limited understanding of the foreign country and culture in which they are working." Second, "our own cultural and nationalistic biases, of which we are often only dimly aware, . . . result in emotional responses that can severely distort our analysis of events." Third, "[we] should have become much more modest about our ability to understand foreign countries and about our capacity to influence them." In fact, the Bush administration's bid to improve the United States' image abroad led to a string of resignations and appointments to the undersecretary post. From Beers through the president's trusted advisor Karen Hughes, many capable appointees have found it difficult to succeed in this mission, which is disproportionately focused—and heavily so—on the Middle East. See David Straub, "Public Diplomacy and the Korean Peninsula," Conference Paper, Session IV, in *First Drafts of Korea: The U.S. Media and Perceptions of the Last Cold War Frontier* (KSP Conference, Stanford, CA, July 13, 2007), 8–9. Also, for an example of the intense criticism levied against Karen Hughes and the administration for its years of public diplomacy efforts, see the editorial by AEI scholar David Frum, "Losing the Battle against Anti-Americanism," *National Post*, November 3, 2007; and Robert Satloff, "How to Win the War of Ideas," Editorial, *Washington Post*, November 10, 2007.

38. Straub (2007), 4

39. Straub (2007), 4–5.

40. Online papers such as OhMyNews and portals such as naver.com have also played crucial roles in mobilizing young people on key policy issues.

41. Personal correspondence, May 12, 2008.

42. Aaron Han Joon Magnan-Park, "Remember Me, Remember Us, Remember Korea: *Hallyu*, Flashbacks, and the Transformation of South Korea Into an Unforgettable Nation," *Toward Sustainable Economic and Security Relations in East Asia: U.S. and ROK Policy Options*, vol. 18 (Korea Economic Institute, February 28 2008), www.keia.org/joint_studies.php (accessed January 8, 2009).

43. Straub (2007), 4–5.

44. "The Search for a Common Strategic Vision" (2008).

45. Straub (2007), 4–5.

46. Straub (2007), 9.

47. Stephen Hess, *International News and Foreign Correspondents* (Washington, DC: Brookings Institution Press, 1996), 32.

48. See Hugh Gusterson, "Paranoid, Potbellied Stalinist Gets Nuclear Weapons: How the U.S. Print Media Cover North Korea," *Nonproliferation Review* 15, no. 1 (March 2008): 21–42.

49. Caroline Gluck, "Reporting North Korea," in *First Drafts of Korea: The U.S. Media and Perceptions of the Last Cold War Frontier* (KSP Conference, Stanford, CA, July 13, 2007).

50. Stephen M. Walt, "Why Alliances Endure or Collapse," *Survival* 39, no. 1 (Spring 1997): 156–79.

51. Cheoleon Lee, "Gallup World Poll: South Korea's Political Dilemma," September 22, 2006, www.gallup.com/poll/24679/gallup-world-poll-south-koreas-political-dilemma.aspx (accessed June 23, 2009).

52. Mutual Defense Treaty between the Republic of Korea and the United States of America (signed October 1, 1953), http://avalon.law.yale.edu/20th_century/kor001.asp (accessed January 8, 2009). Many Americans do not appreciate that from the beginning of the alliance, its goals extended beyond the Korean peninsula. Indeed, the Mutual Defense Treaty specifies a regional purview and does not mention North Korea by name.

53. Victor D. Cha, "Shaping Change and Cultivating Ideas in the US-ROK Alliance," *The Future of America's Alliances in Northeast Asia*, ed. Michael H. Armacost and Daniel I. Okimoto (Washington, DC: Brookings Institution Press, 2004): 129. For further discussion of alliances' ability to extend beyond their original rationales, see Jae Jung Suh, *Power, Interest, and Identity in Military Alliances* (New York: Palgrave Macmillan, 2007): 304.

54. White House press release, "President Bush Participates in Joint Press

Availability with President Lee Myung-Bak of the Republic of Korea" (Camp David, April 19, 2008), www.whitehouse.gov/news/releases/2008/04/20080419-1.html (accessed January 8, 2009).

55. *"New Beginnings" in the U.S.-ROK Alliance: Recommendation to U.S. Policymakers* Korea Society and Shorenstein Asia-Pacific Research Center of Stanford University (2008). http://ksp.stanford.edu/events/new_beginnings_toward_a_new_era_of_ussouth_korean_partnership/ (accessed June 19, 2009)

56. Richard Lawless, "Transforming the U.S.–South Korean Alliance" (Remarks presented at Heritage Foundation, April 24, 2008), www.heritage.org/Press/Events/ev042408a.cfm (accessed January 8, 2009).

57. For example, see Michael Armacost, "New Hope for U.S.-South Korea Ties," *Christian Science Monitor*, April 17, 2008; Foster Klug, "Bush Welcomes Like-Minded South Korean President Friday," Associated Press, April 18, 2008; "Fukuda-Lee Meeting Marks Dawn of New Era," *Yomiuri Shimbun*, April 22, 2008.

58. Barack Obama, "U.S. Presidential Candidate Barack Obama's Views on Relations with Asia," *Comparative Connections* (October 2008), www.csis.org/media/csis/pubs/0803qobama_views.pdf (accessed January 8, 2009).

59. Lee, Jong-Heon, "U.S. May Extend Military Role in S. Korea," (June 17, 2009) www.upiasia.com/Security/2009/06/17/us_may_extend_military_role_in_s_korea/5283/ (accessed June 19, 2009).

60. See Peter Hays Gries, "The Koguryo Controversy, National Identity, and Sino-Korean Relations Today," *East Asia* 22, no. 4 (Winter 2005): 13–14.

61. "President Lee Links Public Anxiety on U.S. Beef to Political Motivations," *Hankyoreh*, May 13, 2008.

62. "U.S. Beef Imports Fuel Online Scaremongering," *Chosun Ilbo*, May 5, 2008.

References

Achin, Kurt. 2005. "South Korea-US Alliance in Difficult Transition." Voice of America, May 2.

———. 2006. "Senior South Korean Official Apologizes for North's Nuclear Test." Federal Information and News Dispatch. Voice of America, October 10.

Albritton, Robert B., and Jarol B. Manheim. 1983. "News of Rhodesia: the Impact of a Public Relations Campaign." *Journalism Quarterly* 60: 622–28.

———. 1984. "Changing National Images: International Public Relations and Media Agenda Setting." *American Political Science Review* 78, no. 3 (September): 641–57.

Althaus, Scott L., Jill A. Edy, and Patricia F. Phalen. 2001. "Using Substitutes for Full-Text News Stories in Content Analysis: Which Text Is Best? Workshops." *American Journal of Political Science* 45, no. 3: 707–23.

Amsden, Alice H. 1989. *Asia's Next Giant. South Korea and Late Industrialization.* New York: Oxford University Press.

Anderson, Benedict. 1983. *Imagined Communities: Reflections on the Origin and Spread of Nationalism.* New York: Verso.

Armacost, Michael H. 1999. "Asian Alliances and American Politics." Asia-Pacific Research Center (APARC) Working Paper, February.

———. 2004. "The Future of America's Alliances in Northeast Asia (Introduction)." In *The Future of America's Alliances in Northeast Asia*, ed. Michael H. Armacost and Daniel I. Okimoto. Stanford, CA: The Walter H. Shorenstein Asia-Pacific Research Center.

———. 2008. "New Hope for U.S.-South Korea Ties." *Christian Science Monitor*, April 17.

Armitage, Richard L. 1999. "A Comprehensive Approach to North Korea." Institute for National Strategic Studies, Strategic Forum, no. 159, National Defense

University, March. www.globalsecurity.org/wmd/library/news/dprk/1999/forum159.html.

Bak, Sang-Mee. 2004. "South Korean Self-Identity and Evolving Views of the United States." In *Strategy and Sentiment: South Korean Views of the United States and the U.S.-ROK Alliance*, ed. Derek Mitchell, ch. 4. Washington, DC: Center for Strategic and International Studies.

Barnett, Michael, and Raymond Duvall. 2005. "Power in International Politics." *International Organization* 59, no. 1 (Winter): 39–75.

Benwell, Bethan, and Elizabeth Stokoe. 2006. *Discourse and Identity*. Edinburgh: Edinburgh University Press.

Bloom, William. 1990. *Personal Identity, National Identity and International Relations*. Cambridge: Cambridge University Press.

Bong, Young-Shik. 2003. "Anti-Americanism and the U.S.-Korea Military Alliance." *Confrontation and Innovation on the Korean Peninsula*. Washington, DC: Korea Economic Institute.

Brians, Craig Leonard, and Martin P. Wattenberg. 1996. "Campaign Issue Knowledge and Salience: Comparing Reception from TV Commercials, TV News and Newspapers." *American Journal of Political Science* 40, no. 1 (February): 172–93.

Brooke, James. 2002. "Threats and Responses: Nuclear Politics; South Korea Criticizes U.S. Plan for Exerting Pressure on North." *New York Times*, December 31.

———. 2003. "South Opposes Pressuring North Korea, Which Hints It Will Scrap Nuclear Pact." *New York Times*, January 1.

Brown, David. 2000. "Never Better! . . . But Can It Last? U.S.-ROK Relations." *Comparative Connections* 1, no. 3 (January) (CSIS Pacific Forum).

Burgos, Russell. 1996. "The Second Hands of History: Partisanship and the Corporate Transformation of American Journalism." Unpublished paper, University of California Los Angeles.

Bush, George W. 2002. Press Release, "State of the Union address." Office of the Press Secretary, January 29. www.whitehouse.gov/news/releases/2002/01/20020129-11.html.

Carpenter, Ted Galen, and Doug Bandow. 2004. *The Korean Conundrums: America's Troubled Relations with North and South Korea*. London: Palgrave Macmillan.

Cha, Victor D. 1999. *Alignment Despite Antagonism: The US-Korea-Japan Security Triangle*. Stanford, CA: Stanford University Press.

———. 2002. "Korea's Place in the Axis." *Foreign Affairs* 81, no. 3: 79–92.

———. 2003. "Mr. Kim Has Our Attention. But He Won't Be Able to Keep It." *Washington Post*, May 4.

———. 2004. "Korea: A Peninsula in Crisis and Flux." In *Strategic Asia 2004–2005: Confronting Terrorism in the Pursuit of Power*, ed. Ashley J. Tellis and Michael Willis. Seattle, WA: National Bureau of Asian Research.

———. 2004. "Shaping Change and Cultivating Ideas in the US-ROK Alliance." In *The Future of America's Alliances in Northeast Asia*, ed. Michael H. Armacost and Daniel I. Okimoto. Washington, DC: Brookings Institution Press.

Cha, Victor D., and David C. Kang. 2003. *Nuclear North Korea: A Debate on Engagement Strategies*. New York: Columbia University Press.

Chang, Jae-Soon. 2006. "North Korean Leader Kim Tours Fertilizer Factory Amid Halt In South Korean Aid." Associated Press Worldstream, November 13.

———. 2006. "South Korean President Pledges to Keep Relations with North Korea 'Friendly.'" Associated Press Worldstream, November 2.

Choe, Sang-Hun. 2006. "Seoul Torn over Response to Test: Critics Take Aim at 'Sunshine Policy.'" *International Herald Tribune*, October 13.

———. 2006. "South Korea Grapples with Competing Pressures as It Weighs Its Response to North Korea." *New York Times*, October 12.

———. 2006. "Seoul Joins Tokyo in Bid to Get Tough with North." *International Herald Tribune*, October 10.

Chosun Ilbo. 2003. "Restoring the Alliance." Editorial. In "ROKG Urged to Put 'National Interest' before 'Pride' Where USFK Alliance Is Concerned." World News Connection, February 17.

———. 2004. "South Koreans Fear American Troop Shift Is Start of Downsizing." *South China Morning Post*, May 20.

———. 2004. "A Miscalculated Attempt to Showoff Roh's Confidence in Diplomatic Relations."November 14. http://english.chosun.com/w21data/html/news/200411/200411140033.html.

———. 2008. "U.S. Beef Imports Fuel Online Scaremongering." May 2.

Cohen, Bernard C. 1973. *The Public's Impact on Foreign Policy*. Boston: Little, Brown.

Connor, Walker. 1994. *Ethnonationalism: The Quest for Understanding*. Princeton, NJ: Princeton University Press.

Cossa, Ralph A. 2004. "US-Japan Defense Cooperation: Can Japan Become the Great Britain of Asia? Should It?" In *The Future of America's Alliances in Northeast Asia*, ed. Michael H. Armacost and Daniel I. Okimoto. Stanford, CA: Asia-Pacific Research Center.

Cumings, Bruce. 1981. *The Origins of the Korean War*, vol. 1. Princeton, NJ: Princeton University Press.

Demick, Barbara. 2002. "South Koreans Shrug Off Nuclear Threat." *Los Angeles Times*, December 26.

Eberstadt, Nicholas. 2004. "Tear Down This Tyranny: A Korea Strategy for Bush's Second Term." *Weekly Standard* 10, no. 11 (November 29): 19–20. www.weeklystandard.com/Content/Public/Articles/000/000/004/951szxxd. asp?pg=1.

Economist. 2002. "George Bush and the Axis of Evil." February 2.

———. 2006. "Awkward Bedfellows; South Korea and America." September 9.

ElBaradei, Mohamed. 2003. "No Nuclear Blackmail." *Wall Street Journal*, May 22.

Entman, Robert M. 1992. "Blacks in the News: Television, Modern Racism and Cultural Change." *Journalism Quarterly* 69: 341–61.

Fackler, Martin. 2007. "First Drafts of Korea—Experience of a Business Journalist." In *First Drafts of Korea: The U.S. Media and Perceptions of the Last Cold War Frontier*, ed. Gi-Wook Shin, Daniel C. Sneider, and Donald Macintyre. Stanford, CA: Asia-Pacific Research Center.

Faiola, Anthony. 2004. "South Korea Weighs Allowing Once-Taboo Support for the North; Debate Reflects Division over Détente." *Washington Post*, November 22.

Fifield, Anna. 2006. "Clouds over South Korea's 'Sunshine Policy'." *Financial Times*, October 10.

———. 2007. "Tales of the Hermit Kingdom: The Challenges of Covering North Korea," in *First Drafts of Korea: The U.S. Media and Perceptions of the Last Cold War Frontier*. Conference, Shorenstein Asia-Pacific Research Center, Stanford, CA, July 13, 2007.

Flake, Gordon L. 2006. Testimony, Hearing on "U.S.-Republic of Korea Relations: An Alliance at Risk?" House Committee on International Relations, September 27.

Freedom Promotion Act of 2002. House International Relations Committee. http://foreignaffairs.house.gov/archives/107/fpa0617.htm.

Frum, David. 2007. "Losing the Battle against Anti-Americanism." *National Post*, November 3.

Gamson, William A. 1992. *Talking Politics*. New York: Cambridge University Press.

Gans, Herbert J. 1979. *Deciding What's News*. New York: Pantheon.

Gellner, Ernest. 1983. *Nations and Nationalism*. Ithaca, NY: Cornell University Press.

Gitlin, Todd. 1980. *The Whole World Is Watching*. Berkeley: University of California Press.

Gleysteen, William H. Jr. 1999. *Massive Entanglement, Marginal Influence: Carter and Korea in Crisis*. Washington, DC: Brookings Institution Press.

Gluck, Caroline. 2007. "Reporting North Korea" in *First Drafts of Korea: The*

U.S. Media and Perceptions of the Last Cold War Frontier. Conference, Shoren-stein Asia-Pacific Research Center, Stanford, CA, July 13, 2007.

Greimel, Hans. 2006. "North Korea Nuke Test Fans Fears of East Asian Nuclear Arms Race." Associated Press, October 9.

Gries, Peter Hays. 2005. "The Koguryo Controversy, National Identity, and Sino-Korean Relations Today." *East Asia* 22, no. 4 (Winter): 13–14.

Grinkler, Roy. 1998. *Korea and Its Futures: Unification and the Unfinished War.* New York: St. Martin's Press.

Gusterson, Hugh. 2008. "Paranoid, Potbellied Stalinist Gets Nuclear Weapons: How the U.S. Print Media Cover North Korea." *Nonproliferation Review* 15, no. 1 (March): 21–42.

Haggard, Stephan, and Marcus Noland. *Famine in North Korea: Markets, Aid, and Reform.* New York: Columbia University Press.

Hahm, Chaibong. 2005. "The Two South Koreas: A House Divided." *Washington Quarterly* 28, no. 3 (Summer): 57–72.

Hamm, Taek-Young. 2006. "North Korea: Economic Foundations of Military Capability and the Inter-Korean Balance." In *North Korea: 2005 and Beyond*, ed. Philip Yun and Gi-Wook Shin. Stanford, CA: Asia-Pacific Research Center.

Hankyoreh Shinmoon. 2004. "Exercising His Right to Express His Views on NK." November 16. www.hani.co.kr/section-001100000/2004/11/001100000200411160354001.html.

———. 2007. "No Reason to Stay in Iraq." July 10.

———. 2008. "President Lee Links Public Anxiety on U.S. Beef to Political Motivations." May 9.

———. 2008. "Religious and Civic Leaders Call for Aid to N. Korea." June 3.

Harle, Vilho. 2000. *The Enemy with a Thousand Faces.* Westport, CT: Greenwood Press.

Harnisch, Sebastian. 2002. "U.S.-North Korean Relations under the Bush Administration: From 'Slow Go' to 'No Go.'" *Asian Survey* 42, no. 6 (November/December): 856–82.

Harrison, Selig S. 2006. "South Korea-U.S. Alliance Under the Roh Government." *Nautilus Institute Policy Forum Online* 6, no. 28A (April 11).

Herman, Burt. 2008. "Chillier Winds Blow across Korean Border." Associated Press, March 6.

Hess, Stephen. 1996. *International News and Foreign Correspondents.* Washington, DC: Brookings Institution Press.

Hong, Soon-Young. 1999. "Thawing Korea's Cold War: The Path to Peace on the Korean Peninsula." *Foreign Affairs*, May/June.

Hong, Young-Lim. 2004. "U.S. More Dangerous Than North Korea? Most Seem to Think So." *Chosun Ilbo*, January 12.

Hwang, Balbina Y. 2003. "Defusing Anti-American Rhetoric in South Korea." *Backgrounder*, no. 1619, Heritage Foundation, January 23.

———. 2004. "Minding the Gap: Improving U.S.-ROK Relations." *Backgrounder*, no. 1814, Heritage Foundation, December 21.

———. 2005. "Spotlight on the North Korean Human Rights Act: Correcting Misperceptions." *Backgrounder*, no. 1823, Heritage Foundation, February 10.

Ikenberry, G. John, Chung-In Moon, and Mitchell Reiss. 2008. "The Search for a Common Strategic Vision: Charting the Future of the U.S.-ROK Security Partnership." U.S.-ROK Strategic Forum, February 18. www.wm.edu/news/?id=8681.

Iyangar, Shanto. 1991. *Is Anyone Responsible? How Television Frames Political Issues*. Chicago: University of Chicago Press.

Jacoby, William G. 2000. "Issue Framing and Public Opinion on Government Spending." *American Journal of Political Science* 44, no. 4: 750–67.

Jager, Sheila Miyoshi. 2006. "Time to End the Korean War: The Korean Nuclear Crisis in the Era of Unification." *Policy Forum Online* 6, no. 93A (November 2). San Francisco: Nautilus Institute for Security and Sustainable Development. www.nautilus.org/fora/security/06 93MiyoshiJager.html.

Kang, Connie K. 2004. "Roh Cautions U.S. on North Korea." *Los Angeles Times*, November 13.

Kang, David C. 2005. "Rising Powers, Offshore Balancers, and Why the US-Korea Alliance Is Undergoing Strain." *International Journal of Korean Unification Studies* 14, no. 2: 115–40.

Kelly, James A. 2001. "United States Policy in East Asia and the Pacific: Challenges and Priorities." Testimony before the Subcommittee on East Asia and the Pacific, House Committee on International Relations, Washington, DC, June 12.

Kessler, Glenn, and John Pomfret. 2003. "North Korea's Threats a Dilemma for China; Ally's Nuclear Gamesmanship Rankles Beijing." *Washington Post*, April 26.

Khang, Hyun-Sung. 2006. "Political Fallout Still Hangs over Seoul; Confusion over Engagement Policy Follows Nuclear Test." *South China Morning Post*, October 26.

Kim, Do-Yeong. 2003. "After the South and North Korea Summit: Malleability of Explicit and Implicit National Attitudes of South Koreans." *Peace and Conflict: Journal of Peace Psychology* 9, no. 2 (June): 159–70. www.informaworld.com/smpp/title-content=t775653690-db=all.

Kim, Key-Hiuk. 1980. *The Last Phase of the East Asian World Order*. Berkeley: University of California Press.

Kim, Seung-Hwan. 2002–2003. "Anti-Americanism in Korea." *Washington Quarterly* 26, no. 1 (Winter): 109–22.

———. 2004. "Yankee Go Home? A Historical View of South Korean Sentiment toward the United States, 2001–2004." In *Strategy and Sentiment: South Korean Views of the United States and the U.S.-ROK Alliance*, ed. Derek Mitchell. Washington, DC: Center for Strategic and International Studies.

Kim, Sun Hyuk. 2000. *The Politics of Democratization in Korea*. Pittsburgh, PA: University of Pittsburgh Press.

Klug, Foster. 2008. "Bush Welcomes Like-Minded South Korean President Friday." Associated Press, April 18.

Kongdan Oh Hassig, and James Przystup. 2007. "Moving the U.S.-ROK Alliance into the 21st Century." Special Report, Policy Research Group, Institute for National Strategic Studies and Institute for Defense Analyses, September. www.spark946.org/bugsboard/index.php?BBS=pds_2&action=viewForm&uid=130&page=1.

Korea Herald. 2004. "Rumsfeld's Curse." September 1.

———. 2006. "Rice's Seoul Visit, Editorial." October 19.

Krasner, Stephen D. 1983. *International Regimes*. Ithaca, NY: Cornell University Press.

Krause, Jill, and Neil Renwick, eds. 1996. *Identities in International Relations*. New York: St. Martin's Press.

Kusnitz, Leonard A. 1984. *Public Opinion and Foreign Policy America's China Policy 1949–1979*. Westport, CT: Greenwood Press.

Lapid, Yosef, and Friedrich Kratochwil, eds. 1996. *The Return of Culture and Identity in IR Theory*. Boulder, CO: Lynne Rienner.

Larson, Eric V., Norman D. Levin, Seonhae Baik, and Bogdan Savych. 2004. *Ambivalent Allies? A Study of South Korean Attitudes toward the U.S.* San Diego, CA: RAND.

Lawless, Richard. 2008. "Transforming the U.S.-South Korean Alliance." Presentation at Heritage Foundation, April 24. www.heritage.org/Press/Events/ev042408a.cfm.

Lee, Chae-Jin. 2006. *The Troubled Peace: U.S. Policy and the Two Koreas*. Baltimore, MD: Johns Hopkins University Press.

Lee, Jae-Kyoung. 1993. Anti-Americanism in South Korea: The Media and the Politics of Signification. Ph.D. diss., University of Iowa.

Lee, Karin J. 2004. "The North Korean Human Rights Act and Other Congressional Agendas." Policy Form Online, October 7. www.nautilus.org/fora/security/0439A_Lee.html.

Lee, Nae Young, and Jung Han-oorl. 2003. "Panmi yŏron kwa hanmi tongmaeng [South Korean Public Opinion on Anti-Americanism and the U.S.-ROK alliance]." *Kukka chŏllyak* [National Strategy] 9, no. 3. www.sejong.org/Pub_ ns/PUB_NS_DATA/kns0903-03.pdf.

Lee, Sook-Jong. 2004. "Generational Change in South Korea: Implications for the US-ROK Alliance." In *Strategy and Sentiment: South Korean Views of the United States and the U.S.-ROK Alliance*, ed. Derek Mitchell, ch.5, pp. 43–49. Washington, DC: Center for Strategic and International Studies.

————. 2005. "Allying with the United States: Changing South Korean Attitudes." *Korean Journal of Defense Analysis* 17, no. 1 (Spring): 81–104.

Levin, Norman D., and Yong-Sup Han. 2002. *Sunshine in Korea: The South Korean Debate over Policies toward North Korea*. Santa Monica, CA: RAND.

Lobe, Jim. 2004. "Now Neo-Con Hawks Push Regime Change in North Korea." *Inter Press Service* 22 (November).

Lugar, Richard G. 2003. "A Korean Catastrophe." *Washington Post*, July 17.

Macintyre, Donald. 2007. "Tales of the Hermit Kingdom: The Challenges of Covering North Korea," in *First Drafts of Korea: The U.S. Media and Perceptions of the Last Cold War Frontier*. Conference, Shorenstein Asia-Pacific Research Center, Stanford, CA, July 13, 2007.

Magnan-Park, and Aaron Han Joon. 2008. "Remember Me, Remember Us, Remember Korea: *Hallyu*, Flashbacks, and the Transformation of South Korea Into an Unforgettable Nation." *Toward Sustainable Economic and Security Relations in East Asia: U.S. and ROK Policy Options*, no. 18, February 28, Korea Economic Institute. www.keia.org/joint_studies.php.

Manyin, Mark E. 2003. "South Korean Politics and Rising 'Anti-Americanism': Implications for U.S. Policy toward North Korea." Report for Congress, Congressional Research Service, May 6.

Marquand, Robert. 2003. "How S. Korea's View of the North Flipped." *Christian Science Monitor*, January 22. www.csmonitor.com/2003/0122/p01s02-woap. html.

May, William F. 2007. "Containing Fear in Foreign Policy." Lecture sponsored by the Kluge Center, U.S. Library of Congress, November 29. www.loc.gov/ today/pr/2007/07-228.html.

McDougall, Walter A. 1997. *Promised Land Crusader State: The American Encounter with the World Since 1776*. Boston: Houghton Mifflin.

McGrory, Mary. 2001. "Shadow on 'Sunshine Policy.'" *Washington Post*, March 15.

McIntyre, Jamie. 1999. "Washington Was on the Brink of War with North Korea Five Years Ago." CNN.com, October 4. www.cnn.com/US/9910/04/korea. brink.

Mearsheimer, John J. 2001. *The Tragedy of Great Power Politics*. New York: W. W. Norton.

Mitchell, Derek. 2003. "Strategy and Sentiment; Korea Economic Institute."

US-Korea Relations: Opinion Leaders Seminar. Washington, DC: Korea Economic Institute.

————. 2004. *Strategy and Sentiment: South Korean Views of the United States and the U.S.-ROK Alliance.* Washington, DC: Center for Strategic and International Studies.

Moens, Alexander. 2004. *The Foreign Policy of George W. Bush: Values, Strategy and Loyalty.* Burlington, VT: Ashgate.

Monroe, Alan D. 1979. "Consistency between Public Preferences and National Policy Decisions." *American Politics Quarterly* 7, no. 1: 3–19.

Morrow, James D. "Alliance and Asymmetry: An Alternative to the Capacity Aggregation Model of Alliances." *American Journal of Political Science* 35, no. 4 (1991): 904–33.

Moon, Chung-In. 2003. "ROK-DPRK Engagement and US-ROK Alliance: Trade-off or Complementary." Presented at the U.S.-DPRK Next Steps Workshop, Nautilus Institute and the Carnegie Endowment for International Peace. Washington, DC, January 27. www.nautilus.org/fora/security/0237A_Moon.html.

Moon, Katharine. 2003. "Korean Nationalism, Anti-Americanism, and Democratic Consolidation." In *Korea's Democratization*, ed. Samuel S. Kim. New York: Cambridge University Press.

Mutual Defense Treaty, Republic of Korea and United States of America (signed October 1, 1953). http://avalon.law.yale.edu/20th_century/kor001.asp.

Myers, B. R. 2003. "The Obsessions of Kim Jong Il." *New York Times*, May 19.

Nau, Henry. 2002. *At Home Abroad: Identity and Power in American Foreign Policy.* Ithaca, NY: Cornell University Press.

Neumann, Iver B. 1999. *Uses of the Other: "The East" in European Identity Formation.* Minneapolis: University of Minnesota Press.

"New Beginnings" in the U.S.-ROK Alliance: Recommendation to U.S. Policymakers. Korea Society and Shorenstein Asia-Pacific Research Center, Stanford University, April 2008.

New York Times. 1993. "Thousands in Korea Are Given Amnesty by New President." March 7.

Niksch, Larry. 2001. "North Korea's Nuclear Weapons Program." Congressional Research Service Report no. IB 91141. Washington, DC: CRS.

North Korea: 2007 and Beyond. Conference, Shorenstein Asia-Pacific Research Center, Stanford University, September 14, 2006. http://iis-db.stanford.edu/evnts/4585/CNAPSTrans.pdf.

North Korea Advisory Group. 1999. Report to Speaker U.S. House of Representatives, North Korea Advisory Group, November 1999. www.fas.org/nuke/guide/dprk/nkag-report.htm.

Nye, Joseph S. Jr. 2004. *Soft Power: The Means to Success in World Politics*. New York: Public Affairs.

Obama, Barack. 2008. "U.S. Presidential Candidate Barack Obama's Views on Relations with Asia." *Comparative Connections*, October 2008. www.csis.org/media/csis/pubs/0803qobama_views.pdf.

Oberdorfer, Don. 2001. *The Two Koreas: A Contemporary History*. New York: Basic Books.

Onishi, Norimitsu. 2006. "Tough Talk from Seoul, If Little Will for a Fight." *New York Times*, October 10.

———. 2008. "South Korean President Pledges Pragmatism." *New York Times*, February 26.

Page, Benjamin I., and Robert Y. Shapiro. 1983. "Effects of Public Opinion on Policy." *American Political Science Review* 77, no. 1: 175–90.

Pai, Hyung Il. 2000. *Constructing "Korean" Origins: A Critical Review of Archaeology, Historiography, and Racial Myth in Korean State Formation Theories*. Cambridge, MA: Harvard University Asia Center.

Park, Doo-shik. 2003. "Media Reps Focus on Anti-US Feelings." *Korea Times*, January 9.

Patterson, Thomas. 1993. *Out of Order*. New York: Knopf.

Perreault, William D. Jr., and Laurence E. Leigh. 1989. "Reliability of Nominal Data Based on Qualitative Judgments." *Journal of Marketing Research* 26 (May 26): 135–48.

Perry, David K. 1987. "The Image Gap: How International News Affects Perceptions of Nations." *Journalism Quarterly* 64: 416–21.

———. 1985. "The Mass Media and Inference about Other Nations." *Communication Research* 12, no. 4 (October 1): 595–614.

Pew Research Center. 2003. "International Public Concern about North Korea, But Growing Anti-Americanism in South Korea Commentary." Pew Research Center for the People and the Press, August 22.

———. 2003. "Views of a Changing World." Pew Research Center for the People and the Press, Pew Global Attitudes Project Survey, June. http://people-press.org/reports/pdf/185.pdf.

Plunk, Daryl M. 1988. "For the Bush Administration, a Policy Challenge on the Korean Peninsula." *Backgrounder*, no. 83, Heritage Foundation, December 9.

Powlick, Philip J. 1991. "The Attitudinal Bases for Responsiveness to Public Opinion among American Foreign Policy Officials." *Journal of Conflict Resolution* 35, no. 4: 611–41.

———. 1995. "The Sources of Public Opinion for American Foreign Policy Officials." *International Studies Quarterly* 39: 427–51.

Rahn, Kim. 2006. "Conservatives Blame Roh, Progressives Blame Bush." *Korea Times*, October 11.

Reid, T. R. 1994. "Dispute Could Hurt U.S.-N. Korea Talks." *Washington Post*, September 15.

Robinson, Michael. 1988. *Cultural Nationalism in Colonial Korea*. Seattle: University of Washington Press.

Rozman, Gilbert. 2004. *Northeast Asia's Stunted Regionalism: Bilateral Distrust in the Shadow of Globalization*. New York: Cambridge University Press.

Rubin, James P. 2001. "Engaging North Korea." *Washington Post*, June 16.

———. 2001. "No Time to Delay on North Korea." *Washington Post*, May 18.

Ruggie, John Gerald. 1998. "What Makes the World Hang Together: Neo-utilitarianism and the Social Constructivist Challenge." *International Organization* 52 (Autumn): 855–85.

Russett, Bruce. 1990. "Doves, Hawks, and U.S. Public Opinion." *Political Science Quarterly* 105, no. 4: 515–38.

Ryu, Jin. 2006. "US-North Korea Enmity Imperils South Korea." *Korea Times*, October 13.

Sands, David R. 2002. "Anti-American Stance Troubles South Koreans; Troops Blame Faulty Intelligence." *Washington Times*, December 18.

Sang-Hun, Choe. 2006. "Seoul Joins Tokyo in Bid to Get Tough with North." *International Herald Tribune*, October 10.

Sanger, David. 1993. "North Korea's Game Looks a Lot Like Nuclear Blackmail." *New York Times*, December 12.

———. 2001. "Korean to Visit Bush, But They Could Be at Odds." *New York Times*, March 7.

———. 2007. "Covering North Korea's Nuclear Program: A Very Different WMD Problem." In *First Drafts of Korea: The U.S. Media and Perceptions of the Last Cold War Frontier*, ed. Gi-Wook Shin, Daniel C. Sneider, and Donald Macintyre. Stanford, CA: Asia-Pacific Research Center.

Satloff, Robert. 2007. "How to Win the War of Ideas." Editorial copy." *Washington Post*, November 10.

Schoenberger, Karl. 2007. "Hot-spot Journalism and the Problem with Coverage of South Korea." In *First Drafts of Korea: The U.S. Media and Perceptions of the Last Cold War Frontier*, ed. Gi-Wook Shin, Daniel C. Sneider, and Donald Macintyre. Stanford, CA: Asia-Pacific Research Center.

Shanker, Thom, and Martin Fackler. 2006. "South Korea Says It Will Continue Projects in North." *New York Times*, October 19.

———. 2006. "South Korea Slides into Political Dispute for Rejecting U.S. Nonproliferation Drive." Yonhap News Agency, November 15.

Shin, Gi-Wook. 1996. "South Korean Anti-Americanism: A Comparative Perspective." *Asian Survey* 36, no. 8: 787–803.

―――. 2003. "The Paradox of Korean Globalization." Asia-Pacific Research Center (APARC) Working Paper, January. http://iis-db.stanford.edu/pubs/20125/Shin.pdf.

―――. 2005. "Asianism and Korea's Politics of Identity." *Inter-Asia Cultural Studies* 6, no. 4: 610–24.

―――. 2006. *Ethnic Nationalism in Korea: Genealogy, Politics, and Legacy.* Stanford, CA: Stanford University Press.

―――. 2007. "Korea Faces Challenges of Multiethnic Society." *Korea Herald*, July 16.

Shin, Gi-Wook, and Daniel Sneider. 2006. "U.S. and Allies Must Stand Up to North Korea's Threat, Opinion-Editorial." *San Jose Mercury News*, October 8.

Shin, Gi-Wook, and Kristin Burke. 2007. "A Mandate with Caveats: Lee Myung Bak's Election, Politics, and Policy." Asia-Pacific Research Center (APARC) Publications, December 28. http://aparc.stanford.edu/publications/a_mandate_with_caveats_lee_myung_baks_election_politics_and_policy.

Shin, Gi-Wook, and Kyung Moon Hwang. 2003. *Contentious Kwangju: The May 18 Uprising in Korea's Past and Present.* Boulder, CO: Rowman and Littlefield.

Shin, Gi-Wook, and Paul Chang. 2004. "The Politics of Nationalism in US-Korean Relations." *Asian Perspectives* 28, no. 4 (December): 119–45.

Shorrock, Tim. 1986. "The Struggle for Democracy in South Korea in the 1980s and the Rise of Anti-Americanism." *Third World Quarterly* 8, no. 4: 1198–99.

Sims, Calvin. 2000. "New (Friendly) Craze in South Korea: The North." *New York Times*, June 20.

Slavin, Barbara. 2007. "Reporting the North Korea Nuclear Crisis and More: Adventures in the 'Axis of Evil.'" In *First Drafts of Korea: The U.S. Media and Perceptions of the Last Cold War Frontier*, ed. Gi-Wook Shin, Daniel C. Sneider, and Donald Macintyre. Stanford, CA: Asia-Pacific Research Center.

Sneider, Daniel. 2006. "The U.S.-Korea Tie: Myth and Reality." *Washington Post*, September 12.

―――. 2007. "Covering Korea in the 1980s: The Democracy Story." In *First Drafts of Korea: The U.S. Media and Perceptions of the Last Cold War Frontier*, ed. Gi-Wook Shin, Daniel C. Sneider, and Donald Macintyre. Stanford, CA: Asia-Pacific Research Center.

―――. 2007. "Strategic Abandonment: Alliance Relations in Northeast Asia in the Post-Iraq Era." Paper presented at the annual symposium of the Korea Institute for International Economic Policy and the Korea Economic Institute, September.

Snyder, Glenn H. 1997. *Alliance Politics.* Ithaca, NY: Cornell University Press.

Snyder, Scott. 2004. "The Role of the Media and the US-ROK Relationship." In *Strategy and Sentiment: South Korean Views of the United States and the U.S.-ROK Alliance*, ed. Derek Mitchell. Washington, DC: Center for Strategic and International Studies.

———. 2007. "The China-Japan Rivalry: Korea's Pivotal Position?" In *Cross-Currents: Regionalism and Nationalism in Northeast Asia*, ed. Gi-Wook Shin and Daniel Sneider, 241–58. Stanford, CA: Asia-Pacific Research Center.

Spaeth, Anthony. 2003. "Roh Moo Hyun Takes Center Stage." *Time*, February 24.

Steinberg, David I. 2003. "Korean Attitudes towards the United States: The Complexities of an Enduring and Endured Relationship." Paper presented at the Georgetown Asian Studies Program Conference, Washington DC, January.

Straub, David. 2007. "Public Diplomacy and the Korean Peninsula." In *First Drafts of Korea: The U.S. Media and Perceptions of the Last Cold War Frontier*, ed. Gi-Wook Shin, Daniel C. Sneider, and Donald Macintyre. Stanford, CA: Asia-Pacific Research Center.

Struck, Doug. 2001. "As Alliances Shift, Japan's Military Role Is Widening." *Washington Post*, September 28.

———. 2003. "Anti-U.S. Sentiment Abates in South Korea; Change Follows Rumsfeld Suggestion of Troop Cut." *Washington Post*, March 14.

———. 2007. "Democracy, Anti-Americanism, and Korean Nationalism." In *First Drafts of Korea: The U.S. Media and Perceptions of the Last Cold War Frontier*, ed. Gi-Wook Shin, Daniel C. Sneider, and Donald Macintyre. Stanford, CA: Asia-Pacific Research Center.

Suh, Byung-Hoon. 2001. "Kim Dae Jung's Engagement Policy and the South-South Conflict in South Korea: Implications for U.S. Policy." *Asian Update*, Asia Society, Summer. www.asiasociety.org/publications/update_southkorea.html.

Suh, J. J. 2004. "Bound to Last? The US-Korea Alliance and Analytical Eclecticism." In *Rethinking Security in East Asia: Identity, Power, and Efficiency*, ed. J. J. Suh, Peter J. Katzenstein, and Allen Carlson. Stanford, CA: Stanford University Press.

———. 2007. *Power, Interest, and Identity in Military Alliances*. New York: Palgrave Macmillan.

Suh, J. J., Peter Katzenstein, and Allen Carlson, eds. 2004. *Rethinking Security in East Asia*. Stanford, CA: Stanford University Press.

Sung Joo, Han. 2000. "Perceived Korean Thaw Draws Diplomatic Challenges." *Korea Herald*, August 8.

U.S.–Korea Relations: Opinion Leaders Seminar. 2003. Korea Economic Institute, Washington, DC, July.

Walker, William. 2002. "Bush's 'Axis of Evil' Warning Sparks Fire." *Toronto Star*, January 31.

Walt, Stephen M. 1987. *Origins of Alliances*. Ithaca, NY: Cornell University Press.

———. 1997. "Why Alliances Endure or Collapse." *Survival* 39, no. 1 (Spring): 156–79.

Waltz, Kenneth Neal. 1979. *Theory of International Politics*. Reading, MA: Addison-Wesley.

Wampler, Robert A., ed. 1992. State Department memorandum, Kartman to Anderson, Subject: Next steps for North Korea. State Department FOIA release, National Security Archive Electronic Briefing Book, no. 164, July 17. www.gwu.edu/~nsarchiv/NSAEBB/NSAEBB164/EBB%20Doc%201.pdf.

———. 1993. State Department memorandum, Tarnoff and Davis to Secretary of State Christopher, Subject: North Korea: Options for next steps. State Department FOIA release, National Security Archive Electronic Briefing Book, no. 164, November 6. www.gwu.edu/~nsarchiv/NSAEBB/NSAEBB164/EBB%20Doc%203.pdf.

Wehrfritz, George. 2003. "Angry at the Yanks." *Newsweek*, January 13. www.newsweek.com/id/62765.

Weisman, Steven R. 2003. "Threats and Responses: East Asia: South Korea, Once a Solid Ally, Now Poses Problems for the U.S." *New York Times*, January 2.

Whitaker, Mark, Zofia Smardz, Thomas M. DeFrank, and Gloria Borger. 1985. "Loud Talk—and a Little Stick." *Newsweek*, July 22.

White House. 1993. Press release. "Remarks by President Clinton in address to the National Assembly of the Republic of Korea." Office of the Press Secretary, July 10.

———. 2008. Press release. "President Bush participates in joint press availability with President Lee Myung-Bak of the Republic of Korea." Office of the Press Secretary, April 19.

Wit, Joel S. 2000. "North Korea: Leader of the Pack." *Washington Quarterly* 24, no. 1: 77–92.

———. 2004. *Going Critical: The First North Korean Nuclear Crisis*. Washington, DC: Brookings Institution Press.

Woodward, Bob. 2002. *Bush at War*. New York: Simon & Schuster.

Yang, Sung-Chul. 2002. "Republic of Korea's Position on North Korea's Nuclear Issue." Speech, University of Pennsylvania, October 17. www.icasinc.org/lectures/yang1.html.

Yomiuri Shimbun. 2008. "Fukuda-Lee Meeting Marks Dawn of New Era." April 22.

Yonhap News Agency. 2000. "Editorials Split on Results of Inter-Korean Ministerial Talks." September 4.

————. 2000. "Hankyoreh Sides with Ruling Camp, Other Dailies Support Opposition." July 14.

————. 2000. "ROK Summit Coverage Rekindles Debate between Liberals, Conservatives." June 15.

————. 2000. *Yonhap Reviews ROK Dailies' View of Prospective N-S Summit.* April 11.

————. 2006. "Let the Sunshine Policy Set." October 12.

————. 2006. "North Korean Nuclear Test 'Far More Devastating' Than Missile Test–Roh." September 15.

Yun, Philip, and Gi-Wook Shin. 2006. *North Korea: 2005 and Beyond.* Stanford, CA: Asia-Pacific Research Center.

Zaller, John. 1999. *A Theory of Media Politics: How the Interests of Politicians, Journalists, and Citizens Shape the News.* Draft copy. www.sscnet.ucla.edu/polisci/faculty/zaller/media%20politics%20book%20.pdf.

Index